DOMESTIC SLAVERY IN WEST AFRICA

JOHN GRACE

DOMESTIC SLAVERY
IN
WEST AFRICA

WITH PARTICULAR REFERENCE TO THE SIERRA LEONE PROTECTORATE, 1896-1927.

BARNES & NOBLE
BOOKS
10 East 53d St., New York 10022
(a division of Harper & Row Publishers, Inc.)

Published in the U.S.A. 1975 by
Harper & Row Publishers, Inc. Barnes & Noble Import Division

Made and Printed in Great Britain
ISBN 0-06-492505-6

Contents

TO BARBARA GRACE

Illustrations

Abbreviations

Abo.	Aborigines
A.P.S.	Aborigines Protection Society
A.S.P.	Anti-Slavery Papers
A.S.S.	Anti-Slavery Society
C.C.P.	Commissioner, Central Province
C.M.S.	Church Missionary Society
C.N.P.	Commissioner, Northern Province
CO	Colonial Office
Col. Sec. or C.S.	Colonial Secretary
Conf.	Confidential
C.P.	Confidential Print
C.R.	Chalmers Report
C.S.P.	Commissioner, Southern Province
C.S.Sp.	Order of the Holy Ghost
D.C.	District Commissioner
ExecCo.	Executive Council (Sierra Leone)
FO	Foreign Office
G.I.L.B.	Government Interpreter's Letter Book
LegCo.	Legislative Council (Sierra Leone)
M.P.	Minute Paper
N.A.	Native Affairs
n.s.	new series
O.A.G.	Officer Administering the Government
O.C./W.A.F.F.	Officer Commanding, West African Frontier Force
P.P.	Parliamentary Papers
P.R.O.	Public Record Office
S.D.N.A.	Secretary, Department of Native Affairs
S.L.A.	Sierra Leone Archives
U.B.C.	United Brethren in Christ

Preface

Despite the highly emotive nature of the word "slavery" I have tried to avoid expressing my personal distaste of the institution in writing this book. However mild it might be in practice, slavery is a system whereby one class of people is deprived of freedom for the benefit of another class. I have preferred to let the facts about West African slavery speak for themselves. Slavery still exists today and it has left its mark on Sierra Leone. I have spoken to men and women who owned slaves or who were slaves less than fifty years ago. For this reason, among many others, it seemed right to investigate the problem of domestic slavery in British West Africa—particularly in the Sierra Leone Protectorate, the last part of the British Empire and Commonwealth where slavery was tolerated.

*   *   *

This book is based on my research at Aberdeen University—research which would not have been possible without the generosity of Aberdeen University and The Canada Council. In addition I would like to thank the staff of the following institutions for their help: Aberdeen University History Department, Aberdeen University Library, Birmingham University Library, the British Museum, Church Missionary Society, the Holy Ghost Fathers in Paris, the Institute of African Studies at Fourah Bay College, the London School of Economics, the Public Record Office, Rhodes House at Oxford, the Sierra Leone Archives at Fourah Bay College, and the Sierra Leone Government—particularly its officials in Bo, Kenema and Pujehun.

I owe a special debt to Mr. N. C. Hollins who served in Sierra Leone for many years and who has told me of his experiences; to Dr. R. Bridges, Mr. C. Fyfe and Professor J. D. Hargreaves for their advice and assistance; and to Dr. C. Visser and Mrs. E. Winter for reading my manuscript; and finally to my wife for her patient help.

CHAPTER I

Domestic Slavery in West Africa during the Nineteenth Century

Most European travellers to West Africa never realized the complexity and richness of its culture. Explorers, missionaries, traders, rulers and administrators were blinded by their cultural arrogance, by their insistence on judging West Africa by European standards. They did not understand that this region was larger than Western Europe and that it included peoples and cultures as sophisticated and as varied as any other part of the world.

Only recently have Europeans begun to realize the inadequacy of the stereotyped image of pre-colonial Africa as a collection of disorganized and lawless small villages dominated by the fear of their neighbours.[1] One of the reasons for the mistakes made by Europeans in West Africa was that they had blindly accepted this view of African life. They could not look at West African society dispassionately nor could they communicate with its leaders effectively; consequently there were many misunderstandings, often with grave consequences for both sides.

Some of the worst mistakes were made over the issue of West African domestic slavery because few Europeans understood its true nature. They failed to see that it was a complex institution closely related to the societies in which it existed. This was partly because previous European experience had been with the very different slavery of the Transatlantic plantations where slaves were isolated from society to perform one particular task—to produce cash crops. The West African slaves, on the other hand, were not isolated from their fellows and the conditions under which they lived were shaped by local considerations, varying greatly from place to place.

At an extreme were those unlucky enough to be slaves in Old

Calabar or Dahomey and thus liable to be sacrificed in great numbers at such important ceremonial occasions as the funerals of leading men.[2] Equally wretched were the Ibo cult slaves, the Osu, who were outcasts (mainly drawn from the ranks of domestic slaves) living under the sentence of death and never knowing when the day of their execution would dawn; the children of Osu, too, inherited their parents' status.[3]

The vast majority of West African domestic slaves lived safer and happier lives. In 1890 a colonial administrator made a typical comment; "as in West Africa generally" the condition of slavery among the Ewe was not degrading. Because the Ewe slave could own property—even other slaves—and because he was treated as a member of the family, Ellis thought his life was easier than that of an English agricultural labourer at the time.[4] Samuel Crowther, an ex-slave who later became a bishop, wrote similarly about the Yoruba in the middle of the nineteenth century:

> The slaves and masters in this country live together as a family; they eat out of the same bowl, use the same dress in common and in many instances are intimate companions, so much so that, entering a family circle, a slave can scarcely be distinguished from a free man unless one is told.[5]

Even Dr. Madden, a keen abolitionist who spoke out against the British toleration of domestic slavery in the Gold Coast in 1842, felt it necessary to admit that the slaves were mildly treated and were comparatively happy.[6] He was referring to the domestic slaves and not to the trade slave, who was treated much more harshly. The trade slave was not bought as a potentially useful member of the household but as an article which could be sold at a profit. Until he was bought as a domestic slave, the trade slave led a wretched life.

As in the rest of West Africa, the life of a domestic slave in the Sierra Leone hinterland could be described as reasonably comfortable and secure—in comparison to the lives of many slaves elsewhere. Human sacrifice was rare and local custom afforded the slave some protection against a cruel master.[7] With some justification John Myer Harris could tell Sir David Chalmers that native slavery in the Sierra Leone hinterland was "not a hard service at all"; but he went on to make the very doubtful assertion that it was a feudal system.[8]

2

There are considerable difficulties in reaching a clear definition of such a complex and varied institution as West African domestic slavery and in some ways it is easier to start by deciding what it was not. Principally it was not a condition of freedom and the lack of freedom dominated the slave's whole existence. His person, his family, his labour, his time and his skill all belonged to his master.

Nor can it be said that domestic slavery was just another form of serfdom, not unlike that which flourished in medieval Europe; this wrongly implies that the slave was participating in some form of social contract whereby he or his ancestors had voluntarily surrendered some personal liberties to a lord or a master in exchange for protection. One obvious difference between slavery and serfdom is that the serf was bound to the land but the slave was bound to his master. A second difference is that even if one could accept the argument that a West African slave lived as pleasant a life as a serf, he had virtually no status as an individual in customary law. The West African domestic slave was a chattel without the right to appeal to the law on his own behalf; others could act on his behalf in much the same way as individuals or societies can bring the owner of an animal before the British courts to answer charges of cruelty. Nieboer saw a clear distinction between the rights of a slave owner and those of a feudal lord:

> The slave-owner may do with his slave whatever he is not by special laws forbidden to do; the master of a serf may require from his man such services and tributes only, as the law allows him to require. The slave-owner has a right of property; the master of a serf has, so to speak, a *ius in re aliena*.[9]

Similarly in his classic work on the Ashanti, Rattray distinguished between the semi-free and the slave:

> It will have been observed already that a condition of voluntary servitude was, in a very literal sense, the heritage of every Ashanti; it formed indeed the essential basis of his social system. In West Africa it was the masterless man and woman who ran the imminent danger of having what we should term "their freedom" turned into involuntary bondage of a much more drastic nature.[10]

3

A second difficulty in finding a concise and comprehensive definition of West African domestic slavery is that during the nineteenth century the institution was continually changing—not necessarily for the better—to meet new circumstances. We have heard much of the benefits Europe brought to West Africa but the damage done was also considerable. Although Europeans finally outlawed domestic slavery the arrival of European slave traders actually led to an increase in the number of West African slaves and to a worsening of the condition of slavery. The capitalist ethic also persuaded West African leaders to think more of the cash value of their people and less of their social value. Although it is extreme to blame the Europeans for the existence of West African slavery it is clear that the arrival of the Europeans in West Africa at first strengthened and encouraged the institution of domestic slavery there. Anene makes this point when he contrasts the prevalence of human sacrifice in Benin in the nineteenth century (after three centuries of the slave trade) with the favourable reports of Benin from Portuguese travellers early in the sixteenth century.[11] Rodney goes even further in blaming the Europeans when he argues that on the Upper Guinea Coast the evils of domestic slavery, and perhaps its very existence, were as much the work of the Europeans as of the tribes of the interior.[12]

A third difficulty in arriving at a definition is the highly emotive nature of the word "slavery"; it conjures up visions of whips cracking across the backs of gallery slaves, of brutal castrations, of being worked to death in Roman mines or American plantations, or of painful death to appease some sadistic god. Because of these associations it is not easy to look at slavery objectively.

A more promising approach to the problem of defining domestic slavery is that of the anthropologist. Rattray found no less than five grades of servitude among the Ashanti, all called slavery in English. The Akyere was the most wretched—like the Osu he or she was under sentence of death until needed as a sacrifice. Better off was the Domum; originally a prisoner of war or a person received as tribute from a foreign state, the Domum could with the chief's consent be killed at funeral ceremonies. Then there was the Odonko, a non-Ashanti man or woman who had been purchased as a slave. Once in Ashantiland he came under the protection of the local chief and could not be killed by his masters, although he would suffer for his crimes at the hands of the chief's executioners. This status was not hereditary because his descendants were virtually freemen. A pleasanter condition of servitude was that of an Awowa, a person who had been pledged for debt or punished for a crime and whose freedom was only temporarily restricted. Finally, there was the virtually free Akoa whose only form of servitude was his obedience to the authority of members of the local society more important than himself.[13] By showing how complex Ashanti slavery was, Rattray has helped towards an understanding of West African domestic slavery. He has also shown how difficult it is to define domestic slavery clearly and concisely.

Mungo Park, the explorer, tried to define slavery in terms of class structure: identifying it when subordination and inequalities of rank and condition were carried to so great a length that the persons and services of one part of the community were entirely at the disposal of another part.[14] M. G. Smith's definition was similar:

> Slavery is a social institution in which one category of persons—the slaves and their descendants—is placed under the control of another—the masters and their heirs.[15]

Looking at slavery as a form of class division reveals little about the institution itself. These two definitions could just as well be describing serfdom or any form of tyrannical hereditary government. Moreover, they would exclude the slaves like the Odonko who were undoubtedly slaves even though their children were free.

Typically British was the use of the concept of property as the key to defining slavery. This was used both by British humanitarians and by the League of Nations. The *Anti-Slavery Reporter* wrote that

> The word "Slave", in its true sense, signifies a person who, in the eyes of the law, is the property of, and wholly subject to the will of another.[16]

In 1906 L. T. Hobhouse defined the slave as "a man whom law and custom regard as the property of another".[17] The League of Nations produced this definition:

5

Slavery is a status or condition of a person over whom any or all of the powers attaching to the right of ownership are exercised.[18]

The trouble with these definitions is that it is very difficult to define property; moreover, West African ideas of property are very different from those of Europeans. If the concept of property implies the right to sell then those domestic slaves whose sale was forbidden by native custom or by the laws of the colonial powers cannot be defined in terms of property. Property is as inadequate as class structure in providing a definition of West African domestic slavery.

Fage's definition of a slave is much more helpful:

> ...a man or woman who was owned by some other person, whose labour was regarded as having economic value, and whose person had a commercial value.[19]

After setting aside the idea of the commercial value of a person, which is mainly applicable to the trade slave, we are left with two of the basic elements of slavery—ownership and the slave's labour. Yet, this still does not go far enough because a man did not own slaves only for the value of their labour but also for military, political and social considerations. The power and influence of the head of a West African household depended directly on the number of his people—wives, children, other relations, clients and slaves—and the easiest way to increase numbers was to take more wives and slaves. Slaves were sometimes kept to impress others with the power and wealth of their masters—they fulfilled a role not unlike that of the liveried retainers of some medieval barons. Fage's definition is incomplete because it omits the idea of slave ownership for military, social and political prestige and power.

From the European point of view definitions which emphasize economic worth, property, class structure and ownership may suffice but they leave out a factor of the utmost importance to the West African. This is the concept of kinship—the most important single factor in determining how a West African lived. Kinship was vital in assessing a person's worth and status even after European influences had encouraged a more commercial view of one's

6

fellow man. Because he was a member of a kin group the free man could enjoy his personal rights; the slave who had no kin was consequently a non-person without any personal rights.

Slaves in West Africa during the nineteenth century can quite simply be seen as persons without kin. By misfortune or by misbehaviour they had lost their status as members of their natural families and had entered into the new and inferior relationship of slave to master. One can combine these different ideas of slavery to define domestic slaves as those no longer enjoying the status of kinship with their natural families but owned by other people for the economic value of their labour and for the power and prestige they brought their owners.

*   *   *

The relationship of the domestic slave to his master, unlike that of the plantation slave to his, usually developed to the slave's advantage. Once in the new household he began to acquire at least some of the status of kin because he would be protected by his master. When he was thought to be of the household, that is domestic, he was unlikely to be sold again. In time slaves and their descendants earned more and more of the privileges of kinship until it was finally forgotten that some members of the household were of servile origin.[20]

Using the degree of kinship enjoyed in the master's household it is possible to outline five stages of the recently acquired slave's progress to full membership of the family. The trade slave was very badly off because he had none of the rights of kinship and he fared little better than a wild animal except that his owner would not want to lose on his investment by harming the slave; he was either in transit or he was being held while his owner looked for a buyer.

Once the trade slave came to a master who intended keeping him, he was regarded as a domestic slave and was therefore entitled to a measure of consideration. This second stage was like one of probation; for a year or two the slave would be closely supervised and strictly treated. If he proved recalcitrant or tried to run away he would probably be sold. If he settled down well he would progress to the more pleasant third stage. Supervision

7

would be lightened and his life would become happier; he might be given some land and a woman.

With long and faithful service the domestic slave would progress to a fourth stage in which he became a trusted member of the household. In particular the younger generation, which could not remember the household without him, would treat him with the respect due to their elders. Unless the slave committed a crime or unless there was a grave economic crisis, customary law regarded the sale of a slave of long standing as shameful. A slave woman could also establish herself more securely in the household by bearing her master's children. These children were particularly important to masters in matrilineal societies because they belonged to him unlike his children by his free wives who belonged to their mothers' families. A wise slave could make himself indispensable by serving his master as confidant and adviser and he could even be appointed guardian of the minor children at his master's death.

Only the children of slaves could progress to the fifth stage— that of slaves of the house. Because they had been born into the family they enjoyed greater kinship privileges. They were brought up as friends and playmates of their freeborn fellows and they were rarely sold. Nevertheless, although they were well treated they were not allowed to forget that they were the children of slaves. By the third and fourth generations servile origins tended to be ignored and forgotten, particularly if—as was so often the case—these descendants of slaves were closely related by blood to the free members of the household. Sometimes these people became clients or dependents of the houshold and enjoyed the same sort of status as a free stranger who had voluntarily sought the protection of the head of the household.

This general pattern was modified by a variety of factors, local and general, which facilitated or hindered the progress of a slave and his descendants towards freedom or semi-freedom. Social, cultural and linguistic similarities would usually accelerate the assimilation of a slave into his new family; differences would retard it. Assimilation could be more difficult for a slave in a relatively stable society with a clearly defined social hierarchy. In times of uncertainty and unrest a slave could rise to the top rapidly, particularly if he was an outstanding warrior or even a good trader.

In discussing the Eastern Delta States in the late nineteenth century G. I. Jones contrasted the more settled Ijo communities of the hinterland where social mobility was difficult to achieve with the principal Oil River States where bought slaves like the Braid brothers and George Amakiri in Kalabar and Jaja Anna Pepple in Bonny rose to positions of great importance.[21] A less spectacular example is that of Dawa of Wunde, a slave who earned his freedom by valour on the battlefield and became such a powerful war chief that he challenged Kailundu of Luawa, the most powerful figure in the eastern Sierra Leone hinterland.[22]

Sometimes when a weak government offered little resistance to the rise of able men from the servile classes, the rich and powerful used secret societies to preserve the status quo. The Egbo or Leopard Society of Old Calabar was the principal obstacle to the attainment of freedom by slaves; it admitted slaves to the lowest grades of membership only and maintained that a slave had no rights against his master. When the rebellious "Blood Men" made peace with their rulers and masters they promised to stop defying the authority of the Egbo in exchange for an agreement to end human sacrifice.[23]

In Sierra Leone the Poro of the Mende admitted slaves to the lowest grades of membership only and tried to keep them in their lowly place.[24] In the twentieth century slaves were admitted to the Human Leopard Society to perform the menial tasks. Even today in Sierra Leone at secret society ceremonies the descendants of slaves are expected to perform the unpleasant tasks, like the butchering of sacrificial animals.[25]

Another powerful influence on slavery was Islam although its willingness to compromise with native institutions was apparently incompatible with its religious message, makes it difficult to assess how great an impact it had on West African institutions like domestic slavery during the nineteenth century. This is particularly true of Sierra Leone where there were few converts to Islam until the late nineteenth century although there had been a strong indirect Islamic influence for many centuries.

Christian missionaries attacked Islam as too ready to tolerate heathen institutions like slavery and polygamy; one thought that this explained why Islam was so much more successful than Christianity in Sierra Leone late in the nineteenth century. Others accused Islam of actively using slavery to increase its numbers.[26] These accusations are unjustified because Islamic leaders had been concerned about the problem of slavery for a very long time. The Koran only tolerated the institution reluctantly; the Timbuktu historian, Ahmad Baba, had pleaded for the humane treatment of slaves.[27] Sir Abubakar Tafawa Balewa's novel, *Shaihu Umar*, shows how concerned enlightened Moslems were about the evils of slave raiding and slavery in West Africa in the nineteenth century.[28]

Some Moslem peoples were prominent slave raiders in West Africa, even against their co-religionists. The Fulani of Northern Nigeria regarded all conquered territory, Moslem and pagan alike, as hunting grounds for slaves. The Fulani of the Guinea highlands relied heavily on slave labour for their basic needs while they turned their attention to the more specialized arts of religious scholarship and war. In Sierra Leone the Moslem Susu and Fula were prominent slavers.[29]

Nevertheless, a Moslem owner would tend to treat his slaves better than pagan or even Christian owners because he accepted his moral obligation to treat them well. He accepted his obligation to educate his slaves and to seek their conversion to Islam "by chastisement if necessary". From the start the slave was seen as a potential follower of Islam—the religion which has transcended the barriers of race and culture far more successfully than has Christianity. If converted the slave was usually entitled to better treatment—as in Zaria:

> Characteristically, the enlistment of slaves among the faithful proceeded by a ritual similar to baptism among us, at which the slaves were given a new name, the owner providing the sheep for the sacrifice, and meeting various other expenses of the ceremony. By means of this ritual the relation between master and slave was assimilated to that between guardian and ward in many important respects. This ritual assimilation was common for slave recruits, and it was obligatory on the master for all slaves born in his ownership.[30]

Moslem slaves were less likely to be sold than pagans and were more likely to gain their freedom; manumission of a Moslem slave was regarded as an act of piety. Slave converts called their masters Baba (father) and would be called son—a clear indication of the quasi-familial relationship of the Moslem slave to his master.

Masters were responsible for arranging their marriages too. Not all Moslem slave owners treated their slaves as well as the Hausa of Zaria but here and elsewhere in West Africa the influence of Islam led to the better treatment of both Moslem and pagan slaves.

*   *   *

In certain parts of West Africa, especially those where the social and political structures were unstable, economic factors had a greater effect on domestic slavery than social, cultural and religious factors. The hinterland of the Sierra Leone Colony in the nineteenth century contained many petty rulers and war-chiefs who rose to power and fell equally suddenly, bringing down with them the "state" which they had created. Under these circumstances of social and political confusion economic and commercial factors were especially influential. Even the relatively strong and stable centre of Temne power at Port Loko in the nineteenth century rested on trade, particularly the slave trade.[31]

Slavery, in Africa was probably generated as much by economic as by social demands. In economic terms slavery was the means by which society organized its labour to suit its needs.[32] The domestic slave fulfilled a wide variety of economic roles—as an agricultural labourer, as a worker for the community, as a house builder, as a domestic servant, as a carrier of goods, as a medium of exchange and as security for debts. It was no exaggeration to write that in West Africa "Partout, à de rares exceptions près, le captif est source de toute richesse".[33]

The extent to which the slave was used as a cultivator of the land depended first on the relative abundance of farming land. In West Africa during the nineteenth century there was still a shortage of people and a surplus of land. Because a man could leave his village and clear and cultivate some virgin bush for his own use, there had to be some form of inducement or compulsion to make him work for another person. Domestic slavery provided the compulsion. Nieboer carried this argument too far when he concluded that "where all land fit for cultivation has been appropriated, slavery is not likely to exist" but there clearly is a link between domestic slavery and the availability of land.[34] It also follows that where there was abundant land a man's wealth would be reckoned not so much in terms of the land he claimed but rather in terms of the labour he had in order to realize the potential riches of the land.

Where land was highly productive there was a more intense demand for labour, and West African slavery there was highly organized in systems not unlike those of the Transatlantic slave plantations. For example, some of the leading Ashanti possessed estates or whole villages of people working for them.[35] By the middle of the nineteenth century the Transatlantic slave trade had been greatly reduced and European demands for palm products and other cash crops were rising; these further encouraged the use of slaves in something like a West African plantation system.[36] In these larger economic units slaves were often less well treated because they no longer had the personal contacts with free people that they enjoyed on the small farms.

The increasing European demands for West African produce also meant more work for the slave in a second role—that of the carrier of goods. Great strains were placed on the rudimentary system of transport. The transport of West African produce and European manufactures over poorly constructed paths and narrow bridges was a slow and an arduous business. Pack animals were unsuitable because of the shortage of animal fodder, which was bulky and difficult to transport anyway, and also because of the prevalence of tsetse flies. Human carriers who were agile and intelligent enough to cope with natural hazards and unexpected difficulties were best suited to the transport of goods to and from the sea and the navigable rivers. The cost of feeding the carriers en route was high and raised prices considerably. The agricultural producers and the traders did not think they could afford to pay the carriers, so slaves had to act as porters—in many parts slave porters were the only means of transporting goods.

Late in the nineteenth century a Methodist missionary in Mende territory in Sierra Leone noted that "Up to the present every bushel of palm kernels we have had from the country has been brought to the riverain towns by slave labour."[37] Similarly in the Sherbro, District Commissioner Alldridge remarked on the great dependence of trade on slave porterage and the expense and inefficiency of the system.[38] Thirty carriers were needed to transport a ton of kernels, which would fetch about £12 in Britain. As it cost about five shillings a day to feed these thirty carriers it could not be profitable to transport the kernels for more than a few days. Consequently palm kernels further inland were left to rot on the trees. The narrow winding paths further increased the distance to be covered; numerous streams and marshes had to be crossed on unsafe stick bridges or oil palm trunks; and the palm kernels were carried in flimsy palm leaf hampers on the slaves' backs.

In view of all these difficulties the volume of trade to the interior was surprisingly large. By the twentieth century the systems of transport developed by the colonial powers transformed the situation. Good roads, bridges and railways made slave porters much less necessary and this presumably made the abolition of slavery easier. The magnitude of the transport revolution in the interior of West Africa is shown by Lord Lugard's estimate that one train of average capacity carried as much as 14,000 carriers at one-twentieth of the cost.[39]

Less strenuously the slave had a third economic role—service as a unit of currency. Even if unlikely to be sold, slaves served as a measure of their masters' wealth. Before the spread of European currency into the interior of West Africa late in the nineteenth century, the slave was one of the most convenient available units of currency. For example, in Sierra Leone the term "head of money"—in other words one slave—had a commonly accepted value.

> At normal times one head of money representing three pounds in merchandise, perhaps consisting of sixteen bushels of palm-kernels or fourteen gin-cases full of husk-rice was the recognised price of a slave in the Gallinas country on the Coast.[40]

A slave had distinct advantages over other units of currency. He needed less food than livestock and was less likely to succumb to the rigours of travel. By the late nineteenth century the cowrie had been so devalued that the cost of a few days' transport could sometimes exceed their value. Rods of brass, copper and iron, cases of gin, country cloths and puncheons of oil were bulky and difficult to carry. On the other hand the slave was a unit of currency which carried itself and which also served the master as a porter.

Fourthly, the slave acted as a pawn or a pledge. He, or free members of the household, could be pledged by the heads of the household as security for a debt or a loan about to be contracted; the debtor could also pledge himself. This system was fairly uniform throughout West Africa. In effect the pawn was in temporary bondage to the creditor until the debt was paid. Sometimes pledges were made for a limited period to repay a debt but it was more usual for the labour of the pawn to serve as a form of payment of interest on the debt which would have to be paid off in full to release the pawn. The creditor had to maintain the pawn but he was not responsible for his actions in the same way as he was responsible for his slaves' behaviour. If free the pawn had to answer for his actions; if a slave the master who had pledged him was still legally responsible for his actions. The pawn who died had to be replaced and pawnship rights and obligations were inherited by the heirs of the creditors and the debtors. A free person who had been pawned had to work as a slave but it was not forgotten that his bondage was temporary and he was treated more respectfully than the domestic slaves.

Pawning was probably originally a gesture of good faith on the part of the debtor but by the nineteenth century it had developed into a more formal type of business agreement which reflected the growing commercial awareness of the peoples of West Africa. Further evidence of this growing commercial awareness comes from the increasing number of masters who sold their domestic slaves for reasons less pressing than those sanctioned by tribal custom. For example, in the 1890s a substantial percentage of the slaves arriving at the British customs post at Kikonkeh on the Sierra Leone coast were running away because their masters were planning to sell them.[41] There is no doubt that European commercial activity in West Africa tended at first to make the lives of the domestic slaves harder, at least until the colonial rulers acted on behalf of the domestic slaves.

*   *   *

Despite the diversity of West African societies, the different political, economic and social influences on domestic slavery and the various roles the slaves fulfilled, it is possible to get a rough picture of how a West African slave lived in the nineteenth century. To begin with, slavery was one of the means whereby the stronger subordinated the weaker and exploited them. Masters were more often than not kind and considerate, and enlightened self-interest, if nothing else, would persuade them to treat their slaves reasonably well because if they did not do so the slaves would work badly or run away. Also, it was obvious that slaves worked better if they had adequate food and shelter.

The fact remains, however, that the rights of slaves were so limited as to be non-existent. They could not own land or other property, although they were allowed the use of them while in servitude. Those who redeemed themselves or who ran away were completely destitute in theory. Slaves could not exercise authority over their children nor could they marry although they might be allowed to settle down with one woman. Some slave owners deliberately stopped their women from having more than one child by the same man in case they became too attached to him.[42] Except for the often uncertain protection of customary law the person who bore the very real stigma of slavery had little support against the caprices of his master.

It is therefore surprising that there is not more evidence of discontent, like that revealed in the rebellions of the West Indian plantation slaves before 1833. This apparent calm was due not so much to the mildness of domestic slavery as to the fact that the domestic slaves were scattered in small groups in different households and were unable to combine effectively against their various masters. In fact there were some rebellions in which domestic slaves were prominent—that of the Blood Men in Old Calabar, for example.[43] In Sierra Leone Yalunka slaves rose against their Fula masters late in the eighteenth century and in 1838 the Koranko slaves rebelled against their Susu masters and defied them for many years. The Sofa warriors were predominantly of rebellious and runaway slave origin.[44]

Although his condition was grim in theory, the domestic slave in practice usually enjoyed certain privileges. His master could look after him and protect him better than he could do so himself. As a non-person he was not legally responsible for his actions, and his master would have to pay the penalty for his crimes. Sometimes customary law strictly controlled the right of an owner to sell, punish or kill his slave. The master was expected to give his slave a wife and land; typically the slave would be given two free days a week to work his land for the benefit of himself and his woman and children.[45] It was also in the masters' interests to provide wives for their slaves. This not only replenished the supply of slaves, but it also helped to keep the slaves with their masters. Slaves with wives and children were less likely to run away.

The institution of slavery assimilated the slaves into society. Polygamy also performed a similar function and there were close links between polygamy and slavery. Wives and slaves increased the labour force and added to the household. Wives, slave and free, worked with the men slaves on the land. The women sowed and weeded while the male slaves did the heavier work like clearing the ground and small children, slave and free, were mainly responsible for scaring the birds away. Sometimes the head of the household would have a number of houses built—each with a number of slaves under the supervision of one of his wives. It was important to maintain the right balance of male slaves and wives. The more men slaves a man had the more wives he needed to work with them on the land and if he had many wives he needed many slaves to clear the ground for them to plant.[46] Obviously changes in one of these institutions would seriously affect the other one. Some observers concluded from this that polygamy and slavery were the same, that all wives were slaves. Mary Kingsley made the distinction that the master controlled his slaves as an absolute monarch but the husband controlled his wives as a constitutional monarch.[47]

Records of woman palaver cases, that is disputes over women, give support to the argument that wives were little better than slaves. The husbands were apparently only interested in the cash value of their wives when they claimed compensation for their unfaithful or runaway wives. In Sierra Leone wives were sometimes used as prostitute decoys. Their job was to seduce a young man which would give the "injured" husband the right to sue for damages; the young man and his family would be faced with heavy damages to be paid to the husband and if the young man could not pay he would be sold into slavery or enslaved to the "injured" husband.[48]

* * *

Clearly West African domestic slavery was a vital part of the West African social structure and it could not be tampered with lightly. The initial reaction of disgust and horror at the institution from administrators and missionaries was usually followed fairly quickly by the realization that it was no simple matter to abolish it. Hasty and ill-considered action against slavery would seriously damage the West African social structure. Then the men on the spot had to persuade their superiors in Europe of the truth of this, which they usually managed to do fairly quickly.

It was, however, unjustifiable to use the real difficulties in the way of reform as excuses for procrastination and inaction. A difficult problem is not necessarily insoluble. The British colonial authorities argued that before deciding on abolition it was necessary to face the problem of providing alternative forms of social, political and economic organization. This was true enough, and it would have been unwise to abolish slavery at a stroke. Yet, it was dishonest to try to have it both ways by arguing also that because of the iniquitous West African institutions like slavery and polygamy, it was impossible to provide alternative forms of social, political and economic organization. This contradiction explains much of the official reluctance to face up to the problem of domestic slavery in British West Africa during the nineteenth century.

NOTES

1. For comments on this see M. Crowder, *West Africa under Colonial Rule* (London 1968), pp. 10–17.
2. J. C. Anene, *Southern Nigeria in Transition* (Cambridge 1966), p. 35; D. Forde (Ed.), *Efik Traders of Old Calabar* (London 1956), p. 117. Richard Burton was told by King Gelele of Dahomey that those executed at the annual customs were the malignant war-captives and the worst criminals, see R. F. Burton, *A Mission to Gelele, King of Dahome* (Memorial ed., London 1893), I, pp. 247–8. Yet, in her article on Dahomey customs Catherine Coquery-Vidrovitch makes it clear that domestic slaves, criminals and war-captives were all sacrificed at these ceremonies. See Coquery-Vidrovitch, "La fête des coutumes au Dahomey: historique et essai d'interpretation", *Annales, Economies, Sociétés, Civilisations*, XIX, 4 (July–August 1964), pp. 699–717.
3. For more about the Osu see D. Forde and G. I. Jones, *The Ibo and Ibibio-Speaking Peoples of South-Eastern Nigeria* (London 1967, reprint of 1950 ed.); T. O. Elias, *The Nature of African Customary Law* (Manchester 1956), p. 98, argues that the Osu were a separate caste.

4. A. B. Ellis, *The Ewe-Speaking Peoples* (The Netherlands 1966, reprint of 1890 ed.), pp. 219–20.

5. C. M. S. CA2/031, Crowther to Venn, 4 March 1857, cited by J. F. A. Ajayi, *Christian Missions in Nigeria* (London 1965), p. 105.

6. G. E. Metcalfe, *Great Britain and Ghana, Documents of Ghana History* (London 1964), p. 169. Hereafter referred to as Metcalfe, *Documents*.

7. In the late nineteenth and early twentieth centuries cannibal societies were active in parts of the Sierra Leone Protectorate and slaves were sometimes sacrificial victims. See below, Chapter V. See K. J. Beatty, *Human Leopards, An Account of the Trials of Human Leopards before the Special Commission Court* (London 1915).

8. P.P. 1899, LX, *Report of the Royal Commission on the Insurrection and Affairs Generally in the Protectorate Adjacent to the Sierra Leone Colony, 1898–99*, II, 2935. Part I (C.9388) consists of the report by Sir David Chalmers (the Royal Commissioner), observations by Sir Frederic Cardew (Governor of Sierra Leone), and a despatch from Chamberlain (the Secretary of State for the Colonies). References to Part I are given as *C.R.I.*, followed by the name of the writer and the paragraph number. Part II (C.9391) consists of oral testimony and documents; it will be referred to as *C.R.II*, followed by the number of the question and answer or by the number of the document in Roman numerals.

   Harris had traded near the Colony for forty years; in 1865 he had told the Select Committee on West Africa that he disapproved of trading licences and of interference with domestic slavery in the Sherbro lest they annoy the inhabitants and harm trade. See C. Fyfe, *A History of Sierra Leone* (Corrected ed. Oxford 1968), p. 338; hereafter referred to as Fyfe, *A History*.

9. H. J. Nieboer, *Slavery as an Industrial System* (2nd ed. 1910), pp. 38–9.

10. R. S. Rattray, *Ashanti Law and Constitution* (London 1956, 1st ed. 1929), p. 33.

11. Anene, *Southern Nigeria*, p. 22.

12. Walter Rodney, "African Slavery and Other Forms of Social Oppression on the Upper Guinea Coast in the context of the Atlantic slave trade", *Journal of African History*, VII, 3 (1966), pp. 431–43. Both Rodney and Anene are too ready to blame European intervention for the faults of West African society but their arguments are valuable antidotes to the writings of those who see only the benefits of European intervention in West Africa and who ignore the destruction and damage it wrought.

13. Rattray, *Ashanti Law*, pp. 34–46.

14. Mungo Park, *Travels in the Interior of Africa* (Edinburgh 1860, 1st ed. 1799), p. 262.

15. M. G. Smith, "Slavery and Emancipation in Two Societies", *Social and Economic Studies*, Vol. 3, Nos. 3 and 4 (December 1954), p. 243.

16. *Anti-Slavery Reporter*, XIV, 4 (July–August 1894), p. 246.
17. L. T. Hobhouse, *Morals in Evolution*, p. 27; cited by C. W. W. Greenidge, *Slavery* (London 1958), p. 20.
18. League of Nations International Convention on the Slave Trade, Slavery and Similar Conditions, 1926, Article I (1); cited by Greenidge, *Slavery*, p. 21.
19. J. D. Fage, "Slavery and the Slave Trade in the Context of West African History", *Journal of African History*, X, 3 (1969), p. 394.
20. This would not apply to groups like the Osu and Akyere, see above pp. 2 and 4. As European influence brought a more settled way of life to West Africa it became harder for the domestic slave to obtain his freedom in some communities.
21. G. I. Jones, *The Trading States of the Oil Rivers* (London 1963), p. 57.
22. K. C. Wylie, "Innovations and Change in Mende Chieftaincy 1880–1896", *Journal of African History*, X, 2 (1969), pp. 295–308.
23. G. I. Jones, "An Essay on the Political Organization of Old Calabar", Forde (Ed.), *Efik Traders*, pp. 116–17; Anene, *Southern Nigeria*, pp. 34–5.
24. Little, "The Political Function of the Poro", Part I, *Africa*, XXXV, 4 (1965); C. B. Wallis, "The Poro of the Mende", *Journal of the African Society*, 4, No. 14 (1905), p. 185.
25. Beatty, *Human Leopards*; information from a lecturer at Fourah Bay College.
26. C.M.S. G3 A1/0 1888, No. 72, Rev. W. Allan, Report on the State of the Church in Sierra Leone, p. 14; C.S.Sp., *Bulletin*, X, no. 99, p. 138, Report by Father Gommenginger, October–November 1873; Max Gorvie, *Our People of the Sierra Leone Protectorate* (London 1944), pp. 10–11.
27. M. Hiskett, Introduction to C. L. Temple, *Native Races and Their Rulers* (2nd ed. London 1968), p. xxvi.
28. Sir Abubakar Tafawa Balewa, *Shaihu Umar* (London 1967).
29. J. S. Trimingham, *Islam in West Africa* (Oxford 1959), pp. 29 and 18; J. Suret-Canale, *La République de Guinée* (Paris 1970), p. 88; S.L.A., Conf. Abo/N.A. Letter Book, pp. 38–9, J. C. E. Parkes, Remarks on Slave Traffic, 23 July 1890.
30. Smith, "Slavery and Emancipation", pp. 249–50.
31. E. A. Ijagbemi, "A History of the Temne in the Nineteenth Century" (Edinburgh Ph.D. thesis 1968), pp. 73, 102, 103, 113.
32. This is not to say that slavery was the most efficient method of labour organization. Adam Smith had no doubt that slave labour was more costly than free labour, see Adam Smith, *The Wealth of Nations* (Oxford 1869), I, pp. 85 and 390–1.
33. D. Bouche, *Les Villages de Liberté en Afrique noire française* (Paris 1968), p. 66.
34. Nieboer, *Slavery*, p. 303.
35. J. D. Fage, *A History of West Africa* (4th ed. Cambridge 1969), p. 94.

36. The effects of "legitimate commerce" on West African slavery will be discussed in Chapter II.
37. W. Vivian, "The Mendi Country", *Journal of the Manchester Geographical Society*, XII, 1 (January 1896), p. 12.
38. T. J. Alldridge, *The Sherbro and its Hinterland* (London 1901), pp. 35–8. Alldridge spent many years as a trader in the Sierra Leone hinterland. In 1890 he was appointed one of the two Travelling Commissioners for the interior and he later became District Commissioner of Sherbro.
39. Lord Lugard, *The Dual Mandate* (5th ed. London 1965), p. 463.
40. Alldridge, *A Transformed Colony. Sierra Leone as it was and as it is* (London 1910), p. 281. See also Alldridge, *The Sherbro*, p. 217; K. Little, *The Mende of Sierra Leone* (Revised ed. London 1967), pp. 30 and 36–7.
41. See Appendix I. In one period 23 out of the 150 runaways believed their masters were planning to sell them. The sale of domestic slaves was obviously by no means rare.
42. An example of this is cited early in Chapter V.
43. See above, p. 9.
44. H. G. Warren, "Notes on Yalunka Country", *Sierra Leone Studies*, o.s. No. 13 (September 1928); Fyfe, *A History*, p. 283; S.L.A., Conf. Abo/N.A. Letter Book, pp. 98–102.
45. CO 267/501/8463, Probyn to CO, 15 February 1908, encloses report on Sherbro District Native Laws and Customs by Mr. Page. See Warren, Note 11, Chapter V and Thomas, *Anthropological Report*, pp. 160–1. Thomas wrote that among the Temne a slave could be free for one, two or three days a week, and that a Susu slave would be free on Thursdays and Fridays.
46. K. H. Crosby, "Polygamy in the Mende Country", *Africa*, X, 3 (July 1937), pp. 249–64.
47. Mary Kingsley, *West African Studies* (London 1899), p. 439.
48. Alldridge, *The Sherbro*, pp. 122–3.

CHAPTER II

The Development of British Policy towards West African Domestic Slavery after 1833

> The unwearied, unostentatious and inglorious crusade of England against slavery may probably be regarded as among the three or four perfectly virtuous acts recorded in the history of nations.[1]

This statement by Lecky is typical of the traditional rather complacent British view of the abolition of slavery in the British Empire in 1833. It is also inaccurate. Abolition was not prompted by humanitarian motives alone. As Eric Williams has shown, the emancipation of slaves in 1833 was actuated largely by economic motives.[2] In the same way British policy towards slavery in West Africa during the rest of the nineteenth century was dominated by economic considerations; except for the decade after 1833 and perhaps briefly in the 1870s expediency and not philanthropy determined British policy towards domestic slavery.

This is to deny neither the importance nor the consistency of the philanthropic ethic in Britain, but practical difficulties dissuaded the British from following their philanthropic inclinations to emancipate the West African slaves. First, the institution was exceedingly complex and varied from society to society; it was not as demonstrably evil as plantation slavery. Second, until late in the century little of West Africa was British territory and so Britain did not have the legal power to interfere with native institutions like domestic slavery. Finally, the British impact on West Africa profoundly affected its various societies and their economies and thus made it more difficult for Britain to follow a consistent policy.

Yet, it is possible to outline three phases in the development of

British policy in West Africa—three different ways of trying to serve the interests of West Africans as well as those of the British. Although one cannot make clear cut distinctions, one can see that during each phase British decisions were greatly influenced by a particular set of values or ethical standards.

At first the abolitionist ethic was very influential—particularly in the decade after 1833. British policy in West Africa tended to be determined by preconceived attitudes rather than by practical considerations and on occasion principles outweighed expediency. It was believed that Britain must get rid of slavery and other obstacles to progress so that the peoples of West Africa would be free to realize their great potential for progress and development. Second came the conservationist argument, worked out in the 1860s, which was very powerful later in the nineteenth century because of the effective propaganda of Richard Burton and Mary Kingsley and because of the increasing awareness of the practical difficulties facing the colonial powers in West Africa. The conservationists argued that British and West African interests would be harmed by rash interference with the institutions that West Africans had evolved to suit their own needs. With some truth a cynic could describe this as a British attempt to find a moral justification for the triumph of practical considerations over moral principles.

By the end of the century, when Britain was staking her claims to the West African hinterland, a new ethic was being developed. This was in some ways a synthesis of the earlier abolitionist and conservationist ethics. The British Colonial Office was greatly influenced by the developmentalists who argued that the best hope for orderly progress in West Africa was to combine a positive economic policy with a conservationist social policy. Chamberlain's "New Imperialism" reflected this ethic.[3]

The rest of this chapter is a discussion of the development of these ethics in more detail and an attempt to show how British decisions on West African slavery were influenced both by ethical values and also by events in West Africa. Also I hope to show how the existence of West African slavery influenced British policy in West Africa between the emancipation of slaves in the British Empire in 1833 and the "Scramble for Africa" late in the century.

*　*　*

The abolitionist ethic had its greatest influence over British policy in the decade immediately after the triumph of 1833 and its impact was further increased by the great prestige and skill of its leading exponent, Thomas Fowell Buxton. He was free to turn his attention to the problem of West African slavery after the successful completion of his campaign against the West Indian apprenticeship system in 1838. Buxton had great faith in human nature, and he believed that once positive action had been taken to relieve the West Africans of their burdens of the slave trade, ignorance, superstition, polygamy, and human sacrifice, they would be able to realize their great potential for progress and civilization with little outside help.

In 1839 Buxton founded the African Civilization Society to put into effect his guiding principle—"the deliverance of Africa, by calling forth her own resources".[4] West African problems were to be attacked on four fronts. The slave trade was to be broken by strengthening the Royal Navy's anti-slave trade squadron and by treaties with coastal and inland chiefs against the traffic. Factories and trade ships would promote legitimate commerce as an alternative to the slave trade.[5] Model farms or plantations would be set up to encourage agricultural progress. The West Africans would be given moral and religious education.

On 1 June 1840 Buxton presented his plans to a public meeting of the society which was attended by many distinguished supporters.[6] The Prince Consort presided; also present were the Duke of Norfolk, seven bishops, many other peers, the Tory leader—Sir Robert Peel, the Whig Home Secretary—the Marquis of Normanby, and an as yet unknown medical student called Livingstone. Shortly after the meeting Lord John Russell, then Secretary of State for War and Colonies, told Buxton that the government would make him a baronet. The government further demonstrated its faith in Buxton—and its need for radical support—by subsidising the Niger Expedition of 1841 which was intended to prove the soundness of Buxton's ideas for civilizing West Africa.

The membership of the expedition showed the breadth of Buxton's interests and aims. There were four commissioners with the power to negotiate treaties against the slave traffic with the chiefs; scientists and observers were to gather scientific, political and commercial data about the River Niger and the surrounding country; Negroes were to be settled on a model plantation—for which £4,000 had been raised; missionaries, including Samuel Crowther, were sent to assess possibilities of establishing missions in the area.

The expedition set sail in April 1841 and at first all seemed well. Some highly satisfactory treaties against the slave trade were made with local chiefs and land was obtained for a model farm at the confluence of the Niger and Benué Rivers. The mounting hopes of success were rudely shattered in September by outbreaks of fever which killed over a third of the Europeans on the expedition and led to the withdrawal of the three ships. The negro settlers, who had not been stricken, were left on the model farm which had to be closed in 1842 on the grounds that in the absence of a white superintendent the farm had become completely chaotic. By 1843 the African Civilization Society was wound up and the abolitionist cause had suffered a severe setback. Buxton's death was supposedly hastened by the failure of the Expedition; clearly he must have been deeply distressed by the hostile reaction against what *The Times* alliteratively referred to as "brainless Buxtonian benevolence".[7]

Although Buxton's direct influence on British policy was short-lived, the fiasco of 1841 had important long term effects. First, West African affairs had enjoyed the limelight as never before and public attention had been drawn to them. Second, missionary interest in the region had been aroused. As Ajayi has written, Buxton's influence lived on and "in spite of immediate disillusionment, the Niger Expedition of 1841 marks the beginning of the new missionary enterprise in Nigeria. The publicity set in motion a train of events which the failure of the expedition could not hold back"; moreover, Ifemesia has shown that this expedition set the pattern for subsequent British operations in the Niger valley.[8]

Third, Buxton and his fellow abolitionists did much to spread the idea of legitimate commerce as a civilizing agent; trade in "legitimate" products like palm oil would provide West Africa with a remunerative alternative to the slave trade. It was also thought that as West Africans developed a taste for European manufactures they would be more amenable to the allegedly civilizing influences of Europe. This idea of legitimate commerce as a civilizing agent had been warmly advocated by Wilberforce in the 1780s but it was Buxton who was largely responsible for its widespread acceptance in the nineteenth century.

Fourth, Buxton had aroused official interest in West Africa and concern over slavery there. Besides sponsoring the Niger Expedition Lord John Russell also gave positions of great importance in West Africa to two prominent abolitionists who forced the Colonial Office to think more deeply about the implications of the British presence in West Africa. In 1840 Sir John Jeremie was made Governor of Sierra Leone and during his short term of office Jeremie used his authority to issue a proclamation on slavery after receiving critical reports of how Maclean was handling this problem on the Gold Coast.[9] This led to a discussion on whether it was lawful for a British subject to hold slaves outside British territory. In the end Russell ruled that, except in a few particular cases, the laws of Great Britain were binding only in British territory; he did not think that a British subject would incur any penalty by holding slaves in territory where slavery was permitted by law. This distinction was of great importance on the Gold Coast where British territory was limited and if countries outside British territory tolerated slavery "we have no right to set aside those laws or usages, except by persuasion, negotiation and other peaceful means".[10]

Russell's ruling against direct interference with native laws and usages was a dominating influence in British policy until the "Scramble for Africa", except at the time of Carnarvon's reluctant abolition of slavery in the Gold Coast in 1874. Practical considerations were persuading the Colonial Office towards a policy of non-interference even though the conservationist ethic was not worked out until the 1860s. Caution was the keynote until late in the century when international rivalries spurred Britain on to intervene more actively in West Africa.

More significant evidence of Russell's worries about domestic slavery in West Africa was his appointment of Dr. Madden in 1840 as West African Commissioner of Enquiry to look into various allegations made against Captain Maclean, the British administrator of the Gold Coast. In 1837 Maclean had managed to clear himself of the charges that he was tolerating and even actively aiding and abetting domestic slavery. He argued that he had stopped the export of slaves from the coast and that he was doing his utmost to prevent the transfer of domestic slaves from one owner to another on land; although he had no authority to do so he had been trying to mitigate domestic slavery in the territory surrounding British settlements on the Gold Coast. He hotly denied returning runaway slaves to their owners; in fact he had investigated these cases carefully and had been so anxious not to reconsign people to slavery that he had erred the other way and had "frequently screened criminals from well-merited punishment".[11]

Continuing his defence he had argued that even though the system of pawning had been abused he could not interfere with it because the Colonial Office had accepted pawning. Although at the time of the emancipation in 1833 no instructions had been sent to the Gold Coast to act against merchants who owned slaves, he had acted against domestic slavery and favoured the slave wherever possible. Now he thought that the time had come for Her Majesty's Government to consider this extremely difficult problem. The great advances already made on the Gold Coast had presuaded Maclean that "it would greatly conduce to the further advancement of civilization were the question under discussion finally set at rest".

As for the difficult question of fugitives, the British and local governments had for many years followed the policy of mutually giving up fugitive criminals and others. It was undesirable not to return criminals although he returned as few as possible; a peremptory refusal to return a party of fugitives to the King of Ashanti would lead to the seizure by him of perhaps double the number of some tribe under the British flag and in this the King would conceive himself fully justified. If it were promulgated that the British authorities would receive any runaways, "our settlements would speedily be inundated by hundreds and thousands of the offscourings of those countries", and how would the British Government control and maintain these people? Maclean pointed out that the most troublesome problem was that of fugitive slaves. The problems of slavery bedevilled British relations with African rulers and defied solution until Britain had forcibly established direct control over the West African hinterland.[12]

It was the revelation that a slaving ship had been supplied with guns and powder that finally led to the Madden commission of enquiry. Madden, whose abolitionist zeal had made him unpopular, was also shocked to discover that Maclean allowed British subjects on British territory to own slaves despite the abolition of slavery in 1833. The particular case that drew

Madden's attention to this was that of Hansen, Commandant of Fort James, who at his death had left hundreds of slaves.[13]

The Madden Report sharply criticized Maclean for tolerating the scandal of domestic slavery on British soil; it also drew attention to the confusion as to what was actually British territory and to the fact that Maclean had been exercising jurisdiction over areas outside the British forts on the Gold Coast. The new Conservative Secretary of State, Lord Stanley, did not accept Madden's report and appointed a Select Committee, known as the 1842 Committee, to consider the whole West African problem. Although the 1842 Committee disagreed with many of Madden's statements and conclusions it did accept his most important recommendation that the Crown should resume control of the Gold Coast forts and that the extent of British jurisdiction outside the forts should be clearly defined.[14] It also suggested that the problems of jurisdiction and domestic slavery should be solved by establishing a form of British suzerainty or protectorate over the neighbouring tribes:

> Their relation to the English Crown should be, not the allegiance of subjects, to which we have no right to pretend, and which it would entail an inconvenient responsibility to possess, but the deference of weaker powers to a stronger and more enlightened neighbour, whose protection and counsel they seek, and to whom they are bound by certain definite obligations . . .
> In this arrangement we should find the solution of our difficulty in regard to domestic slavery, . . .

The following year this form of protectorate was provided for by the Foreign Jurisdiction Act which authorized the Crown by Order-in-Council to exercise power beyond annexed territory in as ample a manner as if this power had been acquired by cession or conquest.[15] In effect Britain could treat territories near its colonies as British possessions when it wanted to, but without having to enforce British law in them. In this way some of the inconvenient consequences of British expansion were avoided; since the protected territories were not British soil there was no need to enforce British law in them—in particular domestic slavery would continue to be legal there.[16]

* * *

The failure of the Niger Expedition and the difficulties on the Gold Coast showed that there was no easy solution to the problems arising from the British presence in West Africa. Britain was not yet strong enough to abolish the West African institutions it disliked. Yet, even though the abolitionist ethic was shown to be impractical and utopian, official and unofficial opinion continued to pay lip service to it. There was no alternative set of values until the formulation of the conservationist ethic later in the century. The general unwillingness to admit the impossibility of the abolitionist solution led to years of confusion; British policy in West Africa was fumbling and inconsistent, apparently without a sense of direction and purpose.

Lord Stanley at the Colonial Office did try to follow the recommendation of the 1842 Committee to protect British interests in West Africa by indirect means—by informally extending British control. Embarrassing problems like domestic slavery could be evaded by keeping British territory as small as possible. But Britain was already deeply involved in West Africa and the informal empire proved more of a pious hope than a practical reality. The abolitionist lobby was still very influential. For example, in 1849 humanitarian protests secured the rejection of a recommendation by a Select House of Commons Committee, the Hutt Committee, that the Royal Navy kept in West African waters to fight the slave trade should be withdrawn. Missionaries had good reason to press for the extension of British power in West Africa; so did businessmen. It would be difficult for Britain to desert the West African rulers who had co-operated with her. The British administrators, the men on the spot, were particularly aware of the force of this argument and they were sometimes keen to make their reputations by adding to British power in West Africa. Usually the British Government had no option but to support the sometimes aggressive actions of their men in West Africa. So, despite frequent British denials of the intention to build a West African empire during the half century before the "Scramble for Africa" British jurisdiction was steadily expanding from four main West African centres—the Niger Delta, the Slave Coast, the Gold Coast forts and Sierra Leone.[17]

African institutions were affected by this growth of British jurisdiction but they also influenced the way in which British jurisdiction in West Africa was extended and made more effective.

This was particularly true of domestic slavery which provoked heated debate in Britain as well as posing many practical difficulties, like those of fugitive slaves, in West Africa itself. In fact the issue of domestic slavery—and the slave trade—was partly responsible for the breakdown of the policy of informal empire.

After accepting the report of the 1842 Committee, the British Government attempted to keep British jurisdiction over territories near the Gold Coast forts to a minimum. Yet, by 1844 Governor Hill was extending British jurisdiction by a series of bonds by which West African chiefs were ceding legal rights to Britain; he was also trying to regulate domestic slavery. In March 1844 the governor reported that neighbouring chiefs feared that Britain intended to free the slaves in the "Protectorate" and that "an attempt to carry any such measure would cause a revolution".[18] He told the Secretary of State that he had reassured the chiefs that it was only the export slave trade which had been prohibited but he had also ordered the chiefs not to maltreat their slaves nor to allow the sale of domestic slaves by an owner who had inherited them—the new master should consider the inherited slaves as members of his family. Hill reported that the chiefs were satisfied, but that he had no right to make regulations about domestic slavery.

Earl Grey, Secretary of State in the Whig government from 1846 to 1852, at first shared the reluctance of his Permanent Under-Secretary, James Stephen, to add to British responsibilities in West Africa but by 1850 this reluctance seems to have been overcome. In 1850 Britain bought the Danish forts on the Gold Coast and thus consolidated her position as the paramount power there. In 1852 she tried to tax the protected Gold Coast states even though they were technically foreign; this was a decisive theoretical extension of British jurisdiction. The recommendations of Governor Winniett and of two important Gold Coast merchants to pave the way for social progress must have contributed to Earl Grey's change of heart.[19]

On the Slave Coast Britain was also more active early in the 1850s. She aimed to limit the power of the slaving state of Dahomey and to strengthen Abeokuta—an important trading partner and a centre of Church Missionary Society activity. Abeokuta needed its own exit to the sea; so in 1851 Consul Beecroft landed a British force at Lagos to instal a ruler who would allow the free flow of legitimate trade to and from Abeokuta.[20] In 1853 a second landing to establish British control more firmly was considered necessary.

Long before the formal annexation of Lagos in 1861 the British were actively concerned with domestic slavery there. Although the demand for slaves for export was declining sharply, internal slavery was apparently flourishing.[21] Some of the men on the spot intervened on behalf of domestic slaves for humanitarian reasons. Lodder, the Acting Consul at Lagos put pressure on masters to allow the redemption of women and children slaves:

> ... their masters often show great unwillingness to part with them, and it is in many of these cases that my interposition is sought, and although, by perseverance, I have in every case succeeded in obtaining the consent of their masters to the mother's manumission of herself and children at an exorbitant rate compared with the price formerly paid, it has been given with reluctance and bad grace and the caboceers and chiefs have set their faces against increasing the number of the free inhabitants.[22]

The motives of Dr. Baikie and Captain Glover who were opening the Lagos-Abeokuta-Niger route in 1858 were less disinterested. They were short of porters so they declared that any slave who volunteered to serve them would be freed. Not unnaturally their Egba masters were angry and ambushed the expedition which they blamed for the loss of their domestic slaves. Ajayi has argued that it was from this time that more attention was focused on domestic slavery in the area and that the sinfulness of the institution was stressed.[23] When Lagos was annexed in 1861 domestic slavery became illegal on what was now British soil, but it took some time for the British to suppress the institution there.

Meanwhile on the Gold Coast, British relations with the powerful Ashanti to the north of the Fanti protected states were embittered by the problem of runaway slaves. The position of the runaway who had reached British territory was clear; he could not be returned to his master. The position of the runaway who had reached territory under British protection, like the Fanti protected states, was not at all clear. Lords Stanley and Grey had rather unhelpfully ruled that the surrender of runaways on protected territories was not illegal but it was contrary to the spirit of British law and should not be sanctioned.[24] Not surprisingly this problem continued to upset the Ashanti who invaded the Fanti states in 1853.[25]

By the middle of the nineteenth century a new generation of Colonial Office officials were looking at West African problems in a new light. Men like H. M. Merivale and Sir Frederic Rogers were less inclined to see domestic slavery as a plain moral issue but rather as a complex problem which called for sophisticated handling.[26] They were more aware of the relationships of the poll tax, domestic slavery and legitimate commerce to each other and to the whole problem of British jurisdiction in West Africa—as well as of the practical difficulties arising from them.

These difficulties, particularly that of collecting the poll tax, which was first imposed in 1852, prompted the Colonial Office to appoint Major Ord in 1855 to enquire into the situation on the Gold Coast.[27] Ord concluded that the poll tax was a civilizing agent which ought not to be abandoned even though it had yielded little and had caused great resentment.[28] Although Lord Palmerston thought "the most effectual means for securing the concurrence of the Natives in the suppression of the traffic in slaves is to substitute for it the occupations of legitimate commerce," he asked Ord to look at the problem of domestic slavery and pawning and told him that "To eradicate the evil of slavery even in this modified form throughout the protected territory should be the policy of those who represent Her Majesty in the Settlements on the Coast."[29] Nevertheless, Ord's report called for greater respect for the native authorities. He made certain recommendations, like the registration of pawns, which he hoped would modify the system; he thought that for some years to come the British Government would have to tolerate domestic slavery in the protected states where the slaves were treated more like clansmen than slaves.

The Secretary of State, Labouchere, told Sir Benjamin Pine, the newly appointed Governor of the Gold Coast, that he could not accept Ord's recommendations which "would be far too direct a recognition of an evil which is only tolerated because we have not the means of suppressing it", but he approved any measures to ameliorate the condition of the slaves provided the government was not involved in direct interference with domestic slavery.[30]

At first Pine did not accept this; he agreed with the 1842

Committee's recommendation that British jurisdiction must not continue when it compelled the toleration of slavery and involved Britain in slavery cases. He concluded that Britain should give up her jurisdiction and confine her efforts to a few small colonies. British attempts to reduce slavery in the protected areas had failed; in fact, by removing some of its worst abuses Britain might even have strengthened slavery and prolonged its existence—"The effect of our interference may have been to smooth and varnish it for its preservation."[31]

Commenting on Pine's despatch Merivale challenged the view of the palm oil trade as "working its beneficial influence in gradually ameliorating the condition of the large proportion of the Population held in a State of bondage, which is gradually becoming nominal".[32] Merivale thought the British encouragement of legitimate commerce was encouraging slavery:

> ...under the circumstances, any increase of commerce or of production, such as the growth of cotton, ... must inevitably entail an increase of slavery and of the internal slave trade.[33]

There is considerable evidence that legitimate commerce did lead to a rise in the numbers enslaved and to the organization of more strongly disciplined slave labour systems not unlike those of the Transatlantic plantations.

In the palm rich states of the Niger Delta and Dahomey, slaves who could no longer be exported were used in the plantations. Dike has shown how the palm oil trade became the mainstay of the economies of the Niger Delta states after the suppression of the slave trade in the 1840s; Ross has shown similar links between the decline of the slave trade and the growth of the palm oil trade on the Slave Coast early in the 1850s.[34] In Dahomey, after a French firm opened at Wydah in 1841, the palm oil trade grew rapidly until the 1870s when nearly half a million pounds' worth of palm products were exported annually; the new royal plantations were tended by slaves no longer needed for export.[35] Sir Frederic Rogers expressed his concern that the spread of legitimate commerce would make chiefs and slave holders more aware of the commercial value of labour and "that an easy serfdom would thus be changed into a punishing slavery".[36] Writing about the situation near Lagos later in the century an economic historian has recently shown how Sir Frederic's fears were justified:

> The rise of legitimate commerce, far from bringing about the abolition of internal slavery, increased the demand for cheap labour in Africa itself, and slave raiding continued in order to meet growing domestic needs. As a result, there arose a relatively small group of large producers controlling a dependent labour force of slaves and serfs which was responsible for a considerable proportion of the palm produce shipped from Lagos in the second half of the nineteenth century. At Abeokuta and Ijebu Ode, the two centres which supplied the greater part of the produce exported from Lagos, the leading chiefs employed several hundred slaves in the creating of an export surplus for the overseas market.[37]

Similar effects were noted elsewhere. In 1871 the Governor of Sierra Leone attributed Britain's flourishing commerce in West Arica to slave labour. Over a million pounds' worth of produce was being exported from West Africa annually but only a thousand pounds' worth was the product of free labour—and all European merchandise to the interior was carried by slave porters.[38] Writing about the Temne of the Sierra Leone hinterland, Ijagbemi concluded that the need for labour to produce legitimate crops led to widespread slave raiding.[39]

Despite all the problems related to the limited British jurisdiction over the protected states of the Gold Coast, Merivale did not think that the British should withdraw; the problem of domestic slavery should in the meantime be left alone.[40] Yet, by the end of 1857 Pine felt sure enough of himself to attempt to regulate slavery and related institutions. He instructed the courts never to make a slave or a pawn return to his or her master, to emancipate slaves where masters had been cruel, not to act in cases where cruelty had not been proved, to allow only the enforcement of debts if the pawn was the debtor himself and to prosecute any British subject implicated in slavery or pawning.[41]

Sir Benjamin Pine made little progress in solving the problem of slavery; when his brother, Richard Pine, became Governor in October 1862 the most pressing problem he had to face was the old one of runaways from Ashanti territory. Richard Pine refused to return runaways to the Ashanti and the Ashanti War of 1863–

1864 followed. The Fanti proved very unwilling to protect their lands perhaps partly because of their grievances. Heading their list of grievances was British interference with domestic slavery which they alleged had greatly weakened authority and harmed their agriculture; they said that if they had been allowed domestic slaves they would have felt able to supply the British forces with men.[42]

This Ashanti War was followed by yet another parliamentary enquiry; the Select Committee of 1865 recommended that there be no further extension of British power in West Africa and looked forward to the ultimate withdrawal of Britain from the whole region except Sierra Leone. These recommendations were accepted by the Colonial Office but had little effect on the men on the spot. British expansion continued on the Gold Coast and Britain took over the Dutch forts in 1872.

The difficulties with the Ashanti continued but in the Ashanti War of 1873–1874 Britain acted with more determination; she destroyed Kumasi and forced the Ashanti to sue for peace. Then it seemed necessary to review the question of British jurisdiction in the Fanti states. Lord Carnarvon, Secretary of State in the Conservative Government which had taken office early in 1874, recognized the failure of the policy of withdrawal and decided on a formal extension of British jurisdiction. The Gold Coast Forts and Settlements and Lagos were joined to form one colony; then, under the authority of the 1843 Foreign Jurisdiction Act, the Gold Coast Legislative Council was empowered to legislate for the protected territories.[43]

With this extension of British law the problem of domestic slavery in the Fanti states had to be faced. In Britain the abolitionists and their opponents engaged battle on this issue. The victory of the former was the last triumph of the abolitionist ethic in the nineteenth century, but the difficulties which ensued as a result of the abolition meant the triumph of a much more cautious approach to native institutions and contributed partly to the development of the new protectorate status later in the century. This was to help the British to avoid dealing with domestic slavery and related problems.

At first Carnarvon opposed a direct attack on slavery in the Fanti states; in May he told the Lords that repugnant as he found the institution, "the difficulties involved in an immediate and compulsory emancipation of slaves" would be greater than those of allowing the institution to continue and that abolishing slavery would mean increased British obligations in the area.[44] Privately Carnarvon was even less sympathetic to the abolitionist argument; he referred to a coming Parliamentary debate as "this unprincipled attempt to make capital out of the supposed abuses of the slave trade" and argued that since the Fanti states would not be British territory, slavery there could only be "discountenanced and indirectly attacked". Immediate emancipation would be interference with property and would require up to a million pounds compensation for the slave holders "or a very large military force to ensure that such a proclamation is not an idle and undignified threat"; he expected trouble—possibly war—to follow from such a policy.[45]

Carnarvon, however, quickly changed his views. Dr Livingstone, who had campaigned so fiercely against the Arab slave traders in East Africa, was buried in Westminster Abbey in April 1874 and abolitionist feeling was particularly strong at this time. In June allegations that the Gold Coast authorities were sanctioning slave dealing and helping in the recapture of runaway slaves prompted the Aborigines' Protection Society to submit a memorial on slavery to the Colonial Office. The signatories, including three Members of Parliament, urged the abolition of the pawn system and no legal recognition of the status of slavery. The memorial brushed aside the difficulties foreseen by Carnarvon and argued that in return for the benefits of British protection the tribes must be made to agree to the abolition of slavery.[46]

Carnarvon was apparently convinced. On 21 August he wrote to the Governor of the Gold Coast calling for action:

> But the time has now come when it appears to me possible to lay aside the somewhat timid attitude which was, in a great measure, imposed upon my predecessors by the force of circumstances, and even to incur some risk, for the sake of removing the dishonour and moral taint which is incurred by a toleration of slavery, when once that toleration ceases to be a matter of absolute necessity.[47]

Since the British Government had saved the Fanti from the Ashanti it required Fanti co-operation in the abolition of slave dealing and the regulation of the master/slave relationship in such a way that slavery would die out in the not too distant future. Carnarvon foresaw two main problems—compensation for slave owners and looking after the emancipated slaves. He proposed making the import of slaves a crime, the emancipation of foreign-born slaves with compensation of eight pounds per adult to be paid to the owner, and a declaration that all children born in the territories after the end of 1874 should be declared free—a measure which would lead to the extinction of slavery in the next generation.

Governor Strahan preferred stronger action; he advocated the complete abolition of all forms of slave dealing, bartering and pledging, no recognition of the status of slavery in British and in native courts, and the declaration of freedom for all born after a certain date. He opposed compensation to the slave owners whose slaves by their labour had already repaid many times their price and he foresaw little disruption because most freed slaves would prefer to stay with their former masters.[48] He enclosed drafts by David Chalmers of two ordinances which were proclaimed in December 1874.[49] The first abolished all forms of slave dealing but the second—"An Ordinance to Provide for the Abolition of Slavery in the Protected Territories"—fell short of complete abolition. Clause III declared all born in the Gold Coast Protectorate after 5 November 1874 free persons to all intents and purposes. Clause IV stated that no claim or alleged right over or affecting the liberty of any person should be allowed in any court or tribunal. Clause V provided for the punishment of any person trying to enslave another.[50]

For the first time Britain undertook to end domestic slavery on what was technically still foreign soil. This important step was due less to the reforming zeal of the Secretary of State and the Conservative Government than to the particular circumstances in 1874 which favoured the abolitionists. British administrators in the Gold Coast had found themselves involved in problems arising from the toleration of domestic slavery; with the failure of the policy of informal empire and the realization that Britain would not be withdrawing from West Africa it seemed practical to deal firmly with the ticklish problem.

The abolition of domestic slavery in the protected territories of the Gold Coast gave rise to new problems and seemed to justify the forebodings of Carnarvon. The native rulers complained that contrary to previous promises their slaves had been liberated.[51] In January 1875 they presented three petitions in which they complained that the old and well-established custom of slavery should not have been overthrown so suddenly. They made various gloomy prophecies that they would be ruined without their slaves, that there would be a shortage of labour, that the freed slaves would become vagabonds and criminals, and that trade would suffer.[52] Finally, they claimed compensation for the slaves they had bought, but neither Strahan nor Carnarvon were sympathetic.

Members of the Basel Mission in the area reported that except in areas where they had been harshly treated few slaves took their liberty, that generally slave owners were not ruined by the loss of their slaves, that there was no shortage of labour, that trade was not suffering and the freed slaves were not becoming criminals and vagabonds.[53] Most missionaries, however, agreed that further official action was needed to make the emancipation effective; among the suggestions made were the posting of officials to the interior tribes to protect ex-slaves from their chiefs, the assignation of land to ex-slaves, more schools, the use of freed labour to build roads, the legal regulation of pawning and measures to care for frail and old ex-slaves.

Sir David Chalmers agreed that abolition had had few ill effects.[54] He reported little social change, no change in the nature of native employment and no material effect on the palm oil industry; he thought that the comparatively small number of slaves who had taken their freedom had done so to join their families in distant parts. The adverse effects he noted were greater difficulties in hiring labour at the coast and the unwillingness of ex-slaves to do more than just enough to support themselves.

Claridge, who wrote a standard history of the Gold Coast in 1915, agreed that comparatively few slaves took their liberty, but he thought abolition harmed the protectorate and asserted that the few slaves who did take their liberty were idle and disorderly people who turned to crime.[55] Also he thought abolition harmed trade with the interior because traders from the interior feared losing their slave porters in the protectorate where they were legally free and they diverted their trade elsewhere. Another writer has noted that chiefs used the loss of their slaves as an excuse to avoid road building and other public works demanded by the British.[56]

Although a number of slaves were liberated without serious economic and social disruption, the abolition of slavery in the protected territories was not considered successful because it gave rise to new problems. These may have contributed to Britain's unwillingness to extend her jurisdiction in West Africa until very late in the century, and they were certainly used as a way to justify the attempts of the Colonial Office to avoid dealing with domestic slavery. By 1880 Governor Ussher of the Gold Coast and Hemming at the Colonial Office were arguing that the 1874 abolition had been too precipitate.[57]

Nor were humanitarians satisfied that the abolition had been successful. For example, in 1890 Fox Bourne of the Aborigines Protection Society made a series of allegations about slavery on the Gold Coast.[58] He alleged that there were still 5,000 child slaves in the protected territories and that recent cases had led him to conclude that in some cases the colonial government was condoning child slavery. The report of the Governor on these allegations almost seemed to condone child slavery on the grounds that it was for the good of the children to be disciplined, that they benefited by being brought into the Protectorate where they were legally free and that they could leave their masters when they wished.[59] Lord Knutsford's reply to the Aborigines Protection Society was brusque; he warned the Society that its unsupported reports and unwarrantable accusations against the colonial government "must tend to impair the authority of the Society, and to diminish the value which, in view of their excellent aims, would otherwise naturally attach to the representations you are instructed to make".[60]

There is certainly a marked contrast between the reactions of the Colonial Office in 1874 and in 1891 to humanitarian representations about West African slavery. In 1874 Lord Carnarvon carefully considered the opinions of the Aborigines' Protection Society, which probably influenced his sudden decision to end slavery. In 1891 Lord Knutsford unceremoniously dismissed the Society's representations and implied that it was making mischief. The abolitionist ethic had far less influence by the 1890s when Britain was set on her course of expansion in Africa and after the events in the Gold Coast had shown that abolition could cause more problems than it solved. This swing to the right in colonial policy was largely the result of practical considerations but it was also justified by the development of a new set of moral standards in dealing with West Africa—these can conveniently be referred to as the conservationist ethic.

* * *

The development of the conservationist ethic can be traced back to the formation of the London Anthropological Society in 1863. Although it was formed to investigate scientifically the racial characteristics of mankind, this society, as Fyfe has pointed out, tended to turn into a society for proving the inferiority of non-Europeans.[61] The famous explorer, Richard Burton, was a Vice-President of the Society, and he argued strongly against the assumption of the humanitarians that all men were equal; he regarded the people of Africa as inferior and childish beings, incapable of assimilating European culture and the message of Christianity. In his *Wanderings in West Africa*, Burton savagely attacked the Westernized Creoles of Freetown:

> ... our Gorilla, or Missing Link, was the son of an emancipated slave, who afterwards distinguished himself as a missionary and a minister ... no man maltreats his wild brother so much as the so-called civilised negro ...[62]

Another Victorian who travelled in Africa, Winwood Reade held similar views about the inferiority of the Africans and also attacked the Freetown Creoles; he also prophesied that through natural selection the African race would eventually die out.[63]

Later in the century the diary of Major Festing's mission to Samori provides an even more forceful example of the "anthropologist's" contempt for the African, especially those "contaminated" by Western influences.[64] Examples from Festing's diary include—"So great is the conceit of these semi-civilized, half-educated natives"; "I am bound to say the negro who has a coating of European varnish, and who thus fancies himself better than his brother in the bush is worse"; "the semi-civilized nigger is the worst type of animal out—conceited, insubordinate, and worthless". Unlike Burton, Festing had no respect for the African

39

of the interior. At Heremakono where he met Samori Festing wrote:

> The African is double by nature, he has two worlds, not one, and I do not think any amount of communication with the white man will ever change him. One might as well expect him to change his skin. Duplicity is ingrained in him, it will always be so.[65]

Although so much of the "anthropologist" writing was negative and racialist some "anthropologists" did take a more positive view of Africa. Burton, for example, argued that the Europeans should interfere as little as possible with the social systems that the Africans had evolved to suit their particular needs, a very different approach from that of the Abolitionists. A greater respect for African institutions was to be the basic principle of the conservationist ethic worked out by Mary Kingsley late in the century.

Mary Kingsley, a heroine in Britain in the 1890s after her travels in the West African interior, was a very effective propagandist who had great influence in official and unofficial circles. She believed that the Africans were not inferior but different. She argued that the white and black races each had "their particular summit in the mountain range of civilization", that European culture should not be imposed on Africans, and

> Both polygamy and slavery are, for divers reasons, essential to the well-being of Africa—at any rate for those vast regions of it which are agricultural, and these two institutions will necessitate the African having a summit to himself.[66]

Mary Kingsley certainly influenced the imperial policy developed by the Colonial Office under Chamberlain from 1895 to 1903.[67] Her conservationist arguments continued to be influential well into the twentieth century; notably in the establishment of Lord Lugard's system of indirect rule in Northern Nigeria. One of Lugard's colleagues, C. L. Temple, forcefully used the conservationist ethic to justify the preservation of slavery:

> I say without hesitancy that they are far better off as they are in their own households, and that we should be well advised to turn our efforts rather to keeping them there than in encouraging them to claim their freedom.[68]

In the hinterland of the Sierra Leone Colony purposeful expansion came comparatively late. By then the power of the abolitionist ethic had grown weaker both because of the problems which decisive action in West Africa apparently caused and the increasing influence of the "anthropologist" and conservationist approach. Naturally policy was determined by the official and unofficial climate of opinion and British experience elsewhere as well as by local factors.

The problems of the slave traffic and domestic slavery had loomed large for many years. Freetown had been founded by humanitarians late in the eighteenth century to accommodate displaced Africans and to demonstrate the blessings of European civilization to the inland tribes. Particularly important was the campaign to wean them from the evils of slavery and the slave traffic by showing them the advantages of legitimate commerce which was expected not only to enlighten the Africans but also to ensure a steady supply of African products to Europe. Here, as in other parts of West Africa, legitimate commerce failed the abolitionists.[69] Many of those who did take up legitimate trade continued to trade in slaves also and European demands for more tropical produce led to an increase rather than a diminution of slavery.

Ijagbemi has argued that during the nineteenth century the need for more labour to cultivate, gather and transport crops to the coast caused slavery to increase in the Sierra Leone hinterland; he attributed much of the fighting in the area to competition for control of the trade routes and to slaving, and he reported that some chiefs found it more profitable to keep their slaves as labourers than to sell them.[70] Since Europe paid such low prices for tropical products, it is difficult to see how the Africans could possibly have afforded not to use slave labour; the payment of wages to their labourers and porters would have priced their produce right out of the European market. Moreover, Freetown had become rich by exporting raw materials from the interior and importing British manufactures. There were fears that if slavery were abolished the price of tropical products would rise sharply and trade would suffer greatly; this colony for liberated slaves apparently had a vested interest in the continued use of slave labour in the interior.

41

In 1885 Governor Sir Samuel Rowe saw this clearly when he wrote of the grievances of those near the Colony:

> They have an idea that they have been neglected; they are beginning to learn that it is the labour of their slaves which furnishes the produce which causes the trade; they believe that it is the profits on the exchange which have enabled traders to build the houses they see in Freetown, and they think that they should have a greater share in the benefits which the collection of the revenue at Freetown has enabled the Government to give the people there.[71]

Another reason for the slowness of Britain to deal with the problem of domestic slavery in the interior of Sierra Leone was that slave raiding and slave trading had to be dealt with first; and she was not able to do this effectively until she had assumed substantial military and political control of the area. At first Britain tackled these problems by including anti-slaving clauses in its treaties with chiefs, but these had little effect and the interior was ravaged by internecine slaving wars until the conclusion of the Yoni Wars in 1887.

Although these treaties were limited in scope, they laid the foundations for further British intervention in the interior where social and political instability also encouraged the extension of British jurisdiction. These rather haphazard annexations were on a small scale, and they were sometimes made for abolitionist principles. Bulama Island had been technically British since the Royal Navy had hoisted the flag there in 1842 but it was not until 1859 that the Colonial Office sanctioned its occupation by the British and their reluctance was overcome partly by the need to end the scandal of domestic slavery there—on what was British soil.[72] In 1861 Governor Hill annexed part of the Sherbro allegedly to keep the French out and to make the suppression of the slave trade in the hinterland easier; the Secretary of State reluctantly agreed because of the importance of Hill's second argument.[73] There were complications in British Sherbro arising from the fact that the domestic slaves there were legally free. Slaves who claimed their freedom were emancipated but otherwise the problem was swept under the carpet.[74] In 1861 Hill also annexed Koya, but it proved difficult to govern and, except for the southernmost strip, it was returned to the chiefs in 1872.[75] The issue of domestic slavery played a minor role in these annexations and in the annexed territories the Sierra Leone Government made only half-hearted efforts to wipe out the institution.

The French were similarly embarrassed by the problem of West African domestic slavery, which in one case led to a withdrawal from annexed territory. When Walo and Dimar in Futa-Toro were placed under direct French administration in 1882 the Senegal authorities began to enforce the liberation of slaves there —technically obligatory since France had abolished slavery in 1848.[76] These regions were almost depopulated by the subsequent exodus of slave owners with their slaves with the result that France abandoned annexation in 1890 and placed them under French protection instead. Slavery again became legal in what was technically foreign soil.

Despite Sir Arthur Kennedy's optimistic assertion in 1870 that the very mild institution of slavery was curing itself without delay, the Sierra Leone Government was plagued more and more by the problems arising from domestic slavery as British jurisdiction in the hinterland was extended.[77] In 1879 when Britain established a Customs post on Kikonkeh Island, near the mouths of the Skarcies Rivers, the local chiefs were so upset by rumours that the colonial government was preparing to abolish slavery in the Skarcies area that they tried to repudiate their treaty with Britain.[78]

In non-British Sherbro, confusion over the nature and extent of British jurisdiction caused further complications. Non-British Sherbro had been annexed by Governor Turner in 1825 but the Secretary of State had repudiated the treaty of annexation. Nevertheless, in 1879 the Crown Law Officers ruled that since Turner's Treaty had never been declared invalid, it was still British territory and British jurisdiction was still in force there.[79] As elsewhere, Britain was faced with two dilemmas in non-British Sherbro. First, although Britain claimed jurisdiction, the Sierra Leone Government lacked the resources to assume active jurisdiction against the will of the local rulers; but if it tried to do so it would have to enforce British laws which would entail the suppression of slavery and other measures which would anger the local rulers so much that they would refuse to co-operate with the Government. Second, slaves were running away to British Sherbro where they were legally entitled to their freedom. This infuriated the chiefs of non-British Sherbro on whom the Government relied for the trade in legitimate produce, and it also deprived them of the slave labour so necessary to increase the trade and revenue of the Colony.[80]

In 1885 the disturbed state of the hinterland and the consequent dislocation of trade prompted the Sierra Leone Association to press for an extension of British jurisdiction; Sir Samuel Rowe thought that domestic slavery would be a major obstacle to such a plan.[81] Samuel Lewis, a leading Creole lawyer, wanted Britain to acquire "a more permanent jurisdiction in and over these territories", but he opposed the use of force and believed "annexation by purchase to be more desirable" than proclaiming a protectorate.[82] He was vague as to how jurisdiction would be established, possibly because of the existence of domestic slavery—an institution which he was prepared to tolerate in a benign form although he was no advocate of slavery.[83]

* * *

During the 1870s the successes of explorers had aroused fresh interest in Africa and the stage was set for the effective European penetration of the continent in the 1880s and 1890s. At first there was confusion and hesitancy over the question of British jurisdiction in West Africa. However, a series of international developments—notably the "Scramble for Africa"—changed the situation. This race of the European powers to take over territory from the allegedly barbarous or semi-barbarous rulers of Africa made it necessary for the Foreign and Colonial Offices to think carefully about the nature of British jurisdiction. Despite general agreement on the need to extend British power there were worries about the difficulties that over-hasty action could cause. Under these circumstances official circles began to work towards the definition of a new form of protectorate over foreign soil.

Early in the 1880s alarm over the danger of French intervention in the Oil Rivers led to a rather desultory discussion at the Foreign Office of the possibility of a British protectorate to keep the French out; there was also a more general discussion of the implications of such a move.[84] By May 1884 it was decided to extend British control and protection over the Oil Rivers and

44

Camerouns by a series of treaties which would also open the interior to British merchants.

The Foreign Office still had only a vague idea of the implications of this new form of protectorate. Memoranda from Sir Edward Hertslet, Librarian at the Foreign Office, show this clearly. In April 1883 Sir Edward repeated the established theories about protectorate status in reply to questions from T. Villiers Lister, Assistant Under-Secretary for Foreign Affairs.[85] He wrote that a protectorate implied an obligation on the part of the protecting state to protect and defend the protected state, which would not normally enter into agreements with other states. The usual form of establishing a protectorate was by treaty, and he mentioned different precedents. The following year, when the Berlin Conference made the need more urgent to clarify the protectorate concept, Hertslet wrote about the formalities necessary for the annexation of territory—again in reply to Lister.[86] His answers were still vague; he wrote that there was no generally recognised form for taking over uninhabited territory, that there was no general rule on how far inland annexations extended and that there were no established formalities for annexation—the consent of the inhabitants was not necessary on all occasions. He concluded that it was very difficult to distinguish clearly between annexation and protection.

At the Berlin Conference in 1884 and 1885 the great powers met to discuss three main issues—the freedom of navigation in the Congo and Niger Rivers, the freedom of commerce in the Congo basin, and "A definition of formalities necessary to be observed so that new occupations of the African coasts shall be deemed effective".[87] Britain, France and Germany settled the first two issues without undue friction. The General Act of the Conference provided for the freedom of trade and navigation in the relevant areas and there was agreement on the slave trade and slavery. The slave trade was banned in the Congo basin, and the signatories committed themselves to strive for the suppression of these evils in other parts of Africa.[88]

On the third issue—that of protectorates and jurisdiction— Britain strongly opposed the view of France and Germany that protectorates would entail jurisdiction—in other words, administrative and judicial responsibility. This was mainly due to the insistence of the Lord Chancellor, Lord Selborne, that there was a clear distinction between annexations and protectorates:

> *Annexation* is the direct assumption of territorial sovereignty. *Protectorate* is the recognition of the right of the aboriginal or other actual inhabitants to their own country, with no further assumption of territorial rights than is necessary to maintain the paramount authority and to discharge the duties of the Protecting Power.[89]

Later in the month he argued that it made little difference to France and Germany whether their overseas territories were protectorates or annexations but that the failure to distinguish them would have undesirable results for the British Empire, notably that "if we annexed any territory, slavery must at once cease to exist".[90]

So Sir Edward Malet, the British negotiator at Berlin, was instructed "to contend that it would be an inconvenient precedent to confound the two systems".[91] The British won the day and there was no compulsion to extend jurisdiction over protectorates. The General Act did contain two significant clauses which showed that the great powers had moved towards a definition of protectorate status and the jurisdiction it implied.[92] Article 34 used the word "protectorate" for the first time in an international agreement and it stipulated that powers acquiring possessions or proclaiming protectorates on the African coast should notify the other signatories to give them the opportunity of making any claims of their own. Article 35 obliged the signatories to

> insure the establishment of authority in the regions occupied by them on the coasts of the African Continent sufficient to protect existing rights, and, as the case may be, freedom of trade and of transit under the conditions agreed upon.

The colonial powers made a series of bilateral agreements demarcating their spheres of influence after the Berlin Act and they met again at the Brussels Conference of 1889 to 1890 to spell out how they were carving up Africa and establishing their authority over the Africans. The Brussels Conference was partly prompted by genuine humanitarian impulses. After public opinion had been aroused by Cardinal Lavigerie's crusade against the slave trade, Britain asked the King of the Belgians to take the initiative in inviting the powers responsible for the control of Africa to a conference at Brussels "to consider the best means for securing the gradual suppression of the Slave Trade on the Continent of Africa, and the immediate closing of all the external markets which it still supplies".[93]

Regrettably the Conference also served to mask the less altruistic motives of the great powers.[94] The Conference, however, did agree on decisive action against the slave trade by land and sea in the General Act of the Brussels Conference Relative to the African Slave Trade which was signed at Brussels on 2 July 1890.[95] Article I provided them with the means of extending their jurisdiction and consolidating their authority over large regions of Africa—to sanction the partition of Africa as well as to suppress the slave trade. It stated that the most effective ways to counteract the slave trade were for the civilized powers to establish administrative, judicial, military and religious services, to build good roads, railways and systems of telegraphic communication, and to restrict the arms and ammunition traffic. Despite this assumption of wide powers the signatories did not commit themselves to decisive action against the slave trade and slavery. Although Article V was an undertaking to legislate against slave traders and raiders within a year, Article III allowed the signatories to proceed gradually with the suppression of the slave trade as circumstances permitted and by any means they considered suitable. Other articles provided for the liberation of slaves being conveyed or traded in, for sanctuary and letters of freedom for fugitives, for refuges for women, and institutions for liberated slave children, for action against the slave traffic by land and sea, and for the control of the liquor, arms and ammunition trades.

At the same time the Foreign Office was considering the enactment of a new Foreign Jurisdiction Act.[96] The last comprehensive Act of this nature had been passed in 1843, and, according to Mr. James at the Foreign Office, it had given Britain jurisdiction in territories under settled rule and its "avowed object was to put a stop to the lawless crimes which were being committed with impunity in the Levant by English subjects, and especially by those who were natives of Malta and the Ionian Islands".[97] Subsequent Foreign Jurisdiction Acts had applied to countries not under settled government. For example, in 1861 the colonial authorities in Sierra Leone had been empowered to exercise jurisdiction in adjoining uncivilized territories.[98] By the late 1880s Foreign Judisdiction Acts were being applied to African territories under the exclusive protection of Britain—territories where British officers monopolized any extra-territorial jurisdiction being exercised. Later in the 1880s the Foreign Office thought the time had come to consolidate the 1843 and subsequent acts into a new and comprehensive Foreign Jurisdiction Act.

There were various reasons for this decision. First, it was realized that the old treaty system was unsatisfactory and so vague that it could lead to disputes and diplomatic complications with other powers interested in Africa. Second, since the Berlin Conference had given the concept of protectorate status international recognition, it had become necessary to define it more clearly, particularly to remove doubts as to the extent of Her Majesty's Government's jurisdiction in protected territories and her power over foreigners there. Third, the establishment of the German Protectorate in East Africa, and more particularly the extension of German protection over the Solomon Islands in 1887, had persuaded the Foreign Office of the need for a new act to protect British interests in her so-called spheres of influence. Ilbert gave an example:

> The establishment on the Somali coast of British courts, having full powers to deal with foreign cases as well as British, would certainly facilitate, and might not improbably bring about, the withdrawal of French consular officers from the same part of the coast.

The 1890 Foreign Jurisdiction Act extended British jurisdiction over all peoples in its protectorates and marked a significant advance in the acquisition of authority over British spheres of influence in Africa. It also marked Britain's acceptance of the view of France and Germany that the existence of a protectorate in an uncivilized country gave the protecting power the right to assume whatever jurisdiction it deemed necessary for the exercise of protection.[99] After the Berlin Conference Britain had moved towards the new idea of a protectorate which could be treated in much the same way as annexed territory, but the legal distinction between the British soil of the colonies and the foreign soil of the protectorates was not forgotten. Britain could assume the powers she thought necessary without having to shoulder the full responsibilities of administering British territory—including the obligation to end slavery.

*   *   *

Two British Protectorates established in the decade between the Berlin Conference and the arrival of Joseph Chamberlain at the Colonial Office in 1895 show how this new concept of protectorate status worked out in practice. The question of the form of government over the Niger Delta area—the Oil Rivers—aroused great interest. Traders, missionaries and officials sought to protect their interests and safeguard their futures in this area which was so rich in palm products. The Berlin Conference and the arrival of the Germans in West Africa made it clear that the decision of May 1884 to make treaties with local chiefs was inadequate to protect British interests there.[100] For this reason and because of criticisms of the Royal Niger Company's handling of affairs there the Foreign Office appointed Major MacDonald in December 1888 to report on the Oil Rivers region.[101] After reading MacDonald's report, Sir Villiers Lister concluded that because the country was rich and had a flourishing trade it could be self supporting with decent management and should be made a Crown Colony.[102] He also thought it desirable to put an end to the uncertainty and intrigues there. Lord Salisbury disagreed because what was suggested would amount to "Queen's Govt with continuance of slavery", which was impossible.[103] Clearly Salisbury's own judgement and not humanitarian pressure influenced his decision; the following year he called the Aborigines' Protection Society "foolish people, without much weight" when they made proposals for the administration of the Oil Rivers.[104]

Lister continued to support the establishment of an Oil Rivers Colony; he thought there would be only two important difficulties.[105] He did not think that the problem of revenue would be very difficult to overcome, but he agreed that the problem of slavery would be somewhat difficult to deal with because the native chiefs would be unwilling to give up their slaves and British philanthropists would clamour for total and immediate emancipation. Even then Lister did not find the difficulties of slavery and the slave trade very great. The export slave trade was ended, slave raids had ceased and the slaves were well treated as a rule; he thought it would be possible to tolerate the institution within a colony while gradually abolishing it. Salisbury did not accept this argument because slavery could not be tolerated on British soil, and so the Oil Rivers did not become a colony but a form of protectorate not unlike a strengthened and extended consular administration. The Foreign Office instructed MacDonald who became the first Commissioner-General to pave the way for direct British rule by developing legitimate trade, by promoting civilization, by inducing the natives to relinquish their barbarous and inhuman customs and by gradually abolishing slavery.[106]

A little later the new concept of protectorate status was more clearly embodied in the Gambian Protectorate. Even after the Anglo-French Conference of 1889 had settled the limits of The Gambia, Britain delayed establishing a system of government over the territory adjacent to the colony.[107] Britain was unwilling to spend the money to establish an effective administration because after half a century of strife the traditional authorities were weak, and because there were difficulties in settling the final details of the Anglo-French boundaries. Slavery also posed problems which could only be avoided as long as Britain did not exercise direct rule. Under these circumstances a protectorate over the Gambian hinterland seemed to be the only answer. In January 1893 two Travelling Commissioners were sent to pave the way for its proclamation. There were clashes with local rulers over domestic slavery and it was decided to tolerate the institution while attempting to modify it. It was hoped that the institution would wither away in the face of official disapproval. In 1894 the Gambian Protectorate Ordinance came into effect. In the same year a Slave Trade Abolition Ordinance made various provisions modifying slavery in the Gambian Protectorate and provided for its end by giving slaves freedom when their masters died. By 1897 Administrator Llewelyn was optimistically reporting that

> Domestic slavery—the only form that now exists—is moribund, as the slaves all know their position, and without any violent measures being resorted to by the Government, the whole fabric of slavery is gradually and rapidly crumbling to pieces.[108]

As the examples of these two protectorates show, officials were more conservationist in their approach to African society than they had been earlier in the century. The strongest argument for conserving or tolerating slavery was that abrupt abolition would lead to social and economic disruption, as it had in the Gold Coast in 1874. It is true that there was disruption after 1874 but it is hard to assess to what extent this can be attributed to abolition and how much to other facets of British expansion. All over West Africa the arrival of Christian missionaries and teachers, the growing numbers of traders penetrating the interior, the influx of European goods and currency, demands for labour and taxes, and interference with the political and judicial prerogatives of the local rulers all weakened and disturbed the religious, cultural, economic, political and judicial systems of traditional organization. British official circles, however, emphasized the suppression or limitation of slavery as a cause of disruption presumably to justify British expansion and to distract attention from the more unsavoury aspects of British expansionism.

A second practical difficulty that faced the Colonial Office was a chronic shortage of men and money. The rapid growth of the Empire and the need to consolidate British power in so many parts of the world made heavy demands on British resources. Not unnaturally the Colonial Office would not be eager to force the abolition of slavery on unwilling chiefs and to take on the responsibility of working out alternative forms of labour organization. Since British armed forces were spread over the globe caution was advisable in treating with African rulers—particularly on the delicate issue of domestic slavery. Britain had worked hard to end the slave trade by sea and by land with considerable success. Since the suppression of the slave trade had cut off fresh supplies of domestic slaves it could be argued that there was no urgent need to attack the problem of domestic slavery.

Unofficial circles were also adopting a more conservationist attitude towards African institutions. This was particularly true of the mercantile interest which had close links with Mary Kingsley, the most effective proponent of the conservationist ethic. Before the last two decades of the nineteenth century the trade in palm products had been very profitable, and the merchants and traders had been content with the minimal protection given to them in the British spheres of influence. When times were bad, however, the various groups comprising the mercantile interest tended to seek official help. There were the numerous independent resident traders who did much to spread British influence in the interior; in 1879 Governor Rowe praised the enterprise of the Aku traders from Sierra Leone who had penetrated deep into the hinterland with European merchandise and brought back palm kernels which would otherwise have rotted on the ground.[109] During the last two decades of the century these traders suffered greatly from the decline of the trade in tropical products as well as from the monopolistic activities of the Liverpool and London firms. This partly explains why the Sierra Leone Association was pressing for the extension of British jurisdiction over the Sierra Leone hinterland in 1885.[110]

By late in the century the independent expatriate traders were no longer an important factor to be reckoned with, because they were being taken over by British firms based in Liverpool, London and Manchester. These firms used their municipal Chambers of Commerce to put forward their views. Particularly vocal as the palm oil trade declined was the Committee of the African Trade Section of the Liverpool Chamber of Commerce, and John Holt served as its Vice-Chairman for eighteen years.[111] Holt had close links with Mary Kingsley who argued so strongly against the sentimentality of the humanitarian and abolitionist view. She called for a new colonial policy based on anthropology, but he quarrelled with her over the nature of this policy. He wanted the minimum of interference, while Kingsley's views were more imperialist.[112] Holt had a happier relationship with E. D. Morel who managed to synthesize the ideas of Holt and Kingsley after the latter's death in 1900.[113]

Although Holt and others with commercial interests in West Africa believed in the minimum of British interference compatible with free trade, they began to press for the extension and development of Britain's West African Empire early in the 1880s. They needed official help to persuade the West Africans to turn to the legitimate trade which would supply commodities for a profitable trade with Europe.[114] Few saw slavery as an obstacle to the development of West Africa's commercial potential. One obstacle that the mercantile interest did persuade the British Government to remove was that of the middleman trading states. For instance, in 1881 Holt wrote to the *Liverpool Daily Post* complaining that Jaja of Opobo, a Niger Delta state, was an obstacle to his trade, and he urged that the British Consul be given greater powers "to deal more effectively with the petty chiefs who at present are allowed to squabble as they wish to the great detriment of trade with this country".[115] Mounting pressure from the mercantile interest led Acting-Consul Johnston to send Jaja to Accra for trial in 1887. This shabby incident—Salisbury said Jaja's "deportation" would be called kidnapping in other places—did not really benefit British trade.[116] Similarly, when Nana, Governor of Benin River, was driven out, tried and exiled in 1894 it was expected that Europeans would then be able to move inland without hindrance and that exports would increase greatly. On the contrary, unrest in the area spread and exports declined by a third; the Europeans who—unlike Nana—could not use slave porters found it prohibitively expensive to travel inland.[117]

Even humanitarian circles lacked the abolitionist zeal displayed by Buxton half a century before. As their influence had declined and as many had accepted the need for compromise in dealing with African problems, their earlier radical enthusiasm had faded. Although united against such obvious evils as witchcraft, fetish, human sacrifice and infanticide they were divided on domestic slavery. They were no longer unanimously convinced that it was a social evil and some even felt that emancipating domestic slaves might do more harm than good. The three principal humanitarian pressure groups putting forward their remedies were the missionaries, the Anti-Slavery Society and the Aborigines' Protection Society.

From the beginning Christian missions in West Africa had been potential agents of disruption. They opposed the traditional religions of the people and threatened traditional authority—that of the father over his family, of the chief over his people and of the master over his slaves. Some earlier missionaries, like Hope Waddell, were conscious revolutionaries:

> Revolution in Old Calabar, recorded Waddell, was inevitable. It was a sign of the progress of the Gospel when in the name of Christianity, slaves disobeyed their masters' orders, children were at loggerheads with their parents and women flouted the authority of the Egbo. It was expected that within nine years the Efik would be completely converted and accept the moral and social codes of Europe.[118]

Clearly Waddell saw Christianity as an agent of political and social reform and he was not prepared to separate the Church and the State in West Africa.

This refusal to distinguish between temporal and spiritual liberty was shared by most early missionaries. That is why so many of the first converts were slaves; in fact, many missionaries saw the slave classes as the nucleus of their membership. As late as 1886 Father Lutz of the Holy Ghost Fathers decided to concentrate on charitable works and converting the slaves at his new mission at Onitsha.[119] Baptisms were confined to the sick, the outcasts and the slaves. His money went on the redemption and education of slave children—a policy which could well have pushed up the price of slaves and led to the enslavement of more children. There was mounting hostility to this mission which encouraged slaves to leave their masters, and in the region Christianity was scorned as a religion fit only for slaves. The mission continued to have little success until it decided to educate free children as well.

Not only did activities like those at Onitsha incur the hostility of slave owners, but the missionaries were at first doubtful whether slave owners were entitled to baptism. It was on this issue that the Christian missions made one of their earliest compromises with West African institutions. The Presbyterian missionaries of Calabar had broken off communion with the American Presbyterians in 1849 because the Americans allowed slave owners in their church, but in 1853 the Calabar Presbyterians argued that they should baptize slave owners who undertook to treat their slaves well and not to sell them.[120] The mission could not be a success if slave holders were excluded and the missionaries had to tolerate the social evil of domestic slavery in the meantime. The Foreign Mission Committee agreed with the Calabar missionaries because

> ... in Calabar it was necessary to tolerate slavery temporarily so that the Christian Church could be established, and when Christians became the majority and could influence laws, slavery could then be abolished.

More cynically it could be argued that the Presbyterians were not prepared to jeopardize the success of their missionary efforts

by taking a firm stand against such an important local institution.
The Church Missionary Society was bothered by the same
problem. In 1879 it drew up regulations prohibiting the acceptance of slave owners as full members of the church, but these did
not work; when the Society reissued these regulations in 1888 the
local Christians refused to accept them and warned that

> . . . anti-slave propaganda in the interior of Yorubaland would
> result in "a wholesale slaughter of the Native Christians, the
> plundering and expulsion of our beloved white missionaries, and
> a total extirpation of Christianity."[121]

When a Church Missionary Society interpreter and a schoolmaster
at Onitsha flogged two slave girls so severely that one of them
died, it became clear that even church agents were keeping
slaves.[122] In 1888 T. J. Sawyerr, a leading Creole merchant in
Freetown, presented a paper to the Native Church Conference
arguing that the Church should tolerate domestic slavery and
polygamy.[123]

Even in London there were signs that Christians were accepting
the separation of the Church and State and the distinction between spiritual and temporal liberty. In 1889 the Archbishop of
Canterbury sent the Foreign Office two resolutions passed by a
meeting of humanitarians at Exeter Hall.[124] The meeting agreed
that domestic slavery was wrong but recognized that its abolition
could not be compelled by external force and confidently hoped
that the advance of Christianity and civilization would in the near
future bring about its entire suppression. With so many problems
arising from domestic slavery it is not too surprising that by the
end of the nineteenth century the Churches wanted to evade the
issue as much as possible. It was not until the twentieth century
when Britain had consolidated her hold on her West African
Empire that the suppression of domestic slavery seemed practicable. It was then that the Churches vociferously began to condemn
the institution again.

The humanitarians of the Anti-Slavery Society and the
Aborigines' Protection Society had lost official sympathy and
presumably also public support by the 1890s.[125] A series of
blunders had made them seem tiresome do-gooders and

troublesome cranks to many; what Fyfe wrote of the two societies earlier in the century was equally true in the 1890s:

> Both suffered by becoming too often the mouthpiece of those more interested in their own than in others' welfare. Ready to support any self-constituted victim, to believe the worst of any colonial government, "Exeter Hall" (so-called from the place where they held their public meetings) tended to weaken the protection it sought to extend by alienating those who might have helped extend it.[126]

The blunders of Exeter Hall, the practical difficulties of abolition and the lack of concern with African rights and interests during "The Scramble for Africa" meant that the humanitarian influence was at its lowest in the 1890s.

Nevertheless, the Anti-Slavery Society did not stop campaigning against slavery. In 1894 it attacked Sir Edward Grey, then Under-Secretary of State for Foreign Affairs, for defending the toleration of domestic slavery in the newly proclaimed Uganda Protectorate. The *Anti-Slavery Reporter* did not agree with Grey's argument that the protecting power should preserve the laws and institutions of a protectorate as far as possible. It pointed out that slavery had been abolished in the Gold Coast Protectorate and that the suppression of the slave trade did not mean a natural death for slavery—only complete abolition would end slavery.[127] But, as the *Anti-Slavery Reporter* shows, during the 1890s the Society was primarily concerned with slavery in East Africa, and surprisingly little attention was given to the institution which was still flourishing in West Africa.

The Aborigines' Protection Society seemed less interested in the speedy abolition of slavery and more concerned with the protection of African societies than their reform. Under the dominating influence of H. R. Fox Bourne, Secretary of the Society from 1889 until its amalgamation with the Anti-Slavery Society in 1909, the Aborigines' Protection Society was apparently guided by the conservationist ethic. Fox Bourne was certainly an advocate of it. In 1900 he told the International Congress on Colonial Sociology that only reasonable persuasion should be resorted to in the abolition of slavery and other barbaric institutions. He also warned the Anti-Slavery Congress in 1900 that premature attempts to abolish domestic slavery before the people were ready for the change could lead to mischief unless the reformers had something better to put in its place.[128]

*   *   *

When Joseph Chamberlain became Secretary of State for the Colonies in 1895 great changes were expected. There was some surprise that such a powerful politician had not taken one of the top-ranking ministries. Great achievements were expected and Chamberlain made his presence felt at the Colonial Office by reorganizing its administration. Moreover, his term of office coincided with a more vigorous programme of British expansion in Africa. In view of Chamberlain's energy and his radical Unitarian background one would have expected abolitionist zeal to inspire him to speedy action against native institutions like domestic slavery. In fact, official papers show that Chamberlain approached African problems with surprising diffidence and that he was quite amenable to persuasion from his Parliamentary Under-Secretary, Lord Selborne, and his permanent officials.

He may not have been aware of his greatest achievement as Colonial Secretary—the formulation of a new ethical approach to the problems of Africa and other allegedly "barbarous" regions. This was a compromise and a synthesis between the abolitionist and conservationist ethics. This new approach, which can conveniently be called the developmental approach, was to be very influential in the British Empire in the twentieth century. Developmentalism sprang from the failure to establish a profitable trade with West Africa on the one hand and from the practical difficulties in the way of radical reform of the "barbarous" societies on the other hand. There were two main elements of the new developmental approach. In the economic sphere a reforming or abolitionist policy seemed to dominate. The African economies were to be Westernized; they were to be given a new economic infrastructure which it was hoped would enable West Africa to establish a profitable trade with Europe. Good roads, bridges, railways and technical help would be needed; the people would have to be taxed and taught the virtues of a cash economy. Under close administrative control the West Africans would thus be able to farm for export on a large scale. At the same time in the social and political sphere the conservationist approach was expected to mould the formation of policy and the administration of West Africa. There was to be the absolute minimum of interference with local governments and institutions. It was hoped that this combination of economic progressivism and social and political conservatism would secure the co-operation of the West African peoples in the development of a vast imperial estate.

The developmental synthesis could not work in practice because it was impossible to isolate economic from social and political considerations in such a way. The West African economies were too closely linked with local societies for such an arbitrary separation to work. The result of the attempt to apply the developmental approach was confusion and contradiction in Britain's colonial policies, especially in West Africa. These confusions and contradictions were particularly evident in the Sierra Leone Protectorate where the British presence was not effective until well into the twentieth century and where Britain continued to tolerate domestic slavery until the beginning of 1928. This gave the Sierra Leone Protectorate the unenviable distinction of being the last part of the British Empire where slavery was abolished.

NOTES

1. Cited by Lady Simon in A.S.P., Misc. Pub., No. 13, *Slave Cargoes —Past and Present* (1939), p. 3.
2. Eric Williams, *Capitalism and Slavery* (North Carolina 1944). Williams carries his argument too far by discounting the genuine philanthropic impulses behind emancipation although he has done a great service by showing that other considerations were more influential.
3. The words "abolitionist", "conservationist" and "developmentalist" are used in a very general sense to describe the ethical standards and their proponents.
4. C. Buxton (Ed.), *Memoirs of Sir Thomas Fowell Buxton, Bart.* (3rd ed. London 1849), pp. 378–80. The society was first called the Society for the Extinction of the Slave Trade and the Civilization of Africa. Buxton took over leadership of the anti-slavery campaign from Wilberforce in the 1820s.
5. Buxton told John Jeremie, a keen abolitionist who was later Governor of Sierra Leone for a few months, that he was going to represent to all powers the immense field for commerce which was closed by the slave trade; *ibid.*, p. 365.

6. *Ibid.*, pp. 432–74, for accounts of the public meeting and the Niger Expedition. See also J. Gallagher, "Fowell Buxton and the New African Policy, 1838–1842", *Cambridge Historical Journal*, X (1950), No. 1, pp. 36–58; this article shows how the Whig government courted the radicals whose support it needed to stay in power —the Whigs fell in 1841 partly because abolitionists opposed their suger proposals.
7. Cited in Metcalfe, *Documents*, p. 160.
8. J. F. A. Ajayi, *Christian Missions in Nigeria 1841–1891* (London 1965), pp. 12–13; C. C. Ifemesia, "The 'Civilizing' Mission of 1841: Aspects of an Episode in Anglo-Nigerian Relations", *Hist. Soc. of Nigeria Journal*, Vol. 2, No. 3 (1962), pp. 291–310.
9. Metcalfe, *Maclean of the Gold Coast* (London 1962), pp. 259ff. Maclean's behaviour will be discussed below. Jeremie died in 1841; as Governor of Sierra Leone he was also responsible for British settlements on the Gambia and the Gold Coast.
10. Metcalfe, *Documents*, p. 164, Russell to Maclean, 14 July 1841.
11. *Ibid.*, pp. 151–3, Maclean to the Committee of Merchants, 14 October 1837.
12. *Ibid.*, pp. 153–5, Maclean to the Committee of Merchants, 16 December 1837.
13. Metcalf, *Maclean*, pp. 259ff. It was the report of Hansen's slaves that prompted Jeremie to issue his proclamation against British slave owners, see above, p. 25.
14. Metcalf, *Documents*, pp. 179–83. Extracts from Report of Select Committee on West Africa, 1842. Since 1828 the Gold Coast forts had been governed by a committee of merchants subject to the supervision of a committee of London merchants trading to West Africa.
15. *Ibid.*, pp. 191–2. The Foreign Jurisdiction Act, 1843, Anno Sexto & Septimo Victoriae Reginae Cap. XCIV.
16. In 1890 when the British Government was reconsidering the status of protectorates it re-enacted the 1843 Foreign Jurisdiction Act and other more limited Foreign Jurisdiction Acts passed since 1843 into a new Foreign Jurisdiction Act.
17. The Niger Delta region was known as the Oil Rivers in the middle of the nineteenth century. The Slave Coast extended from Lagos to the mouth of the Volta River. The Gambia was not a major centre of British expansion.
18. Metcalfe, *Documents*, p. 195, Hill to Stanley, 6 March 1844.
19. *Ibid.*, pp. 219–20, J. Bannerman and B. Cruickshank to Sir W. Winniett, 22 August 1850.
20. John Beecroft was the first British Consul for the Bights of Benin and Biafra; he was appointed in 1849.
21. The number of slaves imported into Brazil dropped from 54,000 in 1849 to 3,000 in 1851. See P. D. Curtin, *The Image of Africa: British Ideas and Action, 1780–1850* (Madison 1964), p. 317. The

decline in the transatlantic slave trade made it more likely that the British would turn their attention to internal or domestic slavery.

22. W. N. M. Geary, *Nigeria under British Rule* (London 1965; first ed. 1927), pp. 36–7, citing duplicate of despatch from Edward Lodder, R.N., Acting Consul at Lagos, to the Earl of Clarendon, 28 March 1858.

23. Ajayi, *Christian Missions*, p. 169.

24. Metcalfe, *Documents*, pp. 220–1, Grey to Winniett, 19 September 1850.

25. *Ibid.*, p. 244, Cruickshank to Newcastle, 18 May 1853.

26. Merivale was Permanent Under-Secretary at the Colonial Office from 1847 to 1859; Sir Frederic Rogers held the same post from 1860 to 1871.

27. CO 96/37/9642, Palmerston to Ord, 31 October 1855.

28. CO 96/40/4316, Ord to Palmerston, 15 May 1856. The attempt to levy the poll tax was abandoned in 1861.

29. See note 27 above.

30. CO 96/40/4316, Labouchere to Pine, 9 November 1856.

31. Metcalfe, *Documents*, pp. 264–7, Pine to Labouchere, Conf. 1 and 10 October 1857.

32. CO 96/39/7800, FO to CO, 28 August 1856, Enclosure, a letter from Consul B. Campbell at Lagos, 14 June 1856.

33. Metcalfe, *Documents*, pp. 267–8, Minute by Merivale, 16 November 1857.

34. K. O. Dike, *Trade and Politics in the Niger Delta 1830–1885* (Oxford 1956), Chapter VI; D. A. Ross, "The Career of Domingo Martinez in the Bight of Benin, 1833–1863", *Journal of African History*, VI, 1 (1956), pp. 79–90.

35. J. D. Hargreaves, *Prelude to the Partition of West Africa* (London 1966), p. 17.

36. *Ibid*, pp. 39–40.

37. A. G. Hopkins, "Economic Imperialism in West Africa: Lagos, 1880–1892", *The Economic History Review*, XXI, 3 (December 1968) pp. 587–8.

38. Cited by Sir Alan Pim, *Economic History of Tropical Africa* (Oxford 1940), p. 39.

39. E. A. Ijagbemi, "A History of the Temne in the Nineteenth Century" (Edinburgh Ph.D. Thesis 1968), pp. iv, 103 and Chapter VI.

40. See note 33.

41. Metcalfe, *Documents*, pp. 270–1, Pine to Labouchere, Enclosure, 29 December 1857.

42. *Ibid.*, pp. 300–1, Grievances of the Gold Coast Chiefs, 9 August 1864.

43. D. Kimble, *A Political History of Ghana: the rise of Gold Coast nationalism, 1850–1928* (Oxford 1963), p. 302.

44. *Parliamentary Debates*, 3rd Series, 219, p. 166, 12 May 1874.

45. Disraeli Papers, XII, Carnarvon to Disraeli, 28 June 1874. Notes from Professor Hargreaves.
46. P.P. 1875, lii, *Correspondence Relating to the Affairs of the Gold Coast* (C.1140), A.P.S. to CO, 18 June 1874.
47. P.P. 1875, lii, *Correspondence Relating to the Queen's Jurisdiction on the Gold Coast, and the Abolition of Slavery within the Protectorate* (C.1139), Carnarvon to O.A.G. Gold Coast, 21 August 1874.
48. *Ibid.*, Strahan to Carnarvon, 19 September 1874.
49. Chalmers, later knighted and the first Chief Justice of the Gold Coast in 1876, was at this time seconded to the Gold Coast from Sierra Leone on special duty. In 1898 he was commissioned to investigate the Sierra Leone risings.
50. C.1139, Strahan to Carnarvon, Enclosures 1 and 2, 17 December 1874.
51. C.1139, Strahan to Carnarvon, 17 December 1874.
52. P.P. 1875, lii, *Further Correspondence Relating to the Abolition of Slavery on the Gold Coast* (C.1159), Strahan to Carnarvon, 3 and 8 January 1875, enclosing the three petitions.
53. Paul Jenkins, "Abstracts from the Gold Coast Correspondence of the Basel Mission, Correspondence on the Slave Emancipation Proceedings in the Gold Coast, 1874–75", various letters from missionaries, June and July 1875.
54. P.P. 1878, lv, *Gold Coast, Report by Sir David Chalmers on the Effect of the Steps which have been taken by the Colonial Government in Reference to the Abolition of Slavery within the Protectorate* (C.2148). This report, dated 12 June 1878, is brief—less than two pages.
55. W. W. Claridge, *A History of the Gold Coast and Ashanti* (2nd ed., London 1964; 1st ed. 1915), pp. 183–4.
56. S. Miers, 'Great Britain and the Brussels Anti-Slave Trade Act of 1890' (London Ph.D. 1969), p. 204. In the twentieth century Sierra Leone Protectorate Chiefs used the same excuse for not supplying labour for public works.
57. Metcalfe, *Documents*, p. 399; footnote 2 refers to the comment Hemming made in 1875. Hemming had a long and distinguished career from his appointment as clerk in 1860; he became Governor of Jamaica in 1898.
58. P.P. 1890–91, lvii, *Correspondence Respecting the Administration of the Laws against Slavery in the Gold Coast Colony* (C.6354), A.P.S. to CO, 20 August and 11 September 1890.
59. *Ibid.*, Governor Griffith to Knutsford, 26 January 1891.
60. Ibid., Knutsford to A.P.S., 4 April 1891.
61. Fyfe, *A History*, p. 335.
62. R. F. Burton, *Wanderings in West Africa* (1863), I, pp. 207, 209. Creoles were descended from African slaves liberated by the British and settled in Freetown.

63. Fyfe, *A History*, pp. 334–5.
64. C. P. African (West), 366, *Sierra Leone. Major A. M. Festing's Mision to Almamy Samodu (1888)*, pp. 19, 57, 70.
65. *Ibid.*, p. 68.
66. M. Kingsley, *Travels in West Africa* (London 1897), p. 680.
67. Her lengthy correspondence with Joseph Chamberlain in 1898 will be discussed in Chapter IV.
68. C. L. Temple, *Native Races and Their Rulers* (2nd ed. London 1968—1st ed. 1918), p. 227.
69. See above, pp. 32–3.
70. E. A. Ijagbemi, "The Freetown Colony and the Development of 'Legitimate' Commerce in the Adjoining Territories", *Journal of the Historical Society of Nigeria*, V, 2 (June 1970), pp. 243–56; Ijagbemi, "A History of the Temne in the Nineteenth Century", pp. iv, 103, 113, Chapter VI, *et al.*
71. P.P. 1886, *Correspondence respecting Disturbances in the Native Territories adjacent to Sierra Leone* (C.4642), Rowe to Derby, 24 June 1885.
72. Fyfe, *A History*, p. 307. Eventually Bulama Island went to Portugal after arbitration.
73. *Ibid.*, pp. 309–10.
74. *Ibid.*, p. 323.
75. *Ibid.*, pp. 311–12, 363–4.
76. F. Renault, "L'Abolition de l'esclavage au Sénégal: L'attitude de l'administration française (1848–1905)", *Revue française d'histoire d'outre-mer*, LVIII, 210 (1971), pp. 5–80; H. O. Idowu, "The Establishment of Protectorate Administration in Senegal, 1890–1904", *Journal of the Historical Society of Nigeria*, IV, 2 (June 1968), p. 253.
77. *Parliamentary Debates*, 3rd series, 220, p. 639, 29 June 1874; Disraeli quoted Kennedy's despatch of 3 November 1870.
78. Fyfe, *A History*, p. 416.
79. *Ibid.*, pp. 417–18.
80. *C.R. II*, 2731. For years the problem of runaway slaves strained relations between the Sierra Leone Government and neighbouring chiefs. Governor Campbell in 1836 made a treaty with the Loko Temne to return runaway slaves from British territory to their owners but the Secretary of State refused to ratify this agreement which was contrary to British law. In 1841 Sir John Jeremie made it clear to these chiefs that their runaway slaves would not be returned to them from British territory.
81. C.4642, Rowe to Derby, 24 June 1885, paras. 10–13. The Sierra Leone Association included leading professional and businessmen in the Colony. Both Creoles and Europeans were members. The Association's Memorial first came to the Colonial Office via the Manchester Chamber of Commerce, *ibid.*, Manchester Chamber of Commerce to CO, 21 May 1885, enclosure. It was only submitted

to Rowe in June, which could hardly have made him sympathetic to its representations.

82. C. P. African (West), 318a, July 1886, *Correspondence respecting Disturbances in the Native Territories Adjacent to Sierra Leone*, Rowe to Stanley, 14 January 1886, enclosure, S. Lewis's Paper to the Sierra Leone Association, 6 August 1885, p. 14.

83. *Ibid.*, p. 16.

84. See Hargreaves, *Prelude*, pp. 303–15, for a full discussion of the Oil Rivers Protectorate.

85. FO 97/562/4825, Conf., No. 6, Memo. by Sir E. Hertslet on the Protectorate of States, 24 April 1883.

86. FO 84/1818, Memorandum on the Formalities necessary for the effective Annexation of Territory, 18 December 1884.

87. P.P. 1884, *Correspondence respecting the West African Conference* (C. 4205), Baron Plessen to Granville, 8 October 1884.

88. P.P. 1885, *Protocols and General Act of the West African Conference* (C.4361), Articles 6 and 9.

89. FO 84/1819, 3 January 1885, Memo. by Selborne (italics by Pauncefote), cited by W. R. Louis, "The Berlin Congo Conference", in Gifford and Louis (Eds.), *France and Britain in Africa* (Yale 1971), p. 209. I have drawn heavily on Louis for this paragraph.

90. FO 84/1820, Selborne to Pauncefote, 23 January 1885, cited by Louis, "The Berlin Congo Conference", p. 211.

91. P.P. 1885, *Correspondence with Her Majesty's Ambassador at Berlin respecting West African Conference* (C.4284), Sir E. Malet to Granville, 21 February 1885.

92. C.4361, Articles 34 and 35. In Article 35 much depends on what is meant by occupation.

93. FO 83/2010, The Marquis of Salisbury to Lord Vivian, 17 September 1888.

94. Clearly shown by S. Miers, "Great Britain and the Brussels Anti-Slave Trade Act of 1890", (Ph.D. thesis, London 1969).

95. P.P. 1892, *General Act of the Brussels Conference relative to the African Slave Trade* (C.6557).

96. The first Foreign Jurisdiction Acts were passed in the sixteenth century giving the English Government certain rights of jurisdiction over its subjects in the Ottoman Empire.

97. FO 97/562, Memo by Mr. James, 16 August 1887. The 1843 Act served wider purposes than this, see above, p. 27.

98. FO 97/562, Conf. Memo., "Indian and African Protectorates", by C. P. Ilbert, 24 January 1889. The rest of this paragraph and the next paragraph are mainly based on this memo. by Ilbert.

99. See above, p. 46, for Britain's views in 1885.

100. See above, pp. 44–5, for the decision of May 1884.

101. For more on the Oil Rivers Protectorate see C. Gertzel, "John Holt: a British Merchant in West Africa in the Era of Imperialism" (Ph.D. Oxford, 1969), pp. 386ff., 419–20, *et al.*

102. FO 84/1997, Minute by Lister, 18 June 1889.
103. *Ibid.*, Minute by Lord Salisbury, undated. Internal evidence shows this was soon after Lister's minute in June.
104. FO 84/2084, Minute by Salisbury on A.P.S. Memorial on the Administration of the Oil Rivers District, 13 June 1890.
105. FO 84/2085, Memo. by Lister, 17 July 1890.
106. FO 84/2110, FO to MacDonald, 1 January 1891, cited by Gertzel, "John Holt", pp. 423–4.
107. See H. A. Gailey, *A History of the Gambia* (London 1964) and J. M. Gray, *A History of the Gambia* (Cambridge 1940).
108. P.P. 1897, *Gambia Annual Report for 1896* (C.8279–19), para. 13.
109. CO 806/151, Rowe to Hicks-Beach, 13 October 1879, cited by N. A. Cox-George, *Finance and Development in West Africa* (London 1961), p. 149. Fyfe's *History* shows how energetic the Sierra Leonean traders were and how much they achieved until late in the century.
110. See above, p. 44.
111. C. Gertzel, "John Holt". The fact that Holt represented Liverpool circles at the Berlin Conference indicates the importance of the Liverpool interest.
112. For more about Kingsley see above, p. 40. For a detailed treatment of the Liverpool interest, Kingsley and Morel read B. Porter, *Critics of Empire. British Radical Attitudes to Colonialism in Africa 1895–1914* (London 1968), Chapter VIII, "Liverpool and Africa". Porter believes that Kingsley was an ineffective propagandist.
113. See Porter, *Critics of Empire*, pp. 254ff. Morel worked as a clerk for Elder Dempster, the shipping line to West Africa, and his writings began to attract attention in the 1890s. In 1901 he resigned from Elder Dempster and, with Holt's help, became a full time reformer and publisher of the *West African Mail*.
114. R. Robinson and J. Gallagher, *Africa and the Victorians* (London 1965, reprint of 1961 ed.), p. 394.
115. Gertzel, "John Holt", p. 222, citing *Liverpool Daily Post*, 2 December 1881.
116. M. Crowder, *West Africa*, pp. 120–1.
117. Gertzel, "John Holt", pp. 464–6. In 1893–94 exports from the Benin River area were worth £100,411; in 1896–97 £66,924.
118. E. A. Ayandele, *The Missionary Impact on Modern Nigeria, 1842–1914* (London 1966), p. 18. He cites Hope Waddell's Journal, 19/22 October 1854.
119. J. P. Jordan, *Bishop Shanahan of Southern Nigeria* (Dublin 1946), pp. 12, 14–16, 35, 69–70, *et al.*
120. Ajayi, *Christian Missions*, pp. 103–5.
121. Ayandele, *The Missionary Impact*, pp. 47–8, 332. He quotes C.M.S. G3/A2/05, C.M.S. Agents to Secretaries, 14 June 1889.
122. Geary, *Nigeria*, pp. 172–4. The murder was in 1877 but the scandal did not break until the trial in 1882.

123. C.M.S. G3/A1/o 1888, No. 76, Paper on Polygamy and Domestic Slavery by T. J. Sawyerr, read by him to the Native Church Conference, 26 January 1888.
124. FO 84/1990, Archbishop of Canterbury to Lord Salisbury, 5 March 1889.
125. The reactions of Lord Knutsford and Lord Salisbury to representations of the Aborigines' Protection Society are good examples of official disfavour; see above, pp. 38 and 49.
126. Fyfe, *A History*, p. 217.
127. *Anti-Slavery Reporter*, XIV, No. 4 (July-August 1894), p. 205.
128. H. R. Fox Bourne, *The Claims of Uncivilised Races* (London 1900), p. 11; *Slavery and its Substitutes in Africa* (London 1900), p. 5.

SIERRA LEONE IN AFRICA
(Courtesy of University of London Press Ltd.)

CHAPTER III

The Events leading up to the Proclamation of the Sierra Leone Protectorate in 1896

As the rivalry for colonial territory grew more intense during the last two decades of the nineteenth century, it was increasingly apparent that Britain could no longer adequately safeguard her interests in West Africa just by making treaties with certain chiefs and stating imprecise claims to spheres of influence. It was necessary to define clearly and precisely the nature and extent of British jurisdiction. This was as true in the hinterland of the Sierra Leone Colony as in other parts of West Africa.

The international agreements reached at Berlin and Brussels smoothed the way for the clarification of European claims in West Africa. In particular the Brussels Act of July 1890 gave international sanction to the occupation of West Africa by the so-called "civilized nations" in pursuit of their selfish aims. At Brussels African rights were ignored and scarcely any attempt was made to establish a legal or a moral basis for the European seizure of West African territory. Little consideration was given to the Africans who were treated in much the same way whether they lived in colonies under direct European control or in protectorates where the colonial powers exercised limited jurisdiction or in spheres of influence where theoretically the local ruler was as much a sovereign in his own country as Queen Victoria was in Britain. The Brussels Act was interpreted to give its signatories *carte blanche* to take what they could get in Africa.

To justify the carving up of Africa the issues of slavery and the slave trade were used at all levels—from the delegates at the international conference table down to the most junior political

67

officer in West Africa. The Sierra Leone Government was no exception although it was the realization that much of its hinterland was going to France by default which was primarily responsible for the extension of British jurisdiction over the Sierra Leone hinterland. The fear that the Sierra Leone Colony would become an isolated enclave too small to support itself led to a more aggressive policy in the interior.

In 1887 Sir Henry Holland, the Secretary of State, wrote to Governor Sir Samuel Rowe about steps to be taken to secure peace and a prosperous trade with the producing areas in order to bring financial stability to the Colony of Sierra Leone, which could not expect financial assistance from the Treasury.[1] Three schemes had been proposed. Sir Henry rejected annexation, proposed by the inhabitants of the Colony, as too expensive for the Colony—and for various other unspecified reasons. He considered the proposal to proclaim a protectorate more carefully but did not feel conditions were as suitable for this method of extending British jurisdiction as they had been in the Gold Coast, and Parliament opposed any extension of British authority over the West African interior. Sir Henry favoured Rowe's plan to appoint Travelling Commissioners to persuade the inland chiefs to allow freedom of trade, to keep the peace and to refer their disputes with their neighbours to the Sierra Leone Government. This had the advantage of not entailing any responsibility for defending the tribes in the district against attack from tribes outside the district and of avoiding any interference with the internal economy and institutions of the people. Sir Henry also approved the enlargement of the police force by one hundred men and an officer and the construction of a frontier road linking the navigable heads of the rivers and leading to Freetown via Songo Town. As was suggested the following year, this road would serve as an effective boundary which could be regularly patrolled and it would benefit the country almost as much as annexation without "incurring the attendant responsibilities of interfering with the social habits and customs of the people".[2] Yet, during the next three years the Sierra Leone Government did little to put these instructions into effect, except for making treaties on the lines suggested by Rowe and approved by the Colonial Office.[3]

These treaties were made largely because of warnings from Governor Hay, Rowe's successor. Late in 1888 Hay warned the

Colonial Office of the need to make treaties with neighbouring chiefs lest other nations obtain the cession of territory which Britain could not afford to lose.[4] Three months later he stressed the importance of settling the Anglo-French border because "the French are as persistently surrounding us and cutting off as far as they possibly can the avenues of trade from the Interior to this place"; so the Colonial and Foreign Offices agreed that Hay should make treaties with the surrounding chiefs to exclude the French as much as possible.[5] In August 1889 the Anglo-French agreement outlined the border between the Sierra Leone hinterland and French territory, leaving the details to be worked out by British and French Boundary Commissioners.[6] This paved the way for Lord Knutsford's instructions at the beginning of 1890 for the more effective control of the interior.[7]

An equally important reason for the more aggressive British expansion in the early 1890s was the disturbed state of the hinterland where local wars and slave raiding had harmed the Colony's trade and revenue—particularly in the mid-1880s. Farmers who feared that their crops would be burnt or that they would be enslaved before harvest time were unlikely to work hard to produce extra crops for exports. Moreover, crops frequently failed to reach Freetown and the coast because marauding bands of warriors, called warboys, had blocked the trade routes.[8] As Lawson, the Government Interpreter, noted, the activities of the warboys also prevented caravans of traders from the interior from reaching the Colony.[9] The Civil Commandant at Sherbro felt unable to estimate the turnover for 1888 because "so very much depends on the pacific state of country".[10] Sometimes disturbances in the interior threatened British territory. When the Yonni raided Songo Town in British Koya in 1885 the Governor warned that if this attack were to pass unpunished "these fellows will become emboldened, and they are quite capable of attacking Waterloo".[11] The Yonni were punished by Colonel de Winton's expedition but the Mende attacks in 1887 on Sulima and Mano Salija, on the coastal strip ceded to Britain in 1882, went unavenged.[12] There was also the problem that the limits of British territory were sometimes vague and Hay thought there would be less chance of raids on British territory if its limits were more clearly defined.[13]

The French threat and the disturbed state of the hinterland

showed how closely linked the Colony was to the interior, on which it depended as a source of export crops and as a market; this dependence was even greater after France severed the trade routes from Freetown to parts of the interior under French control. By 1890 the policy of assuming rights without additional responsibilities was clearly a failure and the Colony of Sierra Leone was in danger until Britain extended her authority over the interior.

It was not merely fears about the unrest of the West African interior and French expansion that led to British expansion. By 1890 there was a more positive and aggressive attitude gaining ground at the Colonial Office; there were less worries at the prospect of assuming additional responsibilities in West Africa. Typical of this new attitude were Hemming's comments that the old dread of increasing British responsibilities by taking on more territory had been proved by experience to be somewhat of a bugbear and that the extension of jurisdiction brought advantages rather than serious difficulties. In the Sherbro District, for example, the extension of authority and protection had been followed by "a state of peace and order hitherto unknown there, and an immense increase of trade".[14]

Notwithstanding Hemming's opinions British expansion did entail the awkward responsibility of solving the problems of the slave traffic and slavery. The solution to the first problem was clear. Both official and unofficial circles agreed on the need to end the slave traffic in the interior. Britain was obliged to do so under the Berlin and Brussels agreements and the slave traffic was harming British interests in the Colony of Sierra Leone and elsewhere in West Africa.

It was more difficult to agree on a desirable solution to the problem of domestic slavery. Little was known about the institution in the hinterland of Sierra Leone even though about half the population were slaves. The main source of information is the evidence presented to Sir David Chalmers in 1898.[15] This shows that in general the institution was comparatively mild and that legitimate commerce had not made the lives of the slaves much harder, as it had done in some parts of West Africa.

Lack of information did not stop the conservationists from concluding that it would be dangerous to interfere with domestic slavery, which was a mild institution evolved to suit local needs. Nor did it stop the abolitionists from arguing that slavery was hindering progress and that for practical reasons, as well as moral ones, Britain should suppress the institution.

One of the practical problems which Freetown had to face was the influx of runaway slaves who were coming to the Colony from the interior in increasing numbers during the 1880s.[16] As the aboriginal population of Freetown grew tension rose, particularly when times were bad and new arrivals could not find jobs and homes. The 1881 census showed that there were 1,534 Temne in Freetown and by 1885 it was thought necessary to appoint a Temne headman in Freetown to assist the police in investigating the many thefts blamed on the Temne.[17] Rowe pointed out the problem that the new arrivals could do little besides unskilled labour:

> Much of the unskilled labour of this place is done by the people of this tribe, and lately petty riots have occurred as a consequence of disputes between them and other labouring sections of the community in their desire to obtain employment when work was scarce.[18]

By 1887 there was so much trouble that Lawson complained, "this beating, stoning and whipping of Timmanis and other aborigines in town is getting worse".[19]

Some of the Creole Press tended to blame all Freetown's troubles on the arrivals from the interior. In 1894 the *Sierra Leone Times* referred to "the countless number of run-a-way slaves at present swelling the burglar's brigade in Freetown" and to the "purposeless, irresponsible, wholly insanitary band of escaped domestic slaves".[20] The *Sierra Leone Weekly News* was more moderate. It opposed proposals to stop aborigines coming into Freetown because "we have no more claim to the Colony than they have", and in 1902 it stated that the hooligans in Freetown were nearly all children of the Creoles—not aborigines from the interior.[21] The exodus of runaways from the interior also infuriated chiefs and slave owners, who sometimes took great risks to recapture runaways, as the Rev. Neville's adventure shows. From the shore he witnessed the plight of twenty-two escaped slaves whose master

... pursued after them in an armed Canoe even to the sea shore of the Colony at the Cape and if the Rev. Mr Neville of Fourah Bay College was not at the Cape at the time it would have ended in a horrible scene. He could not bear it, so he pushed his own boat into the sea and with the assistance of some fishermen hard by, succeeded in capturing the two canoes, master and the slaves.[22]

* * *

All these considerations, local and international, moral and expedient, social and economic, prompted the more decisive policy in the Sierra Leone hinterland from the beginning of 1890, when Lord Knutsford gave instructions for three major steps, which had been under consideration for some time, to make British authority more effective in the interior.[23] First, two Travelling Commissioners were appointed to make treaties with the inland chiefs—Garrett in the north and Alldridge in the south. Second, Knutsford instructed the Governor to go ahead with the construction of a road linking the navigable heads of the rivers. After the clearing of this road, which was longer than the one contemplated by Garrett two years before, the territory between the road and the coast fell more directly under the control of the Sierra Leone Government which assumed responsibility for the maintenance of law and order in this thirty mile wide strip.

Third, the clearest evidence of the increased British presence in the interior was the establishment of the Frontier Police in 1890. This para-military force was intended to keep the peace and to protect trade; to fulfil these functions they patrolled constantly, they tried to prevent attacks by warboys and slave raiders, and they dealt with murders and violent robberies.[24] Although no specific instructions to suppress the slave trade were given to the Frontier Police at the time of their establishment, Governor Hay hoped that the stationing of the Frontier Police in the interior would lead to the eradication of the slave traffic there.[25] In their efforts to preserve peace the Frontier Police soon became active in the suppression of the slave traffic. It began by stopping slave caravans and other aspects of the slave traffic which caused disputes. It was not expected that the Frontier Police would suppress domestic slavery. In drawing up their instructions at the beginning of 1889 Hay had made it clear that they were not to interfere with the rule of the chiefs and with African customs—notably domestic slavery.[26]

As a result of treaty obligations to chiefs further upcountry and because of the fear of French encroachment, the Frontier Police were soon deployed well beyond the frontier road, which was not the original intention. The resources of the force were consequently over-extended and very small isolated police outposts, lacking adequate supervision, had to be established. Not unnaturally some members of these small detachments tended to take advantage of their position as uniformed representatives of the Sierra Leone Government. Some became petty despots who interfered with the rule of the chiefs and with native customs, especially domestic slavery. The local rulers made many complaints about police interference with their domestic slaves. Although some of these complaints may have arisen from genuine misunderstandings (it was difficult sometimes to distinguish between slaves to be sold and slaves to be kept as domestics), it is likely that all ranks of the force tended to exceed their instructions on domestic slavery.

Inspector Lendy, who became the second Inspector-General of the force in 1892, was an impetuous young man who was not prepared to let regulations stand in his way. In 1889 Lendy, then a lieutenant in the West India Regiment, came across Fula slave traders with eighty slaves in chains near Rotifunk. He flogged the slavers and destroyed their towns instead of sending them to Freetown for trial, a step which would have raised the awkward problem of slavery on British soil.[27] The abolitionist zeal of Lendy and his colleagues led to some sharp exchanges with those who favoured the conservationist approach—notably J. C. E. Parkes, Superintendent of the Department of Native Affairs. In 1893 they quarrelled over the right of the Frontier Police to rescue slaves. Although the Governor had recently instructed the Frontier Police to rescue only those slaves being transported for sale, Lendy wanted to rescue those before they were transported; he was confident that there would be no difficulty in recognizing these slaves who were usually manacled. He knew such an extension of police powers would lead to more native complaints about the force but he tried to forestall the expected criticisms of his men by attacking the slave owners:

73

Without the Police we would not hear of the slave traffic at Head Quarters. The moment a slave is released, the owner will, in almost every case, say that it is a domestic slave and then complain, so as to have the Police punished or removed in the hopes of getting men who will take no notice of the traffic.[28]

Parkes disagreed on the grounds that the policemen lacked the intelligence to decide who were to be transported and they might free those being restrained for other quite valid reasons—perhaps a thief, a recaptured runaway or a man accused of woman palaver and unable to pay the damages.[29] He thought the police deliberately interfered with genuine domestic slaves and he knew of no case in which owners of trade slaves had pretended they were domestics. After denying that he was an advocate of slavery Parkes carried his conservationist argument to ridiculous lengths:

In truth the power of the so-called domestics is far greater than their master's and if they chose to rise tomorrow for their freedom their masters could not stop them, but as a rule they prefer this parental form of so-called slavery which entails no thought for the morrow on their part to our wearing, busy, bustling, anxious freedom.

Late in 1893 Parkes continued his defence of domestic slavery as the means of assessing a man's wealth and status.[30] This mild institution was so woven up with the life of the country that it could not be uprooted abruptly. A crusade against domestic slavery would dislocate the whole labour system of the interior and would bring an even larger influx to Freetown. It would take time, tact and patience to persuade the people of the evils of the institution and to abolish it by gradual steps. At this time Parkes's views were very influential; the Colonial Office and Governors Fleming and Cardew listened with respect to the man whose experience and knowledge of the hinterland was unrivalled.

He won this particular argument with Lendy. The Colonial Office agreed that the Frontier Police should wait and watch if they suspected that slaves were to be transported for sale and "interfere as soon as the transport action begins".[31] The Sierra Leone Government then published new instructions to the police, listing the towns and districts where they had the right to stop the transit of slaves and defining the transit of slaves as slaves either

74

chained or shackled being taken or driven along the roads. The police were forbidden to enter the house or yard of anyone to search for slaves and warned against involving themselves in any slave questions where they were stationed.[32]

These instructions worried some British humanitarians; the Anti-Slavery Society wanted to know whether these orders stopped the police from acting against those suspected of employing slaves in British territory, and the Society asked what preventive steps were being taken against slavery in West Africa.[33] The reply was that since the places mentioned were in a British sphere of influence, which was not British soil, British law did not apply there and slavery was legal. As far as the general question was concerned Lord Ripon was convinced that there was no slavery in British Colonies nor in the protected territories of the Gold Coast where slavery had been abolished by special ordinances.

Some members of the Frontier Police did tend to brush aside their orders not to interfere with domestic slavery and others took advantage of inadequate supervision to tyrannize isolated communities but their crimes were unduly magnified by their enemies.[34] The traditional rulers and the slave owners felt most threatened by these uniformed representatives of the foreigners who were taking their country from them. The Frontier Police contributed much to the Sierra Leone Government's successful campaign against slave raiding and slave trading in the interior before the proclamation of the Protectorate in 1896. This did not endear them to the ruling classes of the hinterland. Moreover, although there were no laws restricting domestic slavery in the interior before 1896 the British presence there did tend to limit the slave owners' control over their slaves. The Frontier Police watched for owners transporting a slave to sell him and it therefore became more difficult for the owner to control his unruly slave by threatening to sell him. Runaway slaves could and did seek the protection of the Frontier Police and claimed their freedom by hanging on to the Union Jack flagposts in the British posts. It is one of the ironies of empire that many British humanitarians regarded the Frontier Police as oppressors of the people because of the frequent complaints against them—complaints which in fact were motivated by police intervention on behalf of domestic slaves.

Numerous accusations and counter-accusations, the difficulty of distinguishing between slave trading and domestic slavery, and strong abolitionist and conservationist prejudices make it impossible to decide how much the Frontier Police interfered with domestic slavery. One would expect some police to charge their enemies with slave trafficking and some chiefs would attempt to conceal their guilt by alleging that the slaves concerned were for domestic use and by making counter-charges against their accusers.[35] No doubt there was some substance to complaints made by both sides. Not all the Frontier Police were dedicated to the eradication of slavery; some police even owned slaves themselves. Captain Lendy had to warn them against taking slaves, and in 1907 the District Commissioner of Panguma came across two instances in which members of the force had taken slaves during police actions and sold them.[36] In many cases slavery was a red herring which distracted attention from the real problem— the clash of the old order with the new.

A frequently repeated allegation against the Frontier Police was that it consisted largely of ex-slaves who lost no opportunity to take their revenge on the slave-owning classes. It was alleged that in some cases they even returned in the Queen's uniform to oppress their former masters. K. Little, the anthropologist, wrote that they "were largely recruited from war-refugees and men who were ex-slaves from the very districts of which they were put in charge".[37] It has been pointed out that there is no concrete evidence for the allegation that ex-slaves in the Frontier Police returned to districts where they had been slaves.[38] Yet, it does appear that an increasing number of aboriginals joined the force and a substantial proportion of these recruits would have been ex-slaves. When the force was formed in 1890 nearly twenty-five per cent of its members were from the protected sphere; the rest were Creoles from the Sierra Leone Police Force.[39] The turnover of men was rapid and the composition of the force changed. By 1894 Parkes was worrying about the fact that most of the recruits were from the surrounding tribes and he feared that a member of the force might return to where he had been a slave and influence his old friends there—this would be interference with domestic institutions.[40] He repeated this to Chalmers in 1898.[41] Despite Parkes's opinions it is not clear how many of the Frontier Police were runaway slaves. One correspondent to the *Sierra Leone*

76

Times did recognize one of his runaway slaves in the ranks but because the fellow looked so smart in his uniform the writer felt quite reconciled to his loss.[42]

A leader writer in the *Sierra Leone Times* also believed the Frontier Police returned to areas where they had been slaves:

> The Frontiers should be instructed not to meddle with the domestic slaves of their former masters, nor to unduly interfere with them.[43]

The allegation that ex-slaves returned as members of the Frontier Police and oppressed their ex-masters had circulated widely by 1898 and was repeated several times in the evidence to Chalmers.[44] Officers in the force thought few recruits had been runaway slaves and thought there was little chance of their returning to their old homes.[45] Nevertheless, Chalmers concluded rightly that some of the police had been runaway slaves, whom he rather unfairly branded as the "idlest and worst-behaved of a household". Because there was no system to stop recruits being sent back to their old homes, he reached the highly speculative conclusion that

> ... it must happen that a former slave finds himself in a position to use the authority of the Government against persons of the class to which his former master belongs, and even it might chance, against his former master himself,—an opportunity he would not be likely to neglect.[46]

Although there were many ex-slaves in the Frontier Police and the Sierra Leone Government more than once felt it necessary to repeat the instructions against meddling with domestic institutions this charge is not proven.[47]

Cardew, who became Governor in 1894, took little notice of chiefs' complaints against the police. Whether or not the complaints were justified this must have angered the chiefs. When Bai Sherbro of Samu complained he was told that the Frontier Police had "distinct orders not to interfere with your domestic institutions".[48] That was all the satisfaction he received. Bai Sherbro of Mambolo was rebuked for his complaint that Police Constable Sawyer was encouraging his wives and slaves to run away—"H.E. therefore desires me to caution you against making

77

such reports in the future".[49] Cardew thought, like Lendy, that complaints were made against the Frontier Police because they had been so successful in stopping slave raids and suppressing slavery.[50] He also believed they incurred resentment because they stopped chiefs taking unfair advantage in cases of woman palaver —often attempts to "frame" the man concerned. Even Parkes, no friend of the Frontier Police, credited them with abating this evil and saving many men from ruin.[51]

Undoubtedly their greatest success was the important part they played in the suppression of the slave trade. The turning point in the campaign was the year 1894 which began with the expulsion of the Sofa slave raiders. Then Cardew made his first tour of the interior—for the purpose of stopping the slave traffic, as he told the people at Panguma.[52] Later in 1894 Cardew reorganized the Frontier Police, increasing its numbers from 300 to 500 and greatly improving discipline; consequently it could patrol more regularly and effectively and combat the slave trade with greater success.[53]

Taking everything into account the Frontier Police did as well as could be expected under very difficult circumstances, especially after Cardew's reforms in 1894. The authorities sometimes expected the force to do the impossible—it could not end the slave traffic without interfering with domestic slavery because the two were so intimately connected. For example, sometimes enslavement and slave trading could only be prevented by questioning those concerned who were likely to be domestic slaves. Until after the proclamation of the protectorate the police had no option but to shelter the runaway slaves who came to them. Another difficulty was that the traditional rulers looked on the police as ex-slaves and tended to despise them. Despite all the difficulties the force did make an important contribution to the suppression of the slave trade—an achievement which did not endear them to the traditional rulers.

* * *

British power was being extended over the Sierra Leone hinterland in other ways during the early 1890s and slavery, slave trading and other customs considered barbarous by the British were either the occasion or the justification of these extensions of

British jurisdiction. In Imperri, for example, Tongo Players were invited to investigate a series of murders. They accused thirty victims who were seized and burnt as alleged members of the cannibal Human Leopard Society.[54] To stop these practices Governor Hay in November 1890 proclaimed Imperri part of the Colony, but no new administration was established in the district until 1896, and the chiefs were told that their domestic institutions would be respected—in effect slavery was being tolerated on what was technically British soil between 1890 and 1896.[55]

During Hay's inland tours in 1890 and 1891 he treated the chiefs as subjects rather than independent rulers and he unilaterally greatly enlarged the area where British authority was exercised by mapping out a new frontier road much further inland than the old one. As Fyfe has pointed out:

> Despite Hay's assurances, the chiefs found they were no longer the free agents they had been. Those who ignored Governor's instructions were liable to suffer: Bai Simera, accused to Hay of plundering, only averted arrest by instant apology and restitution. A chief was gaoled for several months by Ordinance because he was said to have contemplated "buying war" from a neighbour. They were warned against using their traditional economic weapon, the Poro, to restrict trade. Nor could promises to respect "domestic institutions" stop slaves or wives running away to the Colony, or bring them back.[56]

The men on the spot were blandly ignoring the rights of the traditional rulers in much the same way as the negotiators at Brussels in 1890. From 1890 to 1896 British authority was being steadily extended over the Sierra Leone hinterland without the consent of the local chiefs.

The most convenient justification for this arbitrary assumption of power was the pressing problem of the slave trade. Even Parkes argued that an extension of British jurisdiction was needed to enable the government to deal with the prime cause of war and devastation in the hinterland, namely plunder:

> ... principally for slaves who were ultimately sold to Soosoo and Foulah dealers who take them to Foutah and the countries beyond and thus keep up a regular system of overland slave trading

79

which under present circumstances it is impossible for the Government even to check as they are generally conveyed by routes outside its limited jurisdiction.[57]

The slave traffic was a problem and there were even allegations that it went on in Freetown; at Konkobar Captain Williams was informed that thirty slaves had been taken to Freetown and sold there by Mandingo traders.[58] Two months later Parkes drew attention to reports that traders from The Gambia were coming to Port Loko to buy children as slaves, bringing them to Freetown ostensibly as their own children and then taking them back to Bathurst by mail steamer.[59] At the beginning of 1892 a Catholic missionary made a series of serious allegations.[60] He wrote that slavery continued in the Colony of Sierra Leone and that it dominated the protected areas. He described how Africans from the French territories came south to buy most of their slaves from the British protected area—mainly Temneland. Every year boats laden with rum, tobacco, powder, guns and other trade goods made their way to the head of the River Sierra Leone and returned crammed with slaves. Even though these convoys passed close to Freetown, the British administrators either knew nothing of them or wished to know nothing because of their powerlessness to end this shameful traffic.

Early the following year Parkes was telling a different story with his description of the success of the measures against the slave traffic in the hinterland.[61] He was probably being too optimistic because later in the year the Foreign Office was concerned about reports of the slave trade in the Sierra Leone hinterland. It reminded the Colonial Office that Britain had incurred obligations under the Brussels Act which meant that a force should be sent upcountry to combat the slave trade, even if it had not been necessary to act against the traffic to secure peace there.[62] The force was sent; despite the unfortunate clash with the French at Waima late in 1893 the expedition achieved its main objective of expelling the Sofas by early 1894.[63] It is likely that one of the important motives for this expedition was the fear that if the British failed to suppress the slave trade the French would have a good excuse to intervene in the British sphere of influence.

* * *

Sir Francis Fleming, Governor of Sierra Leone from spring 1892 until early 1894, was less actively interested in the interior than his predecessor, Hay. He ventured into the interior only once to meet treaty chiefs at what was virtually a durbar at Bandasuma in March 1893.[64] Although his nervous disposition kept Fleming at Freetown—or in Britain on sick leave—during his term of office important decisions were made which committed the Sierra Leone Government more deeply in the hinterland. Fleming himself favoured an extension of active British jurisdiction although he opposed strong arm tactics. In March he and the Chief Justice, Quayle Jones, opposed strengthening and reorganizing the Frontier Police because they preferred to use moral persuasion to inspire confidence in the British sphere.[65] Yet, when Fleming's abolitionist sympathies were aroused he took a stronger line:

> What is more likely to put down slavery than anything else is to take as much of the country as we possibly can under our active jurisdiction and so soon as a separate district for Sulymah is established a commissioner appointed who has time to really consider what part of country might be so taken over I would suggest that as much as possible be so acquired.[66]

In the Imperri, which was British territory, Fleming was not prepared to tolerate customs like slavery and cannibalism nor to allow the natives "to indulge in practices contrary to our ideas of humanity"; there moral influence was not enough to stop regressive practices like domestic slavery and Britain should extend her active jurisdiction.[67] At the Colonial Office Hamilton commented that this was inconsistent with Fleming's views in favour of moral suasion. This was not really a fair comment because Fleming only favoured strong measures to suppress social evils like slavery and cannibalism.

Late in 1892 Fleming tried to persuade the chiefs of Port Loko to cede their territory to Britain because of the threat of French encroachment and because he hoped this cession would make it easier to stop the overland slave trade there.[68] The chiefs did not agree to new treaties of cession because they feared that the Frontier Police would interfere with their chiefly authority and native customs—particularly domestic slavery. Six months later the chiefs were still unwilling to sign a new treaty because of Frontier Police interference with domestic slavery and Acting Governor Crooks notified the Colonial Office of his intention to reaffirm the Port Loko Convention of 1825 in which the chiefs had ceded the Loko territories near Port Loko to Britain.[69] Hemming at the Colonial Office opposed making these British because this would entail the difficulty of having to suppress domestic slavery. Instead he suggested proclaiming a protectorate over the district. This would mean that domestic slavery would not be *ipso facto* abolished and the Frontier Police would not be entitled to interfere with domestic slaves. Nevertheless, in July 1893 the 1825 Convention was reaffirmed by proclamation, although Crooks told the chiefs that the Secretary of State had directed him to inform them that their domestic institutions would not be interfered with—in other words, domestic slavery was to be tolerated on British soil.[70] Although domestic slavery was tolerated this reaffirmation of British sovereignty did deal "a death-blow to the trade in slaves" in the Port Loko area.[71] In the neighbouring territory of Small Skarcies under the rule of Bey Inga the Sierra Leone Government avoided having to deal with domestic slavery by proclaiming a protectorate and promising not to interfere with the chief's authority and native customs beyond what was necessary to enforce the treaty, to maintain peace and order, and to prevent the slave trade.[72]

In the British quarter-mile strip of the Bullom shore a firm stand was taken against the transport of slaves but complications arising from domestic slavery almost led to a British withdrawal from the coastal strip. The trouble began when the Frontier Police arrested Chief Kroobalie for assaulting a runaway slave whom he was trying to recapture in the coastal strip—British since 1847.[73] Supported by Parkes, Kroobalie argued that the cession had been made for fiscal reasons only and that in other ways the chiefs had continued to exercise jurisdiction; therefore the Frontier Police had no right to arrest him. Fleming solved the immediate problem by persuading the complainant to drop charges against the chief but he thought it necessary to settle the problems of jurisdiction raised by the case. Fleming was inclined to agree with Parkes that the coastal strip was British for fiscal purposes only and the Sierra Leone Government had no right to interfere with domestic slavery. He recommended that the Order-in-Council of 1889 which had made the strip part of the Freetown Police District be cancelled. Reluctantly the Secretary of State disagreed. British jurisdiction had been exercised there and slavery could not be allowed in territory ceded to the Queen; the chiefs could be tacitly allowed to exercise jurisdiction as before and, "with respect to the question of domestic slavery, I do not think it necessary that any action should be taken unless a case is brought immediately to your notice".

Five days later, presumably after further considering the implications of the Kroobalie case, Fleming raised the general question of domestic slavery in a despatch to the Colonial Office.[74] The official answer was inconclusive, if not evasive, but the minutes by officials were franker. Hemming thought the Governor should make these decisions on his own responsibility instead of referring it to London which ought not "to have it brought officially to their knowledge that even domestic slavery exists within a British protectorate or sphere of influence". He felt the Colonial Office would be landed "in intolerable difficulties" if it did not follow Parkes's proposal to leave domestic slavery alone. Wingfield agreed that unless Britain was prepared to put down slavery throughout her sphere of influence this was the only thing to do. He could not see how Britain could interfere in cases of refugee slaves outside British jurisdiction where there was no treaty. In drafting the reply Hemming took up Wingfield's argument in a paragraph cautiously deleted by the Permanent Under-Secretary, Meade:

> But H.M.'s Government are not at present prepared to sanction any further system of interference, which would practically involve their undertaking to put down domestic slavery throughout the British sphere of influence.

The problems of jurisdiction in the Bullom coastal strip were still unsolved. The Kroobalie case was just one example of the increase in lawlessness and slave raiding and kidnapping in the area—in the opinion of the Anti-Slavery Society this was the result of withdrawing the small police post from Yongro early in 1892.[75] By the middle of 1893 some progress was being made. In May the Colonial Office agreed that the transport of slaves across the coastal strip, whether in chains and shackles or not, should be stopped, although the police were not to interfere with domestic slaves residing there.[76] The Justice of the Peace in the area, the Rev. Boston, who had had many clashes with the Frontier Police, was removed from office in August 1893; this enabled the Frontier Police post to be reopened.[77]

Early in 1894 Fleming again raised the whole question of British policy towards domestic slavery in the territory near the Colony of Sierra Leone.[78] It was clear to him that there could be no toleration of domestic slavery in any form in the Colony, but he was doubtful to what extent, if any, it could be tolerated in territory ceded to Britain but not administered as part of the Colony, as in the Bullom coastal strip. He also wanted to know "how far we should interfere with domestic slavery" in the British sphere, although he was aware of the instructions not to interfere with native customs beyond what was necessary to maintain peace and order and to prevent the slave traffic. He wanted reassurance that he had been right to refuse to intervene in disputes over slaves between chiefs in the British sphere and right to help escaped slaves forwarded to Freetown from police posts even if their employers were claiming them.

It is not clear what prompted Fleming to raise the slavery issue again; he surely could not have expected a clearer answer than those he had received the year before. Perhaps the Governor —soon to leave Sierra Leone—hoped to persuade the Colonial Office to face up to its responsibility to end slavery in territories under its control but not administered as colonies. Hemming attributed this despatch to Fleming's weakness and inefficiency rather than to any deliberate policy:

> This is one of those awkward questions for the Government at home to deal with which no one but a weak Governor like Sir F. Fleming would think of bringing before us.[79]

The Governor was referred to the Secretary of State's confidential despatch of 19 January 1894 in which it was clearly stated that most of the British sphere was outside British jurisdiction "and it may not be desirable to bring it within such jurisdiction".[80] The British Government had never proposed to interfere with domestic slavery in non-British territory. When matters were more settled it would be the duty of the Sierra Leone Government to warn the people of the Protectorate that slave trading and raiding would have to cease although domestic slavery would not at present be interfered with. The use of the phrase "at present" shows that the Colonial Office contemplated the eventual abolition of domestic slavery and the use of the word "Protectorate" more than two years before the Protectorate of Sierra Leone was proclaimed is significant. The word "Protectorate" was probably used because of a Foreign Office decision a few months before that the British position in the Sierra Leone hinterland was stronger than that in a sphere of influence and whatever territory which had been and would be awarded to Britain must be a British possession.[81]

In this new concept of protectorate status there was little concern with the responsibilities of the protecting power. No longer was the unwillingness or inability of Britain to end domestic slavery seen as a serious obstacle to the proclamation of a Sierra Leone Protectorate. The formal decision to do so was taken in 1893. In 1892 M. D. Davis, a British subject and a trader in the Small Skarcies River area, had complained that native disputes were unsettling trade.[82] The Governor consulted Parkes who pointed out that by setting up Frontier Police posts Britain had already established what was tantamount to a protectorate, and he therefore proposed that a protectorate over the British sphere be proclaimed. He suggested that it be administered by government agents but this plan was vetoed by the Colonial Office when it realized that these posts would have to be filled by Creoles.[83] Parkes thought his scheme would end the slave traffic and that domestic slavery would eventually die out with the end of the slave trade—he did not take into account that the supply of slaves would continually be replenished by the birth of slave children. The Colonial Office postponed its decision until it could consult with Fleming who was due in London on leave.

In August 1893 Acting Governor Crooks, with the unanimous support of the Executive Council, proposed the proclamation of a protectorate, to be accompanied by assurances to the natives that they would not be interfered with excepting so far as might be necessary to suppress armed disturbances.[84] This proposal was not prompted by concern with slavery and the slave trade but by the French decision to cut the trade routes from Sierra Leone to the Niger areas under French control. It was even more urgent after this to secure peace and to encourage agriculture in the hinterland on which the Colony depended so much for its trade and revenue. It was also hoped that the establishment of a peaceful protectorate would relieve the Colony of the influx of people from the interior and stimulate new agricultural ventures in the interior. Again the Colonial Office delayed its decision.

Although Lord Ripon did not think it necessary to proclaim a protectorate this despatch prompted the Colonial Office to consult the Foreign Secretary, Lord Rosebery, who politely replied that he was disposed to defer to the judgement of Lord Ripon.[85] A few days later Lord Roseberry was worrying about reports of the slave trade in the Sierra Leone hinterland and pressing for an expedition to the interior in accordance with British obligations under the Brussels Act to stop the slave trade.[86] This may have tipped the balance in favour of the Colonial Office's decision to make a formal proclamation of a protectorate. There is no record available of the decision which presumably was made informally at some time between Ripon's letter to Lord Roseberry at the beginning of October 1893 and Ripon's letter to Fleming in December 1893 which made it clear that the decision had been taken although it could not be implemented until after the conclusion of a boundary settlement with the French.[87] This was achieved by the Anglo-French agreement of January 1895 which fixed the boundary between the Sierra Leone hinterland and French territory and provided for the appointment of French and British commissioners to settle the final details of the border.[88]

A further reason for the delay in proclaiming the protectorate may well have been the Colonial Office's lack of confidence in Fleming's ability and energy. It may have seemed better to await the appointment of a more capable and energetic governor who was better able to take on the difficult task of effectively extending British sovereignty over the Sierra Leone hinterland. Early in 1894 Fleming decided that he had had enough; he applied for sick leave yet again and left Freetown for the last time.[89]

*   *   *

Colonel Frederic Cardew, the new Governor of Sierra Leone, arrived in Freetown in March 1894. His temperament was quite unlike Fleming's. Cardew was a tough professional soldier who had served twenty years in India and five in South Africa. He did not fear the hardships of the bush, and soon after his arrival he set out on the first of his three extensive tours of the hinterland.[90] He was the brother-in-law of Dean Farrar and an austere Christian who neither smoked nor drank and was a regular churchgoer.[91] His arrival pleased the missionaries and the churchgoing Sierra Leoneans; the Methodist missionary, the Rev. William Vivian, described Cardew as "one of the finest Christian gentlemen it has ever been my joy to meet".[92] The Bishop of Sierra Leone and the Rev. W. J. Humphrey both gladly reported to London that he was a friend of the Church who went to the Cathedral three times on his first Sunday in Freetown.[93] Fired by abolitionist zeal and the desire to spread the blessings of civilization Cardew pursued an active policy in the hinterland, much to the delight of the people of Freetown who had been pressing for such a policy which they hoped would benefit trade.[94] Cardew believed that trade was a powerful civilizing force. Later he was particularly pleased to note the appreciation of European goods in the interior, and he remarked on the fact that the Frontier Police barracks were furnished with curtained beds, tables, crockery and various knick-knacks—adjuncts of civilization which he thought should be disseminated in the interior.[95]

Soon after his arrival in Freetown Cardew heard that Mende warboys were slave raiding and plundering in the Koranko and Konno districts. He planned to investigate on the spot but he already thought it necessary to increase the Frontier Police.[96] Two weeks after his arrival in Freetown Cardew set out on his first tour of the interior from 27 March until 17 May 1894.[97] Cardew and his entourage cut right across the centre of the British sphere to Bandajuma, less than twenty miles from the eastern border. They then followed the border north to Waima and on to Falaba in the northeastern corner of the British sphere, travelled parallel to the northern border to Robat on the Great Skarcies River and returned to Freetown by water. All three tours were intended to pave the way for the proclamation of the protectorate, but in this first tour Cardew was particularly concerned to end the slave traffic which was causing so much disruption.

In his report from Mongheri Cardew told the Colonial Office about his interviews with chiefs en route.[98] He had warned them that the Frontier Police had orders to stop the slave traffic and the transit of slaves under restraint anywhere in the British sphere; those chiefs not previously obliged to stop the slave traffic had bound themselves by treaty to do so in future. Mongheri itself was a centre of the slave trade and he had just intercepted three slaves—a man, a woman and a child. The man and woman had been roped together with halters around their necks and the three slaves were being taken to Susu country by a trader from near Port Loko. The trader had sold cattle at Freetown and with the proceeds he had bought the slaves at Tungea, about twenty miles from Mongheri. Cardew sent the slaves and the trader to Freetown—the former to liberty, the latter for trial. Cardew had concluded that the instructions to the Frontier Police on the slave traffic should be amended to include the whole sphere of influence because by specifying certain places, the proclamation of 12 August 1893 had encouraged slave traders to operate in the places not specifically named.

At Panguma Cardew made it clear to Chief Nyagwa and his followers that he was making the tour to put down the slave traffic, in accordance with Britain's international obligations. When Nyagwa told Cardew he would consult several men before giving an answer about the suppression of the slave traffic, Cardew told him, "It is not a matter of choice: it is the Queen's law."[99] In this despatch from Waima Cardew wrote about his continuing efforts to explain the orders to stop the slave traffic. He had found that the north and the east were the main slave trading areas. The main hunting grounds for slaves included the Gola country in the Liberian hinterland and the Konno, Kuniki and Koranko countries. The main market was the Susu country west of the Great Skarcies River. The principal traders were Fula who exchanged cattle for goods at Freetown and in exchange for these goods which they took upcountry the traders would accept nothing but slaves. It was clear that slaves were being driven right across the British sphere. In fact, Cardew was describing a slave trading triangle; in the western corner was Freetown which supplied trade goods in exchange for cattle, to the east was the British sphere which supplied the slaves in exchange for the trade goods, and in the north was the French sphere which supplied the cattle and took the slaves. On his journey to Waima, Cardew had been horrified to come across an eighteen-year-old girl, who had been sold to a Fula trader by her husband, being driven across the country hobbled by a rough iron staple securing a piece of wood nearly three foot long and six inches in diameter to her ankle. By increasing the police posts and patrols Cardew hoped to make the slave traffic too risky for the traders and thus to prevent such cruelties.

Three subsequent reports were in a similar vein.[100] In the second of these Cardew reported that Bumpan (presumably Bumban in Limba country) was a great centre of the slave traffic, and that he was sending Captain Moore to quell the general unrest there. In the third he enclosed the record of a meeting with chiefs at Sulima; one of them had hoped he would be permitted to buy slaves to keep up the population of his country, but Cardew explained the population would grow faster by natural increase in peaceful times and that much could be done for his people by encouraging trade and agriculture.

Back in Freetown Cardew summed up his impressions of the interior and submitted proposals for its administration after the proclamation of the protectorate.[101] He was especially worried about the slave traffic problem—"the source and origin of all native wars". He had found the chiefs quite co-operative, and he felt that if the Frontier Police were substantially increased the Government would be able to end the slave traffic without any rupture with the chiefs. Optimistically he argued that the extra £7,000 a year to pay for the increase in the Frontier Police would be more than compensated for by the increase in trade which would follow the abolition of the slave traffic. He also proposed restrictions on the arms and ammunition trade, and he concluded that better communications would make it easier to pacify and civilize the hinterland and would encourage legitimate trade. The Colonial Office approved these proposals and Cardew's scheme of administration through the chiefs with the assistance of District Commissioners, although Meade warned that it would be necessary to govern more directly through the colonial administration than Cardew anticipated. However, as Hemming pointed out, the proclamation of the protectorate had to wait until the boundary was settled.

The Colonial Office did not approve of Cardew's policy to suppress domestic slavery as soon as possible, even though he had assured the chiefs "it was not the present intention of the Government to interfere with the domestic institutions of the country".[102] Although Cardew recognized that the institution was so much a part of the people's lives that it could not be uprooted suddenly, he proposed that after the proclamation of the protectorate and the consolidation of British authority, notice should be given that after a year domestic slavery would no longer be allowed. He foresaw few difficulties because the chiefs knew domestic slavery would be suppressed, the year's notice would give them ample time to prepare for the change, and the increase of trade in the interior would more than compensate for the loss of slaves. He also tentatively suggested stipends to help reconcile the chiefs to this reform. At the Colonial Office Hemming, Meade and Bramston all agreed that Cardew's proposals to end domestic slavery were too optimistic. This step, as at the Gold Coast in 1874, would require the consent of the chiefs. For his guidance, Cardew was sent copies of the Parliamentary Papers dealing with the abolition of slavery in the Gold Coast Protectorate in 1874.

Cardew's proposals on domestic slavery were not well received in Freetown either. After praising the Governor's report of his tour and his intended action against slave raiding and trading, Samuel Lewis warned the Legislative Council of the dangers of disorganizing the system of labour in the interior by abolishing domestic slavery. Lewis thought that many would refuse to work if not compelled to do so and that large numbers of ex-slaves would be set adrift.[103] A Freetown journalist thought any upheaval of domestic slavery would harm the Colony; he foresaw instead the gradual and peaceful extinction of the institution once the sources of supply were removed.[104] Both Lewis and the journalist were looking for some sort of compromise between the conservationist and the abolitionist arguments and favoured a gradual and indirect attack on domestic slavery. This line of attack was followed for the first quarter of the twentieth century in the Sierra Leone Protectorate and it fitted in very well with the developmental approach to the West African hinterlands which Chamberlain favoured.

What clearly emerges from Cardew's first tour is his shock and disgust at the nature and prevalence of slavery and the slave trade upcountry. His abolitionist fervour had been aroused and he wanted speedy and radical action to end these twin evils. His outraged humanitarian feelings were as important as the economic and political considerations which he stressed in his correspondence with London. Cardew wanted to help the slaves. For example, he told the Bishop of Sierra Leone that the Government had to do something to educate the rescued slave children, and he proposed that the Government subsidise a school for them, to be run by the Church Missionary Society at Port Loko. Cardew had set aside £200 in the 1895 estimates for this but he asked the Bishop to keep the plan confidential because he had not yet obtained the approval of either the Secretary of State or the Legislative Council.[105] This plan came to nothing but it shows that in pursuit of his humanitarian aims Cardew was prepared to anticipate—in this case wrongly—the decision of the Secretary of State.

After his first tour Cardew was increasingly concerned with the problem of the runaway slaves seeking British protection at the Customs Post on the Island of Kikonkeh, near the mouth of the Great Skarcies River. He accepted various suggestions from Parkes to keep control of the situation.[106] The fugitives were to report to the senior N.C.O. of Police as well as to the Customs Officer, records were to be kept, a monthly return of runaways should be submitted to Freetown, the fugitives were to be allowed to choose where to go and threepence a day would be allowed for their board and lodging. There should be no enticement of wives and domestic slaves away from their husbands and masters.

It is possible to reach some general conclusions about the runaway slaves from the records kept at Cardew's orders until early 1898; the records of runaways forwarded from Kikonkeh to Freetown during a period of fourteen months in 1896 and 1897 are detailed and very useful.[107] The first conclusion is that during the early years of Cardew's term of office there was a steady increase in the numbers of runaways forwarded to Freetown from the British posts at Kikonkeh, the Isles de Los, Tagreen Point, Mahela and elsewhere. In the twelve months from May 1895 to April 1896 there were 76 runaways, of whom 68 came via Kikonkeh; in the fourteen months from April 1896 until May 1897 262 were recorded, of whom 190 came via Kikonkeh. Probably some of the increase was due to more efficient record-keeping, but it is clear that the extension of British authority over the hinterland led to an increase in the numbers of runaway slaves who were realizing that they could leave their masters and seek British protection.

The second conclusion is that the Sierra Leone Government

found that looking after the fugitives was a difficult problem. The children could be apprenticed but it was difficult to find work for the able-bodied and unskilled men when work was scarce in Freetown. Those who were not able-bodied presented an even greater problem. The situation was aggravated by the strong prejudices against the runaways, who were regarded in Freetown as potential vagabonds and criminals.[108] There was considerable support for the allegations made by Temne Chiefs in 1897 that "the greater part of the runaways are those who are lazy and refuse to work".[109] Perhaps as a result of his experiences in the Gold Coast in the eighteen seventies, Chalmers concluded runaways were "generally the idlest and worst-behaved of a household".[110] By running away these slaves showed that they were unhappy as slaves—a fact which tended to weaken the case of the conservationists who argued that domestic slavery was benevolent. If it could be shown that the idle and vicious slaves ran away while the industrious and virtuous slaves stayed put the conservationist case would be strengthened and the abolitionist case would be weakened. This may partly explain the ferocity of the attacks on the runaways who usually found it very difficult to settle down as free men and women in a strange society.

Thirdly the Kikonkeh statistics show that the runaway slaves were not predominantly criminals and vagabonds but a fairly representative cross section of the slave population. Of the 190 runaways in the fourteen months when statistics were most complete 97 were male and 93 female—if the fugitives had been seeking a life of crime and adventure one would expect to find a high proportion of men. Many of the women took their small children with them and there were 34 under the age of five and 9 aged from five to nine. At the other end of the age scale there were 3 runaways over fifty, 7 from forty-five to forty-nine and 25 from forty to forty-four. The greatest number, 48, came from the thirty-five to thirty-nine age group. On the other hand, there were comparatively few young adults, only 10 between fifteen and twenty-four, although one would expect this age group to provide a higher than average number if the runaways had been seeking adventure and excitement. Restrictions by age or sex would have made the vast majority of these runaways ineligible for the Frontier Police and neither would they have been likely to have much success as criminals. The available evidence does not sustain the accusation that most runaway slaves were vicious, idle and criminal.

It is more likely that most slaves ran away because of the behaviour of their masters. Over two-thirds of the 190 runaways gave ill-treatment as the reason for their escape; the rest ran away because they wanted to be free or because their masters had threatened to sell them. The Kikonkeh records also give tribal origins of the runaways. As Kikonkeh was off the Temne coast it is not surprising that more than half were Temne, a quarter were Mende, a tenth were Susu and the rest came from other tribes.[111]

Although most runaways were neither potential criminals nor idle vagabonds, their arrival in the Colony gave rise to serious problems not only in the Colony but also in the hinterland where the chiefs were angry with the Government for protecting the fugitives and even, in the opinion of some, actively encouraging wives and slaves to run away. This was an especially bitter grievance which was not solved by the proclamation of the Protectorate in 1896. The growing resentment of the chiefs over runaways became an important cause of the troubles in 1898. At the beginning of 1898 the Colonial Government decided to stop sending escaped slaves to Freetown and further overcrowding the aborigines' quarters because they could "now have the same protection in the Protectorate as in Freetown".[112] The District Commissioners were made responsible for the problem in their own districts. Later in 1898 the Government stopped maintaining escaped and rescued slaves who had reached Freetown.[113] Still the influx of ex-slaves into the Colony and the complications arising from the problems of runaway slaves in the Protectorate continued to vex the Sierra Leone Government until the final abolition of domestic slavery in the Protectorate at the beginning of 1928.

Within a year of his arrival Cardew was able to report much greater success in dealing with the problem of the slave trade upcountry.[114] In November 1894, after a visit to Sulima and Imperri Districts, Cardew did not think there was any actual slave trading there, although he was perturbed by the custom of "biting" or betting slaves.[115] Parties to a law suit before a native court would often stake a number of slaves on the result and the winner would take all. Mr. Alldridge had recently investigated a case in the Bum District when fourteen slaves had been staked by each side; the Governor had ordered that these slaves be freed or returned to their masters, if they wished. He had warned the chiefs of Sulima and Imperri that the Government could not allow this custom. These chiefs were willing to accept the orders against slave raiding and plundering for slaves but they were worried that if they could not buy slaves they would be left without anyone to work for them. Cardew thought their slaves would stay with them if they were kindly treated, and he reassured the chiefs that the Government did not intend interfering with their domestic institutions but it would not allow the buying, selling or bartering of slaves—including the custom of "biting" slaves.

When Alldridge went to Upper Mende country early in 1895, he rebuked Queen Betsy Gay of Jong for allowing the betting of slaves and reminded her of the seriousness of not obeying the Governor's orders to produce these slaves.[116] Alldridge was generally optimistic although he was displeased with some rulers who, like Chief Koker at Jimi near the Big Bum River, complained of not being able to buy gunpowder and slaves. Alldridge thought the transformation of the country between 1890 and 1895 had exceeded his most sanguine expectations; it was prosperous and peaceful thanks to the effective action of the Government against slave raiding and tribal wars. Although most people were happy with the change there still remained those "who would welcome a return to the former state of things". He also pointed out the need for new industries to give employment to the increasing population and that with permanent peace and the abolition of slavery many more people would be "available for genuine work".

During his second long tour of the interior, early in 1895, Cardew travelled through the rich palm oil belt, more or less along the route the railway was to take. He noted progress in the establishment of law and order. Lord Ripon was pleased to hear from Cardew that the organized Fula and Susu slave traffic had ended.[117] Cardew also reported the successes of Frontier Police posts in towns which had been centres of the slave trade before. He told the Colonial Office that Frontier Police patrols had successfully frightened off the professional slave dealers, although private trading in domestic slaves still continued.[118] Problems remained, particularly in the Kono and Koranko countries which had been recently pillaged for plunder and slaves at the instigation of two powerful Mende chiefs—Nyagwa of Panguma and Vonjo of Kunike.[119] With the help of the Frontier Police, Cardew hoped to recover all the captives who had been taken to Mende country as slaves, including all Chief Suluku's wives.

Back in Freetown Cardew again submitted his proposals for the administration of the hinterland. Except on the question of domestic slavery his views had not been modified to any material extent.[120] He was now prepared to allow the limited import of guns and powder. He suggested the proclamation of a British protectorate over all the territory within the boundary settled by the Anglo-French agreement of January 1895, but he did not feel it was yet time to put into effect the system of administration he had recommended. The Colonial Office approved but preferred that the system of administration and taxation be ready for promulgation at the same time as the proclamation of the protectorate. In the meantime it was agreed that an Order-in-Council should be issued declaring that the Crown had acquired jurisdiction in the foreign territories adjoining the Colony of Sierra Leone and giving the Sierra Leone Legislative Council the right to legislate for these territories in the same way as in the Colony. The Order-in-Council was made on 28 August 1895.[121]

What pleased the Colonial Office most about this despatch was Cardew's abrupt *volte face* on the issue of domestic slavery. With surprising speed the eager abolitionist had adopted many of the conservationist arguments and was now prepared to compromise in view of the many practical difficulties in the way of abolition. From a perusal of the Gold Coast papers sent to him and from personal experience Cardew had realized that abolition would cause unrest and damage trade. Merchants and traders would be angered "if any action were taken which would affect the transport of produce from the Interior"; in other words the slave porters who carried nearly all the goods to and from the interior were necessary. He felt that with increased contact between the Colony and the interior and with the rising demand for labourers to work on the railway, bridges, and roads the problem of domestic slavery would in time solve itself, especially if the Government severely punished all cases of slave trafficking and refused to recognize any rights over slaves in the law courts. He had already observed an amelioration of the system in districts near the Colony, where masters knew they ran great risks of detection and punishment if they sold their slaves and were aware how easily unhappy slaves could gain their freedom by running away to the

Colony. In some cases the relationship between these masters and their slaves had become so free that the slave would go to Freetown to work and then return to his master to whom he would give some of his savings; sometimes the slave would buy his redemption with money earned in Freetown.

Cardew told the Colonial Office again that he had warned chiefs inland of the Government's determination to end slave raiding and trading while promising not to interfere with domestic slavery. He had instructed the Frontier Police not to encourage slaves to come to them for refuge and to protect only those who had been maltreated. Other runaways were to be told to find their own way to Freetown to obtain their freedom. Despite this there is no evidence of Frontier Police turning fugitives away and the 54 out of the 190 slaves forwarded from Kikonkeh to Freetown (see Appendix I) who did not give ill treatment as the reason for their escape were still forwarded to Freetown. In conclusion Cardew pointed out that the canoes which came to trade in Freetown were mostly manned by slaves who did not avail themselves of the opportunity to claim their freedom while on British soil. He thought this showed that their life was not too hard. Although slavery was degrading and it hindered progress, he believed the problem would solve itself in the future as the present master and slave relationship gave way to the master and servant relationship in the future, with the latter willingly giving his services for wages.

Besides pressure from the Colonial Office and Cardew's growing awareness of the practical difficulties which abolition would entail, there were other factors accounting for Cardew's sudden reversal on domestic slavery. Leading Creoles, inland chiefs, officials in the Sierra Leone Government and even missionaries pointed out the practical problems which abolition would cause. Cardew could be impulsive and he may have quickly regretted his vehement condemnation of slavery in 1894. As Fyfe has pointed out, Cardew was flexible enough to change his mind. At first he had wanted to stop the arms and ammunition trade, but when he realized guns were needed for hunting he was prepared to allow the limited sale of arms in the interior. He initially opposed the liquor trade on moral grounds but later decided to allow it on certain conditions because of the revenue it brought in.[122] Similarly, his first generous feelings of sympathy for the slaves were modified by practical considerations and the realization that the institution of domestic slavery was essential to the conservative system of administration he was planning for the interior. Once it had been agreed that slavery was to be tolerated, British jurisdiction could not be directly extended over the hinterland. The existence of domestic slavery thus served to justify the administration of a protectorate through the traditional authorities, even though despatches at the time show that the real obstacle to the annexation of the interior was a shortage of men and money.[123] The Colonial Office refused Cardew's request for a subsidy for the establishment of the protectorate and told him the necessary money had to be raised locally, so he had to economize by using local chiefs as administrators.

In July 1895, when he submitted the scheme for the administration of the protectorate, Cardew repeated his arguments against undue interference with domestic slavery.[124] For the first time in his correspondence with the Colonial Office Cardew referred to "so-called" domestic slavery. This qualification clearly indicates that Cardew had joined those who tried to justify the preservation of the institution by arguing that the word "slavery" was a misnomer for what really was a "domestic institution", "domestic servitude or serfdom", "a system of compulsory servitude" or any other innocuous sounding circumlocution for what plainly was slavery. Cardew also confirmed that laws against slave raiding, slave dealing and pawning would be strictly enforced in the proposed protectorate and that law courts would refuse to recognize claims by masters for property in the form of domestic slaves. The Secretary of State agreed that it would be rash to abolish slavery summarily and stressed that the law courts should not recognize any property claims for slaves; he also referred Cardew to the recent Gambian law on slave dealing and raiding.[125]

Early in 1896 Cardew went on his third long tour of the proposed protectorate. To his own satisfaction at least, he explained to the chiefs and people the changes in administration that would take place after the proclamation of the protectorate and he went through the provisions of the proposed Protectorate Ordinance with the chiefs, who appeared to understand and accept them.[126]

The slave dealing and slavery clauses in Cardew's first Protectorate Ordinance were similar to those in the Gambian

97

Ordinance of 1894.[127] The Sierra Leone Clause XXVIII, like the Gambian Clause I, declared all dealing in slaves and all bequests of slaves absolutely void. This did not mean the end of slavery with the death of existing slave owners because bequests refer to the leaving of property to those who would not normally inherit by native law. The usual inheritance of slaves by the natural heirs of the deceased continued and no steps were taken to prevent the inheritance of slaves in the Sierra Leone Protectorate until 1926.[128] Nor was there a Sierra Leonean equivalent of the Gambian Clause V, which declared that all children born on or after a certain date should be free and that slaves should be freed on the death of their masters. The Sierra Leone Clause XXIX, like the Gambian Clause II, declared that all persons brought into the Protectorate for slave dealing purposes were automatically free. Clause XXX gave the slave or somebody on his behalf the right to redemption for not more than four pounds for an adult and two pounds for a child—less than half the sums of ten pounds and five pounds in the Gambian Clause III. The lower redemption fee was more probably due to the lack of currency in circulation in the Sierra Leone Protectorate than to any humanitarian motive.

In the Sierra Leone Ordinance there was no equivalent to the Gambian Clause IV which empowered the Administrator in Council to proclaim complete emancipation in the Gambian Protectorate. The Sierra Leone Clauses XXXI and XXXII followed the Gambian Clauses VI and VII by providing for the punishment of slave dealers and their accomplices.

As Chamberlain had instructed, Cardew by Clause LXXXI prohibited the law courts from considering any cases of claims on the person of a slave.[129] This made it easier for a slave to keep his freedom, and it protected British officials from the embarrassment of making legal decisions restoring slaves to their owners. Yet, during the twentieth century British officials in the Sierra Leone Protectorate continued to make administrative decisions over the ownership of slaves until the abolition of slavery, and there were many cases in which the District Commissioners refused redemption.[130] Clause LXXXII did afford the slave some additional protection by making it a criminal offence for any native to adjudicate on the person of a slave.[131]

So at the establishment of the Sierra Leone Protectorate there was no provision to end domestic slavery even though various legal provisions afforded some protection to the domestic slaves. This shows how greatly abolitionism had been discredited since the abolition of slavery in the Gold Coast protected territories in 1874. There had been a marked swing to the right at the Colonial Office. In fact the Sierra Leone Protectorate legislation was not as abolitionist as that for the Gambian Protectorate two years before.

There is no simple explanation for this triumph of the conservationist ethic late in the nineteenth century but the Colonial Office was reacting to three main changes. First, in the Scramble for Africa the colonial powers were concerned with international and political problems, and their own interests assumed greater importance than humanitarian considerations. There seemed to be too much at stake to allow sentiment to influence policy. Second, with increasing contacts and experience of Africa, the European Powers were adopting a much more sophisticated approach to the continent and its problems. Issues were no longer seen in terms of black and white in Britain. This was largely due to the influence of the "anthropologists", who had overcome much of their earlier crude racialism. Their activities had led to a growing understanding of the fact that African institutions like slavery had been evolved by African societies to meet their own particular needs. Cardew himself was at first inclined to judge the societies of the Sierra Leone hinterland impulsively and harshly but as he learnt more his judgements became more cautious. Third, the Colonial Office was working out its new developmental approach to Africa and its problems; basically this meant that instead of resorting to direct legislative action to reshape Africa, Britain should concentrate on building up an economic infra-structure which would give the African societies the means with which to reform themselves. Railways, roads, markets, model farms, technical education and other forms of aid would so radically change African societies that institutions like domestic slavery would wither away because they would be so clearly unsuited to the new social conditions resulting from British development programmes. In the meantime it was thought wise to avoid unnecessary interference with African political and social conditions lest this cause chaos and disruption and further delay progress.

At first this new developmental approach failed in the Sierra Leone Protectorate. The traditional authorities quickly realized that this extension of British power would mean their overthrow, and they rebelled in 1898. Afterwards, as British authority was being consolidated in the Protectorate there was still friction between the chiefs and the Sierra Leone Government—particularly because of British taxation and the problem of domestic slavery. The latter was a particularly embarrassing moral and practical problem for the Sierra Leone Government until it was finally abolished at the beginning of 1928.

NOTES

1. C. W. Newbury, *British Policy towards West Africa. Select Documents 1875–1914* (Oxford 1971), pp. 257–9, Herbert to Rowe, 8 March 1887. See also Fyfe, *A History*, p. 454. Sir Henry was raised to the peerage as Lord Knutsford in 1888.
2. C.P. Afr. (West), 350, Further Correspondence respecting Disturbances in the Native Territories adjacent to Sierra Leone, Lt.-Col. Maltby, Administrator-in-Chief, to Knutsford, 7 August 1888, transmits Mr. Garrett's report of his services in Sulymah District, 28 June 1888.
3. E.G.'s in FO 84/1996, Treaty between Governor Hay and Soriebah, messenger of Chief Kallikolleh of Tambacca country, May-June 1889; and FO 84/2008, Treaties with Limba Chiefs, 21 October and 12 November 1889.
4. FO 84/1986, Hay to Knutsford, 5 November 1888.
5. FO 84/1989, Hay to Knutsford, 4 February 1889; also FO 84/1995, Hay to Knutsford, 25 April 1889, for another similar warning.
6. Fyfe, *A History*, p. 486.
7. FO 84/2072, Knutsford to Govr., Sierra Leone, 1 January 1890.
8. C. P. Afr. (West), 318a. This paper by Samuel Lewis has been discussed above, p. 44.
9. S.L.A., Government Interpreter's Letter Book, 10, Lawson to Col. Sec., 5 October 1888. Lawson remarked that during the last quarter roads to and from the interior had been blocked, particularly towards Limba country. This explained the low number of foreign caravans arriving in the Colony.
10. C.P. Afr. (West), 350, Rowe to Knutsford, 27 July 1888, transmits report on Sherbro by Mr. Mosley, Civil Commandant, 15 March 1888.
11. C.P. Afr. (West), 314, Sierra Leone. Native Raid on British Territory; Memorandum by Hemming, 23 January 1886. Hemming quoted Rowe.

12. C.P. Afr. (West), 331, Further Correspondence respecting Disturbances in the Native Territories adjacent to Sierra Leone.
13. C.P. Afr. (West), 346, Further Correspondence respecting Disturbances in the Native Territories adjacent to Sierra Leone, Hay to Holland, 8 November 1887.
14. C. W. Newbury, *British Policy*, p. 206, A. W. L. Hemming, Minute on West African Expansion, 10 November 1890.
15. This evidence will be discussed in Chapter IV. See *C.R.; II*, 764–8, 1880–8, 2724–31, 3327–9, 3435, *et al.*
16. Although most runaways were of servile origin some who came to Freetown were runaway wives, debtors and criminals.
17. C.P. Afr. (West), 318a, Rowe to Stanley, 7 October 1885. Some of these Temne were "indigenous" to Freetown, which had been ceded to the colonists by a Temne ruler.
18. *Idem.*
19. G.I.L.B., 9, Lawson to Col. Sec., 7 November 1887.
20. *Sierra Leone Times*, 27 October and 15 December 1894.
21. *Sierra Leone Weekly News*, 5 February 1898 and 14 June 1902.
22. G.I.L.B., 9, Lawson to Col. Sec., 15 and 17 October 1887; *ibid.*, Lawson for H.E.'s information, 21 December 1887.
23. FO 84/2072, Knutsford to Govr., Sierra Leone, 1 January 1890.
24. For information about the Frontier Police I have drawn heavily on N. H. R. Etheridge, "The Sierra Leone Frontier Police: a study in the Functions and Employment of a Colonial Force", (Aberdeen M.Litt. Thesis, 1967).
25. *Ibid.*, p. 138.
26. *Ibid.*, p. 109, Etheridge cites CO 267/375, Hay to CO, 9 January 1889.
27. Fyfe, *A History*, p. 485.
28. CO 267/400/1560, Governor Fleming to CO, 12 January 1893, Enclosure 2, Lendy to Col. Sec., 4 January 1893.
29. *Ibid.*, Enclosure 3, Parkes to Col. Sec., 9 January 1893.
30. Conf. Abo/N.A. Letter Book, pp. 100–2, Parkes to Govr., 16 December 1893. Similar views were expressed by the Creole Press. Parkes was a Creole himself. See *Sierra Leone Times*, 15 December 1894, 27 April 1895, 28 August 1897; and *Sierra Leone Weekly News*, 23 June 1894, 23 July 1898.
31. CO 267/400/1560, CO to Governor, 17 February 1893.
32. CO 271/6, S.L. Royal Gazette, XXIV, 333 (15 April 1893), p. 72.
33. CO 267/404/12220, British and Foreign Anti-Slavery Society to Lord Ripon, 19 July 1893. Draft reply from CO, 31 July 1893.
34. Perhaps the most spectacular example of oppression by the Frontier Police took place at Sembehun, Upper Bagru. From 1892 there were complaints by the people; these complaints were investigated and the police at fault were punished. Then the complaints died down until Sergeant Coker arrived in the area. In 1897 with government support the sergeant secured the election of his mistress as Paramount Chief. She was Nancy Tucker, a trader from the

Kittam area. See *C.R. II*, 1224–9, 7910–14; Fyfe, *A History*, p. 553. Etheridge, pp. 144–52, discusses this and other cases of Frontier Police in out-stations acquiring undue influence, maltreating local people and committing crimes.

35. These allegations and counter-allegations were often made in the arguments between Parkes and Lendy, see above. Captain Sharpe said those who wished to continue slave trading trumped up charges against the Frontier Police, see *C.R. II*, 3567–8.
36. S.L.A., M.P. 2623/23 June 1907, Anderson to Col. Sec., 28 August 1907.
37. Little, *The Mende*, p. 56.
38. Hargreaves, "Frontier Police Postings: The Growth of a Historical Legend", *Sierra Leone Studies*, new series, No. 3 (December 1954), pp. 186–7.
39. Etheridge, p. 78.
40. Conf. Abo/N.A. Letter Book, pp. 104–5, Parkes to Govr., June 1894. This is apparently the source of the later charges that Frontier Police ex-slaves returned to oppress their former masters.
41. *C.R. II*, 970–3.
42. Etheridge, p. 153, citing *Sierra Leone Times*, 1 September 1894.
43. *Sierra Leone Times*, 27 October 1894.
44. E.G., *C.R. II*, 2752, 4518, 5186.
45. *Ibid.*, 3525–30, 3600–1, 7598–7601.
46. *C.R. I.*, Chalmers, 23.
47. In 1889 Hay included these in the draft instructions, see above, p. 73. In 1891 Parkes informed Lendy of the Governor's orders that the force must not interfere "more than is *absolutely* necessary with any of the domestic institutions of the country ...", Conf. Abo/N.A. Letter Bk., p. 48, Parkes to Lendy, 23 February 1891. In 1893 a similar warning against interference was included in instructions to the force, see above, p. 75.
48. N.A. Letter Book, 1895–96, No. 80, Sanusi to Bey Sherbro, 23 February 1896.
49. *Ibid.*, 1896–98, No. 391, Sanusi to Bey Sherbro of Mambolo, 14 September 1896.
50. *C.R. I*, Cardew, 8, 15.
51. *C.R. I*, Cardew, 8; Conf. N.A. Letter Bk., Parkes to ?. 23 March 1899. Woman palaver has been discussed above, see p. 16.
52. CO 267/408/8998, Enclosure 1, Minutes of a meeting at Panguma, 11 April 1894, between Cardew and Chief Nyagua and followers.
53. Etheridge, pp. 128–9.
54. The Tongo Players were medicine men who were called in to detect murderers and cannibals. They used reports from spies, magic, trial by ordeal and random selection to identify the "criminals".
55. Etheridge, pp. 140–1; Fyfe, *A History*, p. 491.
56. Fyfe, *A History*, p. 490.

57. Conf. Abo/N.A. Letter Bk., pp. 38–9, Parkes, Remarks on the Slave Traffic, 23 July 1890.
58. *Ibid.*, Ag. Col. Sec. to Parkes, 15 July 1892 and Parkes to Col. Sec., 20 July 1892. Captain Williams was the agent of the Sierra Leone Coaling Company, sent to negotiate a treaty with Samori early in 1892. Parkes concluded that these allegation were groundless.
59. *Ibid.*, Parkes to Col. Sec., 14 September 1892.
60. C.S.Sp. Archives, IV, Boîte 199, Dossier A, *Moniteur Universel*, 3 January 1892, article by J. B. Raimbault, C.S.Sp.
61. Anti-Slavery Papers, C152/93, Parkes to Fox Bourne, 12 February 1893.
62. C.P. Afr. (West), 447, Further Correspondence respecting Limits of British and French Jurisdiction in the Territories adjacent to Sierra Leone, FO to CO, 23 October 1893.
63. Fyfe, *A History*, pp. 520–1.
64. Fyfe, *A History*, p. 512; Alldridge, *The Sherbro*, pp. 252–64.
65. CO 267/401/5969, Fleming to CO, 24 March 1893.
66. CO 267/401/6394, Fleming to CO, 28 March 1893.
67. CO 267/401/6953, Fleming to CO, 10 April 1893, Minute by Hamilton, 4 May 1893.
68. CO 267/400/3839, Fleming to CO, 11 February 1893.
69. CO 267/402/11953, Crooks to CO, 28 June 1893, Minute by Hemming, 19 July 1893.
70. CO 267/403/13277, Crooks to CO, 13 July 1893, Enclosure 1, Notes for address to Port Loko Chiefs.
71. C.M.S., Annual Letter from Rev. J. A. Alley at Port Loko, 18 November 1893.
72. CO 267/402/8674, CO to Govr., 8 June 1893; CO 271/6, S.L. Royal Gazette, XXIV, 357 (23 September 1893), p. 200, Article IX.
73. CO 267/400/1552, Fleming to CO, 7 January 1893, draft reply from CO to Fleming, 17 February 1893.
74. CO 267/400/1560, Fleming to CO, 12 January 1893, various minutes and draft reply, 17 February 1893.
75. CO 267/404/10086, Anti-Slavery Society to CO, 15 June 1893.
76. CO 267/402/8675, Crooks to CO, 8 May 1893.
77. CO 267/403/15020, Crooks to CO, 14 August 1893. Difficulties between Boston and the Frontier Police were apparently the main reason for the withdrawal of the latter.
78. CO 267/407/2090, Fleming to CO, 17 January 1894.
79. *Ibid.*, Minute by Hemming, 9 February 1894.
80. *Ibid.*, draft reply, 14 February 1894. The despatch referred to had been written in reply to Parkes's defence of domestic slavery, see above, p. 74. See C.P. Afr. (West), 460, Further Correspondence respecting the Limits of British and French Jurisdiction in the Territories adjacent to Sierra Leone, Ripon to Fleming, 19 January 1894, paras. 17 and 18.

81. C.P. Afr. (West), 447, FO to CO, 5 August 1893.
82. CO 267/400/3841, Fleming to CO, 13 February 1893, Enclosure 6, Parkes to Col. Sec., 18 November 1892. Reply, 6 April 1893.
83. Fyfe, *A History*, pp. 516–17; Newbury, Documents, p. 275, Minute by Hemming, 9 February 1894.
84. CO 267/403/15874, Crooks to CO, 24 August 1893.
85. C.P. Afr. (West), 447, CO to FO, 2 October 1893, FO to CO, 14 October 1893.
86. *Op. cit.*, Note 62.
87. C.P. Afr. (West), 447, CO to Fleming, 13 December 1893.
88. Fyfe, *A History*, p. 524.
89. CO 267/407/1088, Fleming to CO, 18 January 1894.
90. Fyfe, *A History*, p. 522. Cardew was knighted in 1897.
91. *Ibid.*, p. 531.
92. W. Vivian, *Mendiland Memories. Reflections and Anticipations* (London, no date), p. 127.
93. C.M.S. G 3 A1/o 1894, pp. 56 and 57, Letters from the Bishop to Mr. Wigram and from the Rev. W. J. Humphrey to Mr. Baylis, both on 27 March 1894.
94. Both major Creole newspapers commented favourably on Cardew's vigorous policy in the interior; *Sierra Leone Times*, 9 June 1894; *Sierra Leone Weekly News*, 23 June 1894.
95. *C.R. I*, Cardew 120.
96. CO 267/408/6353, Cardew to Ripon, 20 March 1894.
97. For details of this tour see *C.R. II*, 8550–53, Fyfe, *A History*, pp. 522–3, and various despatches from Cardew in CO 267/408 and 409.
98. CO 267/408/8245, Cardew to Ripon, 5 April 1894. The proclamation of August 1893 was virtually identical to that of April 1893, which has been discussed above; see p. 75 and Note 32.
99. CO 267/408/8998, Cardew to CO, 17 April 1894, Enclosure 1, Minutes of a meeting at Panguma between Cardew and Chief Nyagwa, 11 April 1894. This meeting has been referred to above, see p. 78 and Note 52.
100. CO 267/408/9237, Cardew to CO, 26 April 1894; CO 267/409/9238 and 9647, Cardew to CO, 2 and 10 May 1894.
101. CO 267/409/11019, Cardew to CO, 9 June 1894.
102. CO 267/408/8245, Cardew to CO, 5 April 1894.
103. CO 270/33, LegCo Minutes, 30 May 1894, p. 259.
104. *Sierra Leone Weekly News*, 23 June 1894.
105. C.M.S. G 3 A1/o 1894, Cardew to Bishop Ingham, 1 October 1894. When Bishop James Johnson, who was trying to set up an independent episcopate in the Niger Delta, landed in Sierra Leone in 1900 Cardew invited him ot dinner and contributed £5 to his scheme—the only European to do so in Sierra Leone. See Ayandele, *The Missionary Impact*, p. 234.

106. Conf. Abo/N.A. Letter Bk., 118, Parkes to Cardew, 12 September 1894.
107. The conclusions are drawn mainly from Department of Native Affairs Letter Books, 1895–98, and from Native Affairs Minute Papers of 1896 and 1897. From these I extracted records of runaways, including those from Kikonkeh from April 1896 until May 1897, see Appendix I.
108. For the unpopularity of the runaways in Freetown see above, p. 71.
109. *C.R. II*, XVII, Petition of the Timini Chiefs against the Protectorate Ordinance, 28 June 1897.
110. *C.R.I.*, Chalmers 23. For a discussion of the runaway problem in the Gold Coast in the 1870s and of a report by Chalmers see above, p. 37.
111. Yet, twenty-five per cent Mende at Kikonkeh is high; these runaways might have recently travelled along the slave trade route described by Cardew, see above p. 88.
112. CO 270/37, Minutes ExecCo, 4 January 1898.
113. Native Affairs Letter Book, No. 226, Parkes to J.S. Labour (Contractor, Native Affairs Branch), 5 August 1898. Presumably most of these had made their own way to Freetown or had been rescued by those not in government service.
114. The Frontier Police and the campaign against the slave trade have been discussed above, pp. 72–74.
115. CO 267/412/21092, Cardew to Ripon, 15 November 1894.
116. CO 267/416/2843, Cardew to Ripon, 26 January 1895, Report by Alldridge enclosed.
117. CO 267/416/5332, Cardew to Ripon, 16 February 1895.
118. *Ibid.*; CO 267/422/13709, Liverpool Chamber of Commerce to CO, 2 August 1895, Report of address by Cardew.
119. CO 267/417/6681, Cardew to CO, 15 March 1895.
120. CO 267/417/9167, Cardew to CO, 10 May 1895.
121. Fyfe, *A History*, p. 541.
122. *Ibid.*, p. 549.
123. *Ibid.*, p. 543.
124. CO 267/422/12785, Cardew to Chamberlain, 22 July 1895.
125. CO 88/4/902, Llewelyn to CO, 29 December 1894, Enclosure 1, Ordinance No. 12 of 1894, Gambia.
126. CO 267/425/9496, Cardew to Chamberlain, 9 April 1896; *C.R. II*, 8557–58. At any rate, no chiefs voiced their opposition to the provisions.
127. Ordinance No. 20, 1896, Sierra Leone; submitted to CO by Cardew, 16 September 1896, CO 267/426/20474.
128. Before 1926 the only definite evidence I have found of official intervention to stop slaves passing to heirs was in the special case of Nyagwa's heirs, see below, Chapter V, where the general question of inheriting slaves will be discussed. Although in their

judicial capacity British officials could not sanction the inheritance of slaves, they did so in their administrative capacity.

129. For Chamberlain's instructions, see above, p. 97.
130. See below, Chapter V.
131. This clause was re-enacted in the 1897 Protectorate Ordinance as Clause 76, but it was omitted from the 1901 Ordinance, which is discussed below in Chapter V.

CHAPTER IV

The Imposition of British Authority over the Protectorate of Sierra Leone, the Wars of 1898, and Slavery

At first the people of the interior were apparently prepared to accept the Protectorate despite some misgivings. In reality they were only gradually coming to understand the implications of their new status. They were slow to realize that they were neither able to persuade the British authorities to modify the Protectorate Ordinance nor to oppose it effectively. 1896 marked a major new departure in relations between local rulers and Britain. It saw the end of the old treaty system whereby chiefs conceded a measure of control over external affairs in exchange for British patronage and protection—and perhaps a stipend. Despite the legal fiction that the Protectorate was still foreign soil inhabited by foreign nationals the 1896 Ordinance effectively deprived the local rulers of their independent sovereignty. This was made all too clear by the changed attitude of the Sierra Leone Government which began to treat the chiefs as naughty children of limited intelligence rather than as near equals. The chiefs had been native princes; suddenly they became humble subjects.

This situation was not unique to Sierra Leone. The attitude of the Sierra Leone Government reflected the New Imperialism of late nineteenth-century Britain. In many parts of Africa local rulers were puzzled and offended by the sudden sharp decline of their status in the eyes of the British. A petition from Sierra Leone chiefs in October 1897 shows how difficult they found it to understand their new and subordinate relationship to the British after so many years of apparent partnership.[1] The petitioners had loved and esteemed the British for their acts of generosity,

ADMINISTRATIVE BOUNDARY CHANGES
(*Courtesy of University of London Press Ltd.*

humanity and fair play, and they had known that "among all the white races of people, there is none so good as the English Nation". Therefore they had been slow to protest against the Protectorate Ordinance, although last year they had been

> ... not a little set into a state of alarm and apprehension by messengers sent by the Government of Sierra Leone to read and explain to your Memorialists a certain paper said to contain sundry new laws and regulations which the Government intended to bring into their country, most of which your Memorialists did not understand nor believe, being so unlike the spirit of the English people, with whom they have had to deal now over one hundred and ten years. Your Memorialists according to their country fashion thought it best therefore, in order not to appear to be attempting to oppose the wishes of the Government for no cause, to wait and see by facts what the Government actually meant by these new laws.

Alfa Saidoo, a Port Loko sub-chief, made this point rather more succinctly:

> There is a difference between the white people that come now and those before: those who come now do not respect the Chiefs.[2]

From the beginning of the decade traditional rulers near Freetown and the coast had been given warnings of what was to come. There, officials in the Sierra Leone Government had been intervening more actively in local affairs and upsetting traditional rulers by their authoritarian methods and their lack of respect. Years before the proclamation of the Protectorate, chiefs within the British sphere of influence between Hay's frontier roads and the coast had discovered that they were no longer free agents—whether or not they had ceded their sovereignty to Britain.[3] Letters addressed to them by the Department of Native Affairs made this all too clear.[4] Bai Simra of Masimra was told to return the three people of Suri Bunki whom he had sold "or else you will have to take the consequence of your act". Bai Sherbro of Samu's complaint that the Frontier Police were interfering with his domestic institutions were brushed aside on the grounds that the Frontiers had district orders not to do so. Parkes told Bai Kompa of Koya that he objected to his nominee, Bokari Saysay, being made sub-chief of Mahera, and that Charles Smart should be appointed—and His Excellency approved of this.

Not unnaturally these chiefs later opposed the extension of British authority by the proclamation of the Protectorate and were very hostile to the hut tax. In the Ronietta District Bai Simra and Bai Kompa forbade their sub-chiefs to pay the tax; the latter played a prominent part in the initial passive resistance to this tax.[5] In the Karene District Bai Sherbro of Samu proved unco-operative and he protested against his loss of authority and the heavy burden of taxation imposed by Britain.[6]

After 1896 the Sierra Leone Government interfered even more blatantly with the traditional governments of the interior. In parts of the Protectorate it forced the people to accept as rulers its own nominees—men and women who by local law were completely unfitted to rule. This rankled deeply, especially in parts of the Karene and Ronietta Districts where resistance was strong in the wars of 1898.

With Cardew's approval Captain Sharpe, District Commissioner of Karene, selected a man not in the royal line of succession —Santigi Doura—as the new Brima Sanda of Sanda, because he thought the election was taking too long. Sharpe then found it difficult to get the new Brima Sanda crowned in country fashion, and he failed as a ruler because the people would not recognize his authority.[7] Like other government nominees this chief found himself very unpopular, and in 1898 he was forced to flee to the Karene barracks to save his life.[8]

When the acting Regent of Port Loko, Bokari Bamp, refused to co-operate in collecting the hut tax, Captain Sharpe replaced him with Suri Bunki—a trader with no connection with the ruling families of Port Loko and by Sharpe's own admission a nonentity. During the troubles Suri Bunki tried to escape to Freetown but he was caught and drowned by his own people—probably by members of the chiefly family of Bangura.[9] In the town of Karene Yengi Saio was crowned contrary to country law; he was regarded as a tyrant who dared to oppress them because he was supported by the Sierra Leone Government.[10]

In Ronietta District there were similar instances of official pressure being applied to secure the appointment of government nominees unqualified to rule by local law. These rules were very unpopular and in 1898 many of them paid the penalty for collaboration. The Koya Temme found the official choice of a Loko, Charles Smart, to Mahera particularly obnoxious because it threatened their power in Koya.[11] Smart fled to Captain Fairtlough for protection in 1898, and his brother, Pa Kombo, was killed by some of Bia Simra's sub-chiefs. Thomas Neale Caulker, the son of a slave woman, owed his Paramount Chieftaincy to government pressure. He was regarded as a usurper and was killed in 1898.[12]

Two prominent women chiefs in Ronietta also owed their position to official favour. Nancy Tucker of Sembehun became Paramount Chief largely because of her liaison with a sergeant in the Frontier Police.[13] Less outrageous was the choice of Madam Yoko as Paramount Chief of Senehun. She was the widow of the previous Paramount Chief and did not have much trouble in 1898, although she was very unpopular.[14] She was sometimes uneasy, and in 1896 she was worried about the withdrawal of the Frontier Police from Senahu, her town.[15] Despite reassurance from the Department of Native Affairs she was still uneasy and made another unsuccessful application for a police post at Senahu the following year.[16] Towards the end of 1897 she felt it necessary to ask for assistance in collecting the hut tax.[17] After 1898 both these women's chiefdoms were enlarged, but Madam Yoko was later either driven to suicide or murdered.[18] Many collaborators met unhappy ends because of their association with an alien and unpopular government. Some of them had taken advantage of the troubled times to pay off old scores by turning government officials against their enemies.

Another cause of African resentment, especially in the remoter areas, was the lack of information about the changes of 1896. Some of the difficulties may have been caused by the problem of distance and the lack of communications to the interior, but even in areas fairly close to Freetown the people were inadequately prepared for the proclamation of the Protectorate. Although Cardew had told Chalmers that he had fully explained the Protectorate Ordinance during his 1896 tour, it is clear that he and his officials did not explain the Protectorate Ordinance properly.[19] Cardew and his officials did not understand the chiefs very well nor did they realize how deeply conservative the local communities were. Tact and understanding were needed. Cardew and his officers did not possess these qualities. They were poor communicators.

Since the Colonial Office had restricted administrative expenditure and refused to allow the appointment of Creole District Commissioners Cardew had no option but to second Frontier Police Officers to these posts. Cardew did not regret this; he told Chamberlain that he wanted to make Police officers District Commissioners because in such an uncivilized area as the Protectorate he needed men with plenty of common sense and the ability to deal authoritatively with the natives.[20] The appointment of Frontier Police officers as District Commissioners was doubly unfortunate. Not only were they unwilling and unable to persuade the local people to co-operate but they were associated with the Frontier Police which was so violently hated because of the misdeeds of the lower ranks of the force. Already unhappy at having to deal with subordinates the local chiefs were even unhappier when they discovered that they had to deal with Freetown through officers of the hated Frontier Police. The chiefs thought the District Commissioners were not so much blameworthy as misguided "by the Police and Interpreters who in most cases act from personal feeling", and hoping that the Governor would be above such tainted influences they asked for the "ancient privilege of approaching Your Excellency for any redress we may require for advantages taken of us".[21]

Some chiefs found their district headquarters further away and less accessible than Freetown. In Karene District rulers of chiefdoms not far from Freetown complained of having to make three-day journeys to Karene on "every matter"; Bai Kompa of Koya—quite close to Freetown—petitioned against having to take his problems to Kwalu, the headquarters of Ronietta District, sixty miles away and very hard to reach during the rainy season.[22] Bullom chiefs also complained of having to go to Karene which was further away than Freetown and only accessible by travelling through hostile Limba country.[23]

After the Protectorate was proclaimed many chiefs persisted in their attempts to avoid dealing with their District Commissioners and continued to write to the Department of Native Affairs. Captain Sharpe admitted that the people were unwilling to bring their disputes to him and his colleagues and that they had little contact with the people both before and after 1896.[24] The chiefs failed in their attempts to deal directly with Freetown; they were simply told that their letters had been sent on to their District Commissioners, with whom they must in future communicate.[25] No attempt was made to find out why the chiefs persisted in writing to Freetown. If throughout 1897 they were still ignorant of the new state of affairs Cardew and his officials must have been very poor communicators; if there was some other reason for the unwillingness of the chiefs to approach their District Commissioners Cardew should have tried to find out why the District Commissioners were failing in their duty.

Life was particularly difficult for chiefs at loggerheads with their District Commissioners or not trusted by the Sierra Leone government. In many cases chiefs were in disfavour only because their enemies had won official esteem. Freetown had to trust its officials in the interior, and these were not prepared to give a fair hearing to the chiefs who dared to criticize and to complain. Moreover, these officials in some cases relied far too heavily on suspect sources of information, men like Smart and Fula Mansa. These two did much to poison the minds of the British authorities against various chiefs. The Authorities were not prepared to listen to complaints against men like Smart and Fula Mansa. When Bai Kompa complained to Freetown that Smart was attempting to establish a Loko stronghold in the Temne territory of Koya he was merely curtly referred to his District Commissioner. It is not surprising that Bai Kompa was hostile to the Sierra Leone Government in 1898.[26] Even before the proclamation of the Protectorate, Chief Sena Bundu of Furudugu, next to Mahera, learnt that it was futile to complain about Smart's behaviour during a dispute over the ownership of an island. He was warned that if he made more trouble about the island serious notice would be taken of his conduct.[27] This chief also refused to pay the hut tax in 1898.

In 1898 Smart seized the chance to discredit these two old enemies even more. He and Fula Mansa also joined the punitive expedition against various Koya chiefs—including Bai Kompa and Sena Bundu.[28] The Sierra Leone Government was too ready to believe the unsupported evidence of collaborators like Smart and Fula Mansa. It fell into the trap which Lugard saw so clearly, even if he did not always avoid it:

It is my conviction that throughout Africa—East and West—
much injustice and oppression have been unwittingly done by
our forces acting on crude information, and accusations of slave-
raiding, etc., brought by the enemies of the accused to procure
their destruction.[29]

In Bumpe, also a focal point of insurrection in 1898, the British
were similarly heavy-handed in their treatment of traditional
rulers. When Chief R. C. B. Caulker of Bumpe complained of
ill treatment at the hands of the Acting District Commissioner
he was told that the officer's action had been justified by his own
disloyalty and insubordinate behaviour, and:

His Excellency further directs me to inform you that if there is
a repetition of such conduct he will take into consideration the
desirability of desposing you from your Chieftainship.[30]

The next month fresh complaints about Caulker's disloyalty led to
another reprimand and another threat of deposition.[31] There is
no indication that it ever occurred to anybody in Freetown that
Caulker might have had grievances worthy of investigation.

It was no coincidence that Koya and Bumpe were two of the
most troubled parts of the Protectorate in 1898. Those local
rulers who had incurred official disfavour were treated very incon-
siderately by the authorities, and they were quick to realize that
the whole fabric of their society and personal position was being
threatened. The hut tax wars of 1898 were largely the last
desperate attempts of traditional rulers to halt British aggression.

In other parts of the Protectorate too, this aggression was
curiously lacking in finesse. British officials seemed to believe that
the time had come to show the people who was master or perhaps
some of the younger officers wished to provoke a conflict to give
themselves a chance to show their martial skill and courage.
Captain Cave-Brown-Cave, acting District Commissioner of
Karene in 1897, handled the traditional rulers so badly that it is
hard to believe that he was not deliberately being tactless. When
Paramount Chiefs Bai Foki and Bai Kobolo were unwilling to
come to Karene to receive their official staffs of office, Cave sent
Frontier Policemen to bring them by force. Cave refused to listen
to Bai Foki's complaint that he had been shot at by the Frontiers,

and when the Chief complained to Freetown he was referred back to Cave again.[32] There was evidently little point in complaining to Freetown. Parkes had no doubt that Captain Cave's actions had much to do with the rebellion in Karene District:

> ...(the hut tax was)...merely the immediate cause and the arrest of Bai Foki and Bai Kobolo for not going to receive their staves of office the decisions of the District Commissioner in a certain land palaver in which Bai Bureh was concerned and the general treatment of the people in the District by the Frontiers have been the main causes contributing to the rising.[33]

Further evidence of the authoritarian nature of the new system is that the first supplies to District Commissioners recorded in the Native Affairs Department's letter books were one cat-o'-nine-tails and five sets of handcuffs each.[34]

* * *

The Sierra Leone Government was not just tactless in its dealings with the traditional rulers, it was also exceptionally complacent. Cardew took little action either to remedy grievances or to soothe ruffled feelings during the first eighteen months of the Protectorate despite the flood of complaints and formal petitions that poured in. Such inaction at such a difficult time was at least very irresponsible, if nothing worse.

The complaints began soon after a circular letter made it clear to some of the chiefs how much they stood to lose from the establishment of a protectorate.[35] They learnt that they would lose most of their judicial powers. Two new courts would deal with more serious cases, leaving the courts of chiefs only the power to deal with debt cases and small palavers. District Commissioners alone would deal with very serious matters like witch and slave palavers, the slave traffic and inter-tribal disputes. Chiefs and District Commissioners were to sit in judgement on other cases. The chiefs were equally shocked to discover that the Governor was assuming control over the allocation of waste lands, mineral rights and land concessions. With the approval of the Secretary of State the Governor would have the power to depose and replace any chief he considered unfit for office, and subject to the approval of the Governor, District Commissioners could deport people from their districts.

Other provisions of the Protectorate Ordinance were explained in the Circular Letter. The hut tax was to be ten shillings a year for the larger huts and five shillings for the others. Liquor and trading licences would have to be bought. The clauses on the slave traffic and the redemption of slaves were further explained but in general there was little about the institution of slavery. This may have been because Cardew felt that the official policy on slavery was already well enough understood, or because the Governor wished to avoid a written explanation of his policy on what could prove to be a very embarrassing issue. The chiefs, too, in their subsequent petitions did not make the issue of slavery a central one. It was mentioned rather more frequently in relation to other problems like the chiefs' inability to pay the hut tax or the weakening of their authority. Certainly slavery and slave trading were not nearly as important as the Sierra Leone Government made them out to be during the debate on the 1898 troubles.

In London, too, doubts were already being expressed about the Protectorate Ordinance by officials at the Colonial Office. There were fears that Cardew was trying to do too much too soon. Mercer thought it was not obvious to most natives why they should pay the hut tax, and he thought Cardew's arrangements were premature and too ambitious.[36] Antrobus agreed and suggested that at first the tax should be collected in two districts only—"if even it will be possible to enforce the taxes on the whole of these". The Secretary of State instructed Cardew to "commence the new system in a tentative manner and on a comparatively small scale".

The fears at the Colonial Office were justified by the reactions of traditional rulers to the new system. Even before the circular letter some chiefs in Mafwe were protesting their inability to pay the hut tax, and late in 1897 more Mafwe chiefs joined them in a repetition of their protest.[37] Bai Simra of Masimra thought that he would lose control over his wives and slaves, and that he would be quite unable to pay the heavy taxes due in 1898 because of the closure of trade routes to the interior.[38]

Not surprisingly Madam Yoko effusively welcomed the new system, but even she felt some amendments might be needed and asked for time for her people to adjust to the new state of affairs.[39] More typical and more honest were Temne chiefs protesting against the Protectorate—including Bai Bureh of Kassi, who later led the Temne rising, and Bai Foki, who clashed with Captain Cave in 1897 and supported Bai Bureh in 1898.[40] They accepted the laws against slave dealing but begged the District Commissioner to dissuade the Governor from taking their lands from them, saying that they could not pay the hut tax because:

> Now the whole of the domestics we got before all stubborn and refuse to work for us. Now we have no power to force them to work do, we beg you, Captain Sharpe, to tell Governor that we are not able to observe the new laws and to pay house taxes.

They ended their petition by asking that the right to handle their own palavers and to control their waste lands be restored to them, and they stressed their poverty now that they could not get their slaves to work for them. In this important and significant petition official action against slavery and slave dealing was mentioned repeatedly, but it is made clear that this was only a sceondary cause of real or imagined hardship to the chiefs. The chiefs were more concerned with the loss of their powers to govern their people.

At about the same time Vei and Mende chiefs from Sulima and Gallinas expressed their shock and surprise at the provisions of the Protectorate Ordinance:

> We never were informed of such ordinance before or previous till we see it all of a sudden, it give such a terrible cry and noise over the Country . . . but now we see ourselves in bondage, we are not free, we know that our country did not take by conquest only we gave the queen to protect it, we find now that she took it from us, but not only protection. If we know that such will be the case we might not agree to sign treaty with His Excellency Governor Havelock, . . .[41]

They also complained they were too poor to pay trading licence fees or the hut tax. Slavery is not mentioned in the printed version.

Thanks to W. T. G. Lawson, an ex-civil servant related to the rulers of Koya, the next Temne petition against the Protectorate Ordinance was more elegantly phrased.[42] Some Temne Chiefs in

Freetown for the Diamond Jubilee celebrations told Parkes of the changes which worried them most. First, they were to have no more power over their country. Second, the tax brought back memories of the dreadful days when Koya had been annexed and the people had been exploited by unscrupulous tax collectors.[43] Third, fourth and fifth were complaints about the provision for punishing chiefs who were handling cases outside their jurisdiction, about trade licences and controls over the liquor trade. Sixth, although they recognized that slave dealing was forbidden, they begged that the few domestics still with them should not be encouraged to run away to Freetown. While admitting that some slaves ran away because of ill treatment, the chiefs argued that most of the runaways were lazy. Rather inconsistently they went on to express their fears that since two-thirds of the people were slaves and fulfilled so many vital economic and social functions their exodus to Freetown would ruin and depopulate the Protectorate. Many officials accepted the validity of this argument. Captain Sharpe, for example, fined a Sierra Leonean woman after a local chief had complained that she was encouraging his slaves to run away.[44]

The whole problem of runaway slaves in her African protectorates faced Britain with an embarrassing dilemma late in the nineteenth century. By encouraging slaves to leave the masters or declining to dam the flow of slaves seeking liberty under the British flag Britain risked incurring the hostility of the traditional rulers on whom she depended so heavily for the tranquil administration of her protectorates. On the other hand failure to assist runaway slaves could lead to a storm of humanitarian protest in Britain. More than once the government of the day was embarrassed by revelations that British officials in African protectorates were not giving fugitive slaves their liberty. J. A. Pease, M.P., had documentary evidence that in East Africa British officials had been compelling British subjects to return runaway slaves they had been sheltering.[45] In 1897 and 1898 the British Resident at Ibadan was in trouble for returning three fugitives to their masters at Ijesha.[46] Governor McCallum at Lagos wrote a long report about the problem of runaways in December 1897.[47] This clearly showed how complex the problem was, particularly when dealing with two types of runaways. There were those who ran away to Lagos and claimed their freedom and later returned home; McCallum thought they should not be protected from the native authorities unless they had paid the prescribed compensation to their masters and believed they should be warned of this. Then there were those who ran away from one state in the Protectorate to another—possibly their homeland. McCallum suggested telling all native rulers that runaways must be surrendered unless compensation had been paid. The Colonial Office disagreed. Although it accepted that an abrupt collapse of slavery would mean considerable social and economic disorganization the Colonial Office thought McCallum's proposals were injudicious because copies of his letters might reach Britain and the Colonial Office would not be able to defend such proposals in Britain. Clearly officials were thinking of the difficulties caused by Mr. Pease's revelations about British officials restoring slaves to their owners in East Africa.

So neither the Sierra Leone Government nor the Colonial Office could act to prevent the exodus of domestic slaves from the Sierra Leone Protectorate for fear of the consequences this might have in Britain. The Temne chiefs may well have been aware of this because in the five specific requests they made at the end of their petition they did not mention slavery. They wanted the restoration of their country, the abolition of the hut tax, the abolition of trading licences, the right of appeal to the Governor and the exemption of traditional rulers from the possible disgrace of handcuffing and flogging.

After the completion of the Diamond Jubilee celebrations, the Temne chiefs defiantly stayed on in Freetown, waiting for London's reply to their petition and the return of Cardew from leave in Britain.[48] Whitehall's reaction to this petition was cautious and reasonably tactful. Certainly it was much better received than protests from the Freetown and Manchester Chambers of Commerce against the hut tax. The Colonial Office was not greatly impressed by representations from people who had had no direct experience of the Protectorate, and Antrobus commented:

The Manchester and Liverpool Chambers of Commerce, like the Aborigines Protection Society, seems to pass on to us the complaints of irresponsible persons without first trying to ascertain whether there is anything in them.[49]

119

The Colonial Office thought that the Temne petitioners laboured "under some not unnatural misapprenhensions which can only be removed by personal explanations by the colonial officials".[50] The petitioners should be told that the hut tax was necessary for the development of the country, that the new system would promote trade and make it easier for the people to pay the taxes and that their worries about having to give up their traditional rights and customs were exaggerated—in particular the Crown did not intend taking over private land. Wherever possible the Officer Administering the Government was to take pains to remove the misapprehensions of the natives. The Colonial Office did not realize the inadequacy of the District Commissioners as communicators—especially those who were influenced by untrustworthy collaborators. The official who understood the people of the Protectorate best was Parkes, and he could have done much to smooth the way in the first years of the Protectorate. Yet, he and the Department of Native Affairs were given only an unimportant role in the administration of the Protectorate.

Parkes met the petitioners and reported their views. French duties were hindering trade and the price of palm produce was low and the people could not afford the hut tax. Parkes warned that if the hut tax were collected "considerable tact and patience will have to be exercised".[51] The next day Parkes sent the chiefs the gist of London's reply to their petition.[52]

The chiefs were still unhappy, and they stayed on in Freetown to submit another petition a few days later. They reiterated their inability to pay the hut tax and again asked for the restoration of their rights of jurisdiction. More strongly than before, they expressed their concern at the numbers of domestic slaves running away:

> Moreover, among the many things which greatly affect our mind and draw forth tears from our eyes is what relates to our domestics, upon whom we at present solely depend. All of them are daily escaping to the Isles of Tasso and Kikonki, leaving us to do what we are unable and unaccustomed to, the carrying of loads and cleaning of roads.[53]

Meanwhile it was confirmed that one of the chiefs' grievances had been settled. In December 1896 the Secretary of State had ordered the repeal of Part IV of the 1896 Protectorate Ordinance, which dealt with lands; Cardew carried this out in Ordinance 34 of 1896—"The Protectorate Ordinance Amendment Ordinance (No. 2) 1896".[54] When the revised Protectorate Ordinance was submitted, No. 11 of 1897, it did not include the land clauses—among them the very unpopular clause giving the Governor the power to dispose of waste lands.[55]

The debate on the Protectorate Ordinance of 1897 also gave Creole members of the Legislative Council the chance to voice their protests. T. C. Bishop made some telling points. He argued that because the people of the Protectorate were facing great changes the Government should suspend the hut tax, in lieu of compensation for those who were losing their slaves—their main source of wealth.[56] Later Bishop told Chalmers that intelligent people generally approved of the Protectorate Ordinance but thought it premature in parts, especially the hasty imposition of the hut tax when people were trying to get used to the abolition of slavery and the doubtful benefits of replacing chiefly authority with that of the District Commissioners.[57] Sir Samuel Lewis also approved of the principles behind Cardew's policy but had doubts about the ways in which it had been carried out; he thought Cardew did not understand the people of the Protectorate.[58]

The Creole Press had initially supported Cardew's forward policy in the interior but with reservations about his attacks on domestic slavery—"a subject which requires delicate handling"—and on the liquor and arms traffic because these adversely affected the revenue of the Colony.[59] In 1895 many Creoles turned against Cardew because of his interference in the case of Spaine, a Creole Postmaster who was twice acquitted by Freetown juries and convicted at his third trial by a judge and assessors on charges of embezzlement.[60] Consequently in 1896 the *Sierra Leone Times* attacked Cardew and denounced the Protectorate Ordinance as despotic. The following year the newspaper was attacking the principles behind the proclamation of the Protectorate and doubting "the prudence and justice of unduly interfering with the domestic institutions of natives, living in their own countries and under their own chiefs".[61] This Creole paper was apparently more openly concerned about the preservation of domestic slavery than the chiefs themselves.

The more moderate *Sierra Leone Weekly News* also gave

Cardew a warm welcome and supported his policies at first, but it also turned against Cardew after the Spaine case.[62] Its doubts about Cardew's policies grew, and in 1897 it opposed the hut tax and called for major amendments to the Protectorate Ordinance.[63] Nevertheless, during 1897 the Sierra Leone Government remained strangely unperturbed by the mounting tide of criticism. Cardew spent much of the second half of the year in Britain and the Acting Governor did very little.

He certainly did not satisfy the Temne chiefs who still obstinately remained in Freetown and drew up yet another petition against the Ordinance—this time to the Sierra Leone Legislative Council.[64] When Cardew arrived back in Freetown in November the chiefs pointed out that they had been waiting for him for five months and asked him to "give a merciful ear to us".[65]

Briefly it seemed that Cardew might give the chiefs "a merciful ear" and set their minds at rest, but at this crucial stage something went wrong—apparently Cardew lost his temper. Cardew asked Parkes to tell the chiefs about the concessions that he intended making the day before he announced them officially.[66] The chiefs were reasonably pleased and Parkes gathered that most of them were prepared to accept the concessions. The next day the Governor told the chiefs that the tax would be reduced to five shillings or a bushel of palm kernels or husked rice per hut irrespective of size, that temporary huts and villages of less than twenty huts would be exempt and that the chiefs would be given a commission of threepence per hut for collecting the tax.[67] He stressed the advantages of the tax:

> It will tend to the civilization of your people by placing education within their reach, and by providing funds for improving roads and constructing railways, it will open up your country and enable you to send its products more cheaply to the markets, and thus increase the wealth and prosperity of your people.

He told the chiefs that most of their complaints were based on misconceptions and that they could not be left alone to govern themselves because slaving and tribal wars would start again. He told them to address any complaints to their District Commissioners, who would forward them to Freetown as long as they were neither frivolous nor factious.

Then, according to Parkes, the spirit of the meeting turned sour.[68] When a Temne chief from Karene District, Pa Suba of Magbele, said they wished to consider the concessions, Cardew became impatient and told the chiefs that he would give them no more time to decide and that he was not prepared to make any further concessions.[69] Cardew should have known that the Temne very seldom gave a direct answer immediately, and if he had handled them with tact and patience instead of trying to bully them, the chiefs at the meeting might well have agreed to co-operate in the collection of the tax.

Instead the chiefs left the meeting unhappy and angry and immediately drew up another petition.[70] First to sign was Pa Suba, who had been so rudely interrupted by Cardew and who began to collect money to repay his government stipend so that he would be free to contract out of the Protectorate.[71] This fresh petition repeated the chiefs' grievances, but they later made it clear to Sir David Chalmers that they had been aggrieved less by the substance of the meeting than by the way in which Cardew had conducted it.[72] Cardew's reply to this latest petition was curt; he told the petitioners that his decision was final and that they were mistaken in thinking villages of less than eighty huts would be exempt from the hut tax—the limit was twenty.[73]

Cardew was disturbed by the outcome of this meeting with the Temne chiefs. He began to take the possibility of unrest seriously. He gave instructions to District Commissioners and in particular stressed the need to retain enough police to prevent and suppress disturbances. He also announced that Koinadugu and Panguma Districts would be exempt from the hut tax in 1898.[74]

As 1897 ended tension was high throughout the Protectorate, and in 1898 this tension manifested itself in risings in all the districts except Koinadugu which was far from Freetown and exempt from the hut tax. Even Koinadugu was on the brink of rebellion early in 1898, as a report by Captain Birch shows.[75] There had been two serious incidents. At Farandugu in Koranko country an armed mob had surrounded a Frontier Police barracks, and some of them had forced their way inside to recapture a slave woman or wife who had taken shelter there. The corporal in charge had decided that discretion was the better part of valour and had surrendered the woman. There had been serious trouble after the Chief of Bafodeyah had enticed slaves away from Lago.

123

Birch warned that the natives knew of the weakness of the Company at District Headquarters in Falaba and that they thought the time ripe to cause trouble. Out-stations had been reduced, two had been withdrawn and he had only seven Frontiers —one of them a boy bugler—at Falaba.

Yet, there was no rising in Koinadugu in 1898 and the various theories to account for this depend on the theories about the risings in the other four districts. Some argued that the dominant tribal group in the district, the Limba, owned few slaves and had themselves been victims of slavers, and that the Limba owed a debt of gratitude to the British Government which had delivered them from Samori's slave raiders. Others thought the district had been peaceful because it had been exempted from the hut tax. It is also arguable that being so far from Freetown the people had not felt the weight of British authority as much as those nearer Freetown had. Captain Birch preferred to think that the district had accepted British authority because "people in that district are quite different to the other natives, much superior and better dressed", a superiority he attributed to the Moslem influence, and he also thought it a great advantage to have several tribes in the district.[76] There is no single explanation for the comparative peacefulness of Koinadugu, but it seems likely that because it was further away from Freetown than the other districts Koinadugu did not have to make quite such a sudden adjustment to the new system as the others.

*　　*　　*

It was in the Temne towns of Karene and Port Loko in the Karene District that discontent first flared into open rebellion in 1898. It is convenient to call this the Temne Rising although other Temne, notably the Mabanta and Koya Temne in Ronietta District, also rebelled later in the year. The Temne Rising, which began first and lasted the longest, posed the most serious challenge to British authority. Yet, it was apparently provoked by the Sierra Leone Government and its officials, in particular by the District Commissioner of Karene, Captain Sharpe.

Early in February Sharpe began collecting the hut tax in the wealthy and important centre of Port Loko. By his own account he was ready to use strong arm methods of collection.[77] On the

9th he made his first mistake when he arrested Bokari Bamp, Acting Chief of Port Loko, and four other important chiefs because they had refused to promise to order their people not to molest Sierra Leoneans who were paying the tax. Sharpe was not merely over-reacting in a dangerous situation, but he was also, as Chalmers pointed out later, acting illegally by arresting the chiefs.[78] It was not an offence to refuse to promise not to molest nor to refuse to collect the hut tax—the Protectorate Ordinance only obliged the chiefs to pay the tax and not to collect it. Sharpe's readiness to arrest Bokari Bamp was possibly due to the personal antagonism between the two men since they had clashed over the election of the Brima Sanda of Sanda in 1897.[79]

Sharpe's second mistake was to appoint Suri Bunki to replace Bokari Bamp as acting ruler of Port Loko; it is hard to understand why Sharpe chose a man completely unfitted to rule by traditional law and by his own account a nonentity.[80] His third mistake was to believe Suri Bunki's hysterical and unsupported allegations that Bai Bureh was coming to attack Suri Bunki for paying the hut tax. Without any attempt to find out whether the accusation was true or not, Sharpe decided to try to arrest Bai Bureh.[81] Again, Sharpe's readiness to arrest this chief may have been partly due to earlier clashes with him. In 1894 Sharpe had failed to carry out his orders to arrest Bai Bureh and in 1896 the two men had quarrelled when Bai Bureh had been unwilling to help build the barracks at Karene. Sharpe always thought him a troublesome chief.[82] Sharpe's fourth mistake was to under-estimate Bai Bureh's strength and to ask for a force of only twenty Frontier Police to arrest him.[83]

Sharpe must bear a large share of the blame for provoking this very capable chief into rebellion against Britain and also for the humiliating failure to arrest him. This marked the beginning of months of fighting ended only by the arrest of Bai Bureh on 16 November 1898. As La Ray Denzer has pointed out, Bai Bureh took the initiative against the British for four months with a small and poorly equipped army, and he held out against them for six more months after that. He was able to hold out for so long because he skilfully employed guerrilla tactics against the British.[84] Cardew must also share the blame because he was quick to support Sharpe and, when sending Major Tarbet with the twenty men requested by Sharpe, Cardew commented:

I consider Captain Sharpe has acted with great decision and promptitude under very difficult circumstances, and I approve of the action taken by him and of his recommendations.[85]

In a similar manner resistance among the Koya Temne in Ronietta District was provoked by the blunders of British officials. In fact there were no less than three different District Commissioners in charge of Ronietta in the first quarter of 1898. Dr. Hood, the District Surgeon, acted until he was replaced by Captain Moore on 21 January. Moore, chosen because Cardew thought the tense situation called for a military man, knew that he had been sent to collect the tax by force and to crush any resistance.[86] When Captain Fairtlough, previously District Commissioner of Panguma, returned from leave he took over Ronietta —on 17 March.[87]

When trouble came in Ronietta official circles were quick to blame the Koya chiefs who had previously clashed with the authorities. In particular Bai Kompa, Paramount Chief of Koya, Pa Nembana, Chief of Koya and Bai Kompa's second in command, and Almami Sena Bundu of Furudugu were singled out as troublemakers. Bai Kompa and the Almami had clashed with the Sierra Leone Government over the appointment of Charles Smart to Mahera and all three chiefs had been prominent signatories to various petitions against the Protectorate Ordinance.[88]

At the end of 1897 Dr. Hood had politely asked the chiefs in Ronietta to pay the tax quickly and willingly.[89] At the beginning of 1898 Bai Kompa wrote to Parkes saying he could not pay the tax.[90] On 10 January 1898 Hood reported that most Ronietta Chiefs were making no effort to pay the tax.[91] There were disturbances among the Mabanta Temne and in Bagru, Nancy Tucker's country. Hood believed that the Koya sub-chiefs would have been prepared to pay if they had not been intimidated by Bai Kompa and Pa Nembana. This belief was apparently based solely on the unreliable evidence of Smart who also alleged that he had been so intimidated that he feared for his life. Hood did not think he had enough Frontier Policemen to arrest the Paramount Chiefs of the district, and so he sent for Bai Kompa and Pa Nembana.

When the two chiefs did not answer Hood's summons, the first of the four expeditions to crush resistance in Koya during 1898 was organized.[92] Armed and accompanied by Smart, Captain

Warren of the Frontier Police arrested Pa Nembana and then went to arrest Bai Kompa at his home. Bai Kompa said he was ill and refused to get up, but Warren dragged the chief off his bed. Bai Kompa complained that Warren had kicked him and refused to go to Kwalu. As there was some doubt whether Bai Kompa's compound was in the Colony or the Protectorate Warren agreed to let Bai Kompa go to Freetown, escorted by two Frontiers. Meanwhile in Kwalu, Pa Nembana was tried by Captain Moore, and convicted of intimidating Smart and refusing to pay the Hut Tax. He was sentenced to deposition, twelve months' imprisonment with hard labour and thirty-six lashes, although Cardew did not confirm the lashes.

Towards the end of January Captain Moore continued his hard line policy by summoning sixty to seventy leading chiefs to Kwalu and detaining several of them until some attempt was made to pay at least some of the tax their chiefdoms owed. Within some weeks the arrested chiefs paid the tax, including Bai Simra of Masimra and Bai Sherbro of Yoni.[93] Meanwhile Bai Kompa had spoken to Cardew in Freetown and promised to report to Moore at Kwalu and to start collecting the tax. When Bai Kompa failed to report, Moore dispatched a second armed expedition into Koya to find the recalcitrant chief. This expedition failed to find Bai Kompa and its leader, Dr. Hood, reported that armed bands were on the move in Koya.

In March, after receiving information from Smart that Bai Kompa was organizing resistance and collecting an army, Captain Moore led the third expedition into Koya, accompanied also by Captain Fairtlough and Smart himself. Shots were exchanged with warboys—the first fighting in Koya in 1898—but the expeditionary force suffered no casualties although several Koya men were killed. Bai Kompa still eluded capture, and in April Captain Fairtlough led the fourth expedition into Koya, accompanied by Captain Warren, Smart, the Frontiers and Yoni warriors under the command of Fula Mansa.[94] The targets this time were Almami Sena Bundu of Furudugu and Suri Kamara, accused by Smart and Fula Mansa of blocking trade on the Rokel River.[95] Neither man was caught but the expeditionary force looted, destroyed and killed so effectively that the Koya leaders either fled or submitted. Unchecked by Fairtlough, Fula Mansa and his Yoni did most of the fighting and plundering. Fairtlough then appointed Fula Mansa to act as Paramount Chief of Koya and late in April he reported that the country was quiet. This was an uneasy peace, imposed by terror. As Chalmers later pointed out, the harshness of the two later Koya expeditions could not be justified on military grounds. They aroused resentment, they encouraged Bai Bureh to continue his resistance in Karene District, and they were partly responsible for the Mende outbreak at the end of April.[96]

*   *   *

It is clear that the risings of the Temne in Karene and in Koya in the Ronietta District were largely provoked by British aggression, but this does not appear to be true of the Mende outbreak in 1898. The risings of the Mende, Sherbro and Gallinas peoples over wide areas of Bandajuma, Panguma and Ronietta Districts took Freetown by surprise, and there is some truth in the official view of the Mende Rising as a conspiracy.

At first it looked as though Mende resistance to the hut tax would be passive only. Early in 1898 Carr, District Commissioner of Bandajuma, had felt it necessary to go to Mafwe to speak to various chiefs, including some who had recently written to Freetown to say that they could not pay the tax.[97] Carr gave them "a long harangue, and talked quietly and softly to them" but made no progress.[98] Carr sensibly dismissed the chiefs and told them to return in a week bringing what they could manage to pay, just to show their willingness to co-operate. The chiefs returned empty-handed and Carr arrested four of their leaders and dispersed the waiting crowd of four or five thousand. Although he was glad to report that no blood had been shed he was still "not one inch nearer the collecting of the tax", and so he was writing officially to ask how to deal with the chiefs. Freetown approved Carr's actions so far and the Acting Attorney General advised that the four chiefs be given severe sentences, which could be reduced if their people proved co-operative.[99] Cardew took the precaution of telegraphing London for permission to send a company of troops to Bandajuma, if necessary. He then consulted Carr, who expected little trouble and advised that half a company be sent to garrison Bandajuma so that he could use all the Frontiers to collect the tax and to maintain order.[100]

Then Bandajuma apparently calmed down. The imprisoned chiefs' people began paying the tax and by the end of April Carr had collected £2,624 in the district. As a result, Cardew decided that there was no need for troops after all.[101] Although Carr was satisfied with the way in which he had handled an explosive situation and collected the tax, Chalmers was more critical.[102] He considered the arrest of the four chiefs illegal and thought Carr had been slow to realize the dangers of the situation.[103] In particular Carr should have taken warning from the events of 4 January when Dr. Arnold had been mobbed at Gbah while trying to collect the tax.[104] Carr was still satisfied with the situation in his district little more than two weeks before the outbreak of the Mende Rising. He reassured Cardew:

> You may rest perfectly assured, sir, and make your mind easy that there will be no bother or fighting in this district, trouble of course there is, and there may be a little hitch and friction here and there. This is only to be expected in the first year.[105]

In his reply to the Chalmers Report Cardew supported Carr but privately he held different views.[106] In 1899 Cardew wrote to Nathan, Acting Governor of Sierra Leone, to express his pleasure that Carr was being moved from Bandajuma where he had handled the hut tax badly. He suggested to Nathan that if there had been another man there it might have been a different story.[107] Carr was not cast in the same aggressive military mould as his colleagues and the Governor. Perhaps Cardew's opinion of Carr was coloured by suspicions about his morals. In 1900 Carr, then Commissioner of Panguma, was charged with openly cohabiting with certain black women to the scandal of his district and to the detriment of his own influence as Chief Officer of the District.[108] Morals apart, Carr had misjudged the state of affairs in Bandajuma so badly that he gravely weakened the district headquarters by sending most of the garrison to collect tax in a remote area.[109] Yet, Carr was by no means the only official in Sierra Leone who was taken aback by the suddenness, ferocity and wide extent of the Mende Rising.[110] Besides the Mende the Sherbro, Gallinas, Bulom and Temne people in the southern half of the Protectorate rebelled. The rising covered most of Ronietta and Bandajuma Districts and the western half of Panguma. It even extended into the Colony. This rising was comparatively speedily crushed by two military expeditions led by Colonels Woodgate and Cunningham, and peace was restored to the southern half of the Protectorate by the end of June. Although it was more easily suppressed the Mende Rising was much more disturbing than the Temne Rising. The Temne were fighting for their independence against the British but the Mende seemed to be embarking on an orgy of destruction and slaughter of all foreigners. It was not only those associated with the hated Freetown Government who suffered: Creoles and Europeans, traders and missionaries and their associates were robbed, tortured, raped and murdered just because they were aliens living in the Protectorate.

Although it is clear that the Mende and their allies attacked first, there is some doubt as to how and where the rising started. The balance of evidence points to R. C. B. Caulker's chiefdom of Bumpe as the centre of the conspiracy. Two other important chiefs, Bai Sherbro of Yoni (Gbana Lewis) and Nyagwa of Panguma were thought to be instigators and Fawundu of Mano was also suspected.[111] The evidence against Bai Sherbro and Fawundu is by no means conclusive and was partly based on their earlier openly expressed opposition to the extension of British authority over the Protectorate. They had both protested against the Protectorate Ordinance in February 1897, and Bai Sherbro probably organized the boycott of trade in Sherbro in 1897. Cardew admitted that the precise combination that led to the Mende Rising was not traced, but this did not hinder official circles from having "strong suspicions and various opinions".[112]

The role of Nyagwa in the rising is uncertain, and the official case against him was not strong. Yet, both the Governor and the District Commissioner of Panguma, Captain Blakeney, were convinced that he was deeply involved. This may have been wishful thinking because for a variety of reasons it suited the Sierra Leone Government to show that Nyagwa had led the rebellion. First, he was a very powerful chief who could possibly have halted the extension of British power into Panguma. Second, proof of his involvement would lend support to Cardew's theory of the rising as a widespread conspiracy. Third, Nyagwa had previously clashed with Cardew; he had refused to co-operate in the abolition of the slave traffic and he had encouraged slave raids on Kono and Koranko territories.[113] Fourth, because Nyagwa had been a prominent slave raider, proof of his involvement would support Cardew's claim that his campaign against slavery and the slave trade had much to do with the origins of the rising. Fifth, Panguma was exempt from the hut tax and Cardew could argue that Nyagwa's involvement showed that the hut tax was not an important cause of the outbreaks. Sixth, Captain Blakeney had acted rather hastily against Nyagwa, and he needed to show that he had been justified in so doing.

During the first half of 1898 Blakeney's aggression was largely responsible for the unrest in the district.[114] After learning from an escaped slave—whose evidence he should have treated with caution—that Nyagwa was plotting an insurrection against the white man, Blakeney sent two Frontiers in disguise to investigate. The two Frontiers supported the slave's story, according to Blakeney, but strangely enough they were not available to give evidence before Chalmers; they were reported missing but were in fact at Panguma. On the strength of this Blakeney threatened Nyagwa with arrest. Nyagwa agreed that his people should give up their arms. The following month, May, Blakeney arrested Nyagwa although there was no additional evidence against him. In June an attempt was made to rescue Nyagwa from imprisonment in Panguma, and the town was under siege. There was no further attempt to attack government forces in the district but early in 1899 British forces marched into Panguma to crush a coalition of chiefs—including Nyagwa's son—against Fabunde of Luawa. Nyagwa was later sent to the Gold Coast as a political prisoner and died there in 1906.

* * *

After the end of the risings a new struggle began. This raged between the various groups of people who felt it vital to get their version of the 1898 risings accepted. The Colonial Office did not take kindly to Governors who failed to keep their colonies running smoothly, and the futures of Cardew and his officials would be bleak unless they could prove they were beyond reproach. The nature of the official verdict was also a matter of great concern to various other groups in Freetown—to the Creole Press, the rebels, the loyal Africans, the Frontier Police, expatriate and Creole traders and the missionaries. In Britain too, political, mercantile, religious and humanitarian interests were at stake.

The reaction of the Secretary of State, Chamberlain, was at first one of embarrassment at criticism in Parliament and uncertainty as to what line he should adopt. The matter was first raised in the Commons on 21 April (before the Mende outbreak) by an Irish Nationalist, Michael Davitt.[115] He wanted to know by what authority the tax was being collected and "whether, in view of the bloodshed that has been caused in the efforts to enforce the tax, it will be given up". Chamberlain promised a further inquiry as soon as the rebellion was quelled and in answer to a supplementary question agreed that the hut tax had caused the rebellion:

> Yes, I think it can be taken for granted that the opposition of the chiefs to the enforcement of the tax caused the rebellion; but I may add I do not think it in any way justifies the rebellion any more than resistance to any other tax would justify it.

Chamberlain's frankness later caused him some difficulty. When pressed he replied differently and lamely excused his earlier answer:

> It is an unfortunate result of supplemental questions that one has to give an answer without perhaps sufficient consideration,...[116]

Four days later Davitt asked more questions about the rising. Now that it was acknoweldged that the tax had caused the rebellion, he wanted to know if measures would be taken as soon as possible to tell the natives affected that the tax would be discontinued.[117] Chamberlain replied that the Governor did not consider the tax oppressive, but that large exemptions had been made where it was thought that the tax would press heavily on the natives.[118] He warned of the danger of establishing the principle that taxes considered oppressive by the taxpayers should not be levied. A decision to abolish the hut tax would make it very difficult to collect revenue from African colonies which were expected to bear the cost of their own administrations.

When the news of the Mende Rising reached Britain Davitt

moved the adjournment of the House to call attention to the alarming state of affairs in the Sierra Leone Protectorate.[119] He spoke of the hatred of the hut tax and of the offensive manner in which it had been collected—"The collecting force employed was made up of emancipated slaves who offered insult to their previous masters". He viciously attacked Cardew—"A more criminal policy could not be carried out, if, instead of Sir Frederick Cardew, a Governor had been selected from Colney Hatch". In his reply Chamberlain put the issue of the British action against slavery and the slave trade forward as an explanation for the risings. He defended Cardew and attacked Bai Bureh as "a slaver and a rather turbulent person". He referred to the opinion of W. J. Humphrey, a missionary murdered by the insurgents, that the revolt had started with the Creole traders, and he quoted the opinion of the Bishop of Sierra Leone that Bai Bureh was a drunken slaver who had rebelled because he knew that an English takeover would put an end to the slave trade.[120] In conclusion Chamberlain asked the Commons to wait for the outcome of an official inquiry. This effectively forestalled any fierce criticism from the Liberal Opposition, whose spokesman on colonial affairs, Sydney Buxton, was inclined to agree with Chamberlain's diagnosis:

> It was very probable that the original cause of the revolt was the action taken by Sir Frederick Cardew in the direction of interference with domestic slavery, rather than to the proposals with regard to the hut tax. If it is shown that this revolt was caused by an attempt to impose new regulations, with the object of putting down slavery, we shall do all we can to strengthen the Colonial Office in dealing with that question; but so far it is shown that it was due to the hut tax, we shall have to press for its abolition.[121]

Buxton obviously expected the inquiry to find that action against slavery was at the back of the risings. Such a finding would mean that Chamberlain could rely on the support of most of the Commons on this particular issue and also to a certain extent for his methods of extending British authority over West Africa. In June Parliamentary criticism was stilled by the appointment of Sir David Chalmers to inquire into the insurrection in the Protectorate and into the general state of affairs in the Colony and the Protectorate.[122] Extra-Parliamentary criticism did not abate.

The mercantile interest, notably the Chambers of Commerce with West African connections, was very vocal but surprisingly ineffective in their attempts to win Chamberlain over to its interpretation of the Sierra Leone risings. This was despite the fact that Chamberlain himself had been a businessman and despite the powerful propaganda of Mary Kingsley.

Mary Kingsley, who was closely associated with Alfred Jones and John Holt of the Liverpool Chamber of Commerce, attracted attention by arguing that the hut tax was repugnant to the African legal principle that if one made a regular payment for the use of something it would become the property of the recipient of the payment.[123] In other words, by paying the hut tax the people of the Sierra Leone Protectorate were by their own laws acknowledging that their huts belonged to the Sierra Leone Government. Her letter about this to the Spectator led her into "direct communication wih Mr Chamberlain, and now once a week I get a letter from him and he gets a massive answer. He doesn't stick to this hut tax only now."[124] Her comments to Chamberlain were reasonably tactful but she wrote much more trenchantly to E. D. Morel, a clerk in Alfred Jones's Elder Dempster Shipping Company who was making a name for himself as a freelance writer on West Africa:

> From my point of view the amount of the tax and the massacres connected with it did not affect the case. Which was that England had promised those Africans to respect their country law and their private property, by putting on the hut tax she disgraced herself . . .[125]

Morel agreed with Mary Kingsley. Both writers had so much respect for African institutions that they were led to argue for the retention of domestic slavery as a vital part of the social system—a conservationist argument of some influence in Sierra Leone for the next two decades.[126]

The Manchester Chamber of Commerce was lucky to have the *Manchester Guardian* to put the mercantile view so clearly, even though the 1898 risings did not figure prominently on the pages of this newspaper. It argued that the hut tax was the direct cause of the risings because it was an obnoxious tax collected by the Frontiers, who were mostly manumitted slaves; the cost of collection was ruinous and therefore the newspaper thought that the tax should be withdrawn.[127] After the appointment of Chalmers there was little editorial comment, and by the time the Chalmers Report was published West African affairs were overshadowed by the crisis in South Africa.

Chambers of Commerce also made formal representations to the Secretary of State, but they tended to betray the ignorance of their authors rather than to convince Chamberlain. J. Arthur Hutton, Chairman of the African Committee of the Manchester Chamber of Commerce, wrote Chamberlain a very odd letter early in May 1898.[128] He thought that fifty to a hundred thousand troops, of whom a quarter would probably die of fever, would be needed to quell the rebellion and that the cost would be enormous. He advised the Colonial Office to withdraw the tax at once and to sack Cardew. Chamberlain replied courteously that he was most anxious to have the views of the commercial men acquainted with the locality and suggested a meeting with deputations from Chambers of Commerce interested in Sierra Leone. Privately he thought the letter absurd. To talk of fifty thousand white troops was preposterous and to clamour for the dismissal of a governor who had made no mistake was cowardly. Yet, the Colonial Office had to work with the mercantile interest, which might possibly have some good advice to give. All in all, this stupid letter from Hutton angered Chamberlain and destroyed any influence the mercantile interest might possibly have had over the formation of official policy on the risings.

Nearly a year later, on 3 May 1899, Chamberlain met deputations from the Birmingham, Manchester, Liverpool and London Chambers of Commerce and from the West African Trade Association.[129] By then Chamberlain had made up his mind about Sierra Leone and was more concerned to persuade the men at the meeting to accept the official view. He assured them that the British Government did not want to impose its laws and customs on the tribespeople but only to prevent slavery and gross cruelty and injustice and that to give up the hut tax would be regarded as a sign of weakness. Those at the meeting gave up their opposition to the hut tax and agreed to support the Secretary of State's views.

The religious and humanitarian interests were also comparatively ineffective. They were divided, many of them accepted the argument of most white missionaries in the Protectorate and

135

the Colony that the rebels were resisting the attempts of Britain to lead them into the ways of righteousness—particularly the eradication of slavery and the slave trade. Savage attacks on missionaries gave added weight to this view of the rebels as savage slavers.[130] The Anti-Slavery Society could hardly attack the government for provoking a rising by its anti-slavery policy.

The only wholehearted humanitarian support for the rebels came from Fox Bourne of the Aborigines' Protection Society. He attacked the Creoles, the Frontier Police, the recent Governors of Sierra Leone and Cardew. The only recent Governor he sympathized with was Cardew's predecessor, Fleming, whom he called Freeling throughout his article.[131] He opposed the hut tax and condemned the despotic methods used in forcing "the blessings of civilization" upon people too ignorant to appreciate them. The Aborigines' Protection Society could logically argue for the conservation of African social systems, but the Anti-Slavery Society and the missionaries felt bound to support the New Imperialism in its role as an agent of civilization and progress.

In view of the weakness of the various lobbies it is not surprising that it was the permanent civil servants' view of the 1898 risings that Chamberlain finally adopted. As Mary Kingsley pointed out, "things are in the hands of the permanent officials at the F.O. and C.O. offices".[132] Although she thought that Chamberlain was "a strong man in power", it is clear from a study of official papers that Chamberlain was powerfully influenced by his permanent officials and by his Under-Secretary, Lord Selborne, who was also the Prime Minister's son-in-law. Lord Selborne held strongly authoritarian views which prevailed in the Colonial Office despite some initial opposition from moderately tender-hearted officials, like Mercer and Cox. These two opposed Cardew's request for a special commission to try the insurgents, but Selborne supported Cardew—"I would deal with this matter differently. These Coast natives require a firm hand, . . .[133] Mercer at first disagreed with Cardew's claim that the deeply rooted cause of the risings was the suppression of slavery and the desire for independence.[134] He argued that there had been no slave raiding recently and that it had been the Sofas, not the Protectorate natives, who had raided for slaves in the old days. Antrobus, however, disagreed and maintained that the Protectorate tribes had been continually raiding each other for slaves.

Wingfield had no doubt that the disloyal Sierra Leoneans and the hankering after slave raiding had something to do with the disaffection. By June Mercer was supporting his superiors' views that the prevention of slave raiding and Creole incitement had much to do with the risings.[135] Even before Chalmers went to Freetown Lord Selborne and top permanent officials at the Colonial Office had decided the outcome of his inquiry. When Chalmers disagreed with their preconceived ideas they were not at all pleased.

Chamberlain had also apparently made up his mind by the time he and Wingfield briefed Chalmers shortly before his departure for Freetown.[136] Chalmers was told that taxation was necessary to open the hinterland to trade and civilizing influences, that although a free press was all very well in England this was not the case in savage or semi-civilized countries, and that he should inquire into articles in the Sierra Leone Press. Chamberlain wholly differed from the views of the Liverpool and Manchester Chambers of Commerce who were very ignorant and who got their information from agents, many of whom were natives or half-breeds. After all that Chalmers was told to go into the inquiry with a perfectly open mind and assured that Chamberlain's views were subject to what Chalmers reported and might be quite altered by his report.

When Chalmers met representatives of the Chambers of Commerce he was more favourably impressed by their arguments than Chamberlain had been.[137] When he arrived at Freetown on 18 July, Chalmers was flattered by an enthusiastic unofficial welcome from the people of Freetown.[138] In Freetown he was impressed by the dignity and fluency of some of the chiefs from the interior as they testified, and his sympathy for the local inhabitants was aroused by his growing conviction "that an enormous deal of mischief has been done".[139] He clashed with the Governor whom he thought was hindering his inquiry, and the chilly exchange of notes at the end of September over the production of witnesses shows how strained relations between the two men were.[140] What worried Chalmers more was his growing suspicion that the Colonial Office did not want an impartial report from him:

It is very hard to say what games the C.O. is really up to, but I am certain they began by wishing a bona fide report upon a

137

real investigation, and whether the C.O. now wants it or not I mean to try to give such.[141]

In Freetown Chalmers was subjected to considerable pressures from the various groups interested in the outcome of his inquiry. Most powerful were the Governor and his officials who stood to lose a great deal if Chalmers returned an adverse verdict on them. They were able, as the dispute over the production of witnesses shows, to make life very difficult for Chalmers. Moreover, since Chalmers declined to travel to the interior—presumably because of age and ill health—the officials could argue that their first hand experience of the Protectorate gave their views more weight than those of Chalmers. The officials in Sierra Leone had to convince them that the risings had occurred not because of their blunders but because of the wickedness of their opponents. Cardew found many scapegoats. He told Chalmers how disturbed the country had been by slave raiding wars, and he alleged that the suppression of this evil was the principal grievance of the chiefs.[142] He also attacked the Creoles as the inciters of the risings and blamed both Europeans and Creole traders for recklessly disposing of gunpowder in the interior—even during the troubles.

The only important official to disagree with Cardew was the Colonial Secretary, Lieutenant-Colonel Gore, who thought the hut tax should have been halved and not collected so soon.[143] The District Commissioners loyally supported the Governor's arguments. Dr. Hood, Captains Carr, Sharpe and Fairtlough all argued that the rebels had been angered by official action against slavery and incited to rebel by disloyal Creoles.[144] Captain Moore even implied that Sir Samuel Lewis was guilty of incitement; naturally Lewis denied the charge.[145]

Parkes, the only Creole head of a government department, was unsure of his attitude. Although he had at first opposed the hut tax, he told Cardew in May 1898 that he did not blame the tax for the risings.[146] He thought the principal causes were the increasingly independent attitude of wives, children and slaves towards chiefs and headmen who had not the same powers over their people as before, the misbehaviour of inadequately supervised Frontiers, the entire stoppage of the slave trade, and the loss of jurisdiction and income at the appointment of District Commissioners. On the other hand, Parkes told Chalmers that the slaves were happy (presumably not defying their masters) and that the hut tax was greatly resented because the owners felt that by paying the tax they were giving up their huts to the government.[147] W. T. G. Lawson, the Temne of royal descent who had held official posts in Lagos and Freetown, had a very low opinion of the Creoles upcountry, who cheated and maltreated the natives and owned slaves.[148] He thought that the discontent aroused by official action against slavery and slave trading was insignificant, and he attacked the hut tax and the Frontier Police.

Not unexpectedly the "loyal" chiefs toed the official line. Madam Yoko emphasized that official action against the slave trade, slavery and woman palaver were prime causes of discontent.[149] Nancy Tucker alleged that her people refused to pay their tax unless their slaves were returned to them, that they feared the English would take all their slaves away and that she had never heard any complaint against the Frontier Police.[150] Fula Mansa said the main Mende grievances were the hut tax and the fact that they could no longer buy slaves nor flog their wives.[151] Smart testified that the risings sprang from:

> The laws about slaves, making war and raiding, freeing slaves, and no more country customs, no more woman palaver. They dislike all the Protectorate Ordinance.[152]

The missionaries in Sierra Leone were divided on the issue. Nearly all the expatriates supported Cardew and nearly all the Creoles opposed him. The Bishop of Sierra Leone supported Cardew in his testimony to Chalmers and in letters to friends in Britain, in which he argued that the Temne Rising was "a last stand for slavery by some of the Chiefs who are backing up a drunken rebel slaver named Bai Bureh".[153] The Rev. C. H. Goodman, a Methodist missionary who had been imprisoned by the rebels at Bumpe, held similar views and accused the Creole traders of incitement.[154] James Trice, an American Negro working for the Soudan Mission, thought the Marampa Chiefs were unrepentant slave dealers; he held a low opinion of the Creole traders upcountry and said the Frontiers had been unjustly accused of interfering with women.[155]

The Creole missionaries in the Protectorate told Chalmers quite a different story. The Rev. Joseph Johnson, a pastor for the

United Brethren in Christ, thought the hut tax was the main reason for the effort to drive the English out of the Protectorate.[156] F. M. Stewart, an agent of the African Methodist Episcopal Church, testified to the misbehaviour of the Frontiers and the shock caused by the appointment of Suri Bunki as Regent of Port Loko.[157] Josiah Nicolls, a Creole catechist for the Wesleyan Mission at Bandajuma and himself once a corporal in the Frontier Police, told of the misconduct of the Frontiers and said that the rebels' greatest grievances were the hut tax and the Frontiers; he also defended the Creole traders.[158]

With few exceptions the merchants and traders in Sierra Leone —Creole, tribal and expatriate—were agreed in their condemnation of Cardew and his policies. Thomas Buckley, Manager of the Bank of West Africa, was one of the few exceptions. He favoured the direct taxation of the people of the Protectorate, perhaps because this would stimulate the circulation of money there.[159] Most businessmen accepted the arguments put forward by William Pittendrigh, manager of Paterson, Zochonis and Company and President of the Sierra Leone Chamber of Commerce.[160] They dismissed the desire for slaves as a cause of the risings and blamed the hut tax, the misconduct of the Frontiers and the ineptness of the District Commissioners for the troubles. They refused to accept that the Creole traders incited the rebellion, although Pittendrigh did have reservations about the "very stupid comments" made about the Port Loko rising by the Freetown Press.

Naturally those whom Cardew had accused—the Creole traders, the Creole Press and the disaffected local leaders tried to shift the burden of blame from themselves. The Creole traders blamed the hut tax and the Frontiers.[161] James Fitzjohn of the *Sierra Leone Times* and Cornelius May of the *Sierra Leone Weekly News* denied that their newspapers had incited resistance to the Government but their evidence to Chalmers does not sound very convincing.[162] Disaffected local leaders denied that they were barbarous slavers and affirmed that they had accepted the end of the slave trade and were not challenging the restrictions on slavery; they blamed the hut tax, the Frontiers and the government's mistakes.[163]

While Chalmers was gathering evidence in Freetown Cardew continued to bombard the Colonial Office with documents in support of his own view of the risings. In June he sent Carr's report on the Bandajuma disturbances, drawing attention to the claim that it was no hardship for the natives to pay the hut tax with a bushel of palm kernels or husked rice but saying that it was the suppression of slave dealing which was responsible for the risings.[164] Three days later Cardew forwarded a statement from another supporter, an American Negro missionary, the Rev. J. A. Evans.[165]

In July he forwarded Madam Yoko's letter as well as one from the Rev. Price, a member of the Soudan Mission, whose opinion that the hut tax was just the occasion of the outbreak and English interference with slavery was the real cause was noted with pleasure at the Colonial Office.[166] The Colonial Office was not pleased with Dr. Edward Blyden's letter.[167] He thought the hut tax was only one of the causes—others were "the arbitrariness of young and inexperienced officials" and "the frontier police, consisting for the most part of pure savages, dressed up in English uniform, and often the ex-slaves of the very Chiefs whom they are called upon to punish and humiliate".

In August Cardew forwarded the results of a questionnaire on the risings which he had sent to his District Commissioners.[168] These all confirmed Cardew's views, and Fairtlough's report particularly impressed the Colonial Office. Cox thought it confirmed the Secretary of State's view that the hut tax was not the real cause of the risings. Chamberlain wanted it to be published in the Press at once to discount criticism from the Manchester Chamber of Commerce and others and to justify further military operations. His comment—"If, as I fully expect, Sir D. Chalmers's report is of the same general character it will also where published affect public opinion"—shows that he had come to regard the inquiry as a means of forestalling criticism of British policy in the Sierra Leone Protectorate. By the autumn of 1898 Chamberlain was worried by the possibility of criticism of the extended military operations against Bai Bureh, although the only instance of this in the official papers is a letter from the Aborigines' Protection Society expressing concern about plans for further military operations.[169]

In Freetown Chalmers was expressing similar doubts about the wisdom of further military operations and proposed easing the terms of surrender offered to Bai Bureh. Cardew was furious at this interference and forwarded his correspondence with Chalmers on the subject to the Colonial Office.[170] At first Chamberlain was prepared to support Chalmers on the grounds that he had approached Cardew in his private capacity and because Cardew was "inclined to be hard on the Natives & does not take sufficient pains to ascertain their views or to remove their suspicions". Lord Selborne leapt to Cardew's defence. He pointed out that the Governor had a very difficult situation to deal with, that he had acted on principles approved by Chamberlain, that neither the attacks on Cardew nor the reports favourable to Bai Bureh had been proven, and that up to now Cardew had deserved the support Chamberlain had given him. In a second minute Chamberlain explained that he was not doubting Cardew's present actions and intentions, although he felt the hut tax had been insufficiently explained to the people when it was imposed.

Meanwhile in Freetown Chalmers was nearing the end of his hearings and coming to certain conclusions. In November he reported that he would conclude that the hut tax and the way of collecting it had caused the disturbances.[171] The following month, in anticipation of his report, Chalmers made four recommendations—a general amnesty with few exceptions, the repeal of the Insurgents Temporary Detention Ordinance, the suspension of the hut tax, and the avoidance of further military activity.[172]

On 21 January Chalmers sent his report to the Colonial Office.[173] He attacked Cardew, the District Commissioners and the Frontier Police and exonerated the Creoles from the charges of incitement. He did not accept the idea that British action against slavery and slave dealing had been significant causes of the disturbances. The causes were the hut tax, the provisions of the Protectorate Ordinance and the failure of the Sierra Leone Government to make adequate provision for the implementation of the Ordinance. Chalmers made two basic errors in this report. He concentrated on superficialities and he was impelled by his personal dislike of Cardew to attack practically everything the Governor had done instead of concentrating his attacks on the Governor's real errors. The force of his report was weakened by his personal bias against Cardew.

Chalmers failed to make it clear—and presumably failed to grasp—that the hut tax and the Frontier Police were merely particularly irritating symptoms of a much more fundamental problem, namely the British presence in the Protectorate and whether it was either desirable, necessary or morally justifiable. In fairness to Chalmers, it must be admitted that in the late nineteenth century there were few who challenged the assumptions behind the New Imperialism, particularly Britain's right to extend its authority over countries considered uncivilized. If Chalmers had challenged this assumption it is doubtful whether his report would have been taken seriously at all. Yet, the 1898 risings were basically wars of independence against the British and Sierra Leone Governments which by a combination of force, trickery and deceit had taken the hinterland of Sierra Leone from its rightful owners. Chalmers went some way towards realizing this when he wrote that the provisions of the Protectorate Ordinance "went far beyond any historic basis existing at the time of the enactment."[174]

Although Chalmers did not and probably could not openly attack the principle of the extension of British authority over the Protectorate, he did effectively attack the implementation of the forward policy by Cardew and his officials. He was on particularly strong ground in showing how inadequately they had prepared for the Protectorate. He pointed out the fact that "only in 1896 were the subjects more fully shadowed out which were afterwards embraced in the subsequent Protectorate Ordinance, including the intended taxation".[175] Moreover, Cardew seems to have attached little importance to the consent of the chiefs, "nor to have thought he obtained any active assents, although he states that apparently there were no dissentient voices".[176]

Chalmers also attacked other failures to prepare adequately for the Protectorate:

> .... yet I cannot help thinking that the Local Legislature and the Governor would have acted more prudently if they had taken very much more deliberate and effective measures than they did take for familiarising the minds of the Chiefs with the intended changes in their broad and principal tenor, and obtaining their assent, not merely after the Ordinance was passed and in operation, but in anticipation, as was indeed directed by the Secretary of State in dealing with the proposals of Sir F. Cardew. If that had been done there would have been less of the shock of surprise than, I believe, ensued.[177]

Here Cardew was most vulnerable. Captain Sharpe, Acting District Commissioner of Karene when the proclamation of the

Protectorate was promulgated, could not even remember this happening nor whether anything had been done to publicize it, although he did remember the publication of the Protectorate Ordinance with the explanatory letter in October 1896.[178] Fairtlough, District Commissioner of Panguma in 1896 and 1897, never saw this explanatory letter and gave the chiefs his own explanation of the Protectorate Ordinance, which he admitted they did not grasp very well.[179] Nor was Freetown very efficient. The Protectorate Ordinance was so badly drawn up that it had to be amended three times; this was at least partly the fault of the legal officers and partly because the Protectorate Ordinance was rushed through the legislative process in less than a month.[180]

If Chalmers had concentrated his attack on Cardew along these lines it would have been difficult to refute his report, but he weakened his credibility by showing his personal animosity against Cardew and by accepting uncritically the evidence of Cardew's enemies, notably many Creoles and the discontented Protectorate leaders. A glaring example of his bias was his comment on "a remarkable convergence" in the answers of the District Commissioners to the Governor's questionnaire on the risings.[181] There is absolutely no evidence to support this insinuation of collusion to produce similar replies.

One useful point that Chalmers made was the unsuitability of military men as District Commissioners in many cases. Instead of just pointing out that military training was not the best preparation for serving as a District Commissioner, Chalmers went on to rail against all military men in colonial administration. This was unfair to Cardew, himself a military man, who had little choice but to rely heavily on military men to fill the administrative posts in the Protectorate.[182]

*　　*　　*

Chamberlain was impressed by this report, whatever its faults. He was also concerned because it faced him with an awkward dilemma. If the report was accepted the Governor would have to be recalled (or allowed to resign) and the hut tax and the Protectorate Ordinance would have to be repealed, all of which he was unwilling to do. He was equally unhappy at the prospect of repudiating the Royal Commissioner, whom he had chosen, and his report.[183] Lord Selborne did not feel that the report posed much of a dilemma:

> This report does not produce on my mind the same powerful effect which it has apparently produced on Mr. Chamberlain's.[184]

Selborne went on to point out Cardew's fine qualities and to argue that an administrative system was needed to open up the Protectorate and for this purpose a direct tax was necessary. If the Colonial Office gave up the tax this would indicate to West Africa that if you did not like a tax you could rebel. Chamberlain agreed that the power of direct taxation could not be abrogated. In the consideration of the report which followed permanent officials generally agreed with Cardew. Mercer wrote:

> The summing up on the question of slavery is rather one-sided. There is evidence that this matter 'bulked largely' and was a 'material factor'. No doubt it would be correct to say that in itself it would not have been made a cause of quarrel; but it is flying in the teeth of scores of answers to say that it was not a material factor in the rising.[185]

Antrobus also supported Cardew despite some reservations— "We must admit that Sir F. Cardew went too fast".[186] Still searching for a compromise Chamberlain then tentatively suggested replacing the hut tax with some form of tribute.[187]

Looking for a way out of his impasse Chamberlain then wrote to Chalmers in Edinburgh hoping that they would be able to meet to discuss his report and vaguely suggesting that Chalmers might modify his report. Chalmers replied that he was too sick to meet Chamberlain and offered little hope of altering his report to suit the Colonial Office:

> In these circumstances I could have wished that Mr. Chamberlain had seen his way to designate with more particularity the expressions in my Report which he considered it might be desirable and practicable for me to modify. I do not see that it is possible that controversy can be avoided as to the subject matter,...[188]

Chalmers attacked Cardew even more fiercely than he had in the report. He was convinced that the Governor and his officials had committed very grave errors on their own initiative and he accused Cardew of misleading the Colonial Office both before and after the Protectorate Ordinance. He wrote confidentially:

> .... I was strongly led to the conclusion that Sir F. Cardew considered his prestige as a Governor inextricably bound up in the success of the Protectorate Policy which he had recommended, and when he found it was about to fail on the crucial point of finance, determined on compelling success by a policy of peremptory force, not anticipating the terrible mischiefs to which that policy would lead.[189]

Chalmers's unwillingness to compromise and his failure to suggest an alternative to the direct taxation which he wanted to abolish disturbed Chamberlain. He would have liked to discuss with Chalmers

> .... especially the situation which would be created if the Hut Tax were repealed unconditionally after the insurrection, & without any sufficient alternative being substituted.[190]

So Chamberlain looked for another way out of his dilemma. He decided that Cardew should come back to London on leave and be given a chance to refute the charges made against him by Chalmers. Meanwhile Major Nathan would go out to Sierra Leone to administer the government and to make a full report of the situation there.[191] He told Nathan that he did not want to set aside the report of the Commissioner he had selected nor did he want to reverse British policy in Sierra Leone. He also said that he would not act until he had a report from Nathan.[192] He suggested that Nathan consider the advisability of reinstating Bai Bureh, and said that if the revenue from the native chiefs were sufficient the hut tax could be scrapped, but if it were maintained it ought to be extended to the Colony as well as the Protectorate. He thought it necessary to reorganize the Frontier Police "so as to prevent black men levying blackmail and generally ill treating the natives under the aegis of the Government".[193]

Soon after arriving in Freetown Nathan wrote a long letter which finally enabled Chamberlain to make up his mind.[194] Despite certain criticisms of Cardew's abrasive personality Nathan firmly backed his policies. Even though the hut tax and the way in which

it was collected were the "moving causes", Nathan believed that
the stoppage of slavery and the establishment of British tribunals
to protect the people from their chiefs were "powerful contribu-
tory causes". He approved of the principle of the hut tax but
suggested it might be easier to collect if it could be partly paid for
by labour. He thought the Creole influence in fomenting the
rebellion had been considerable, even if not as great as Cardew
thought. Although the Frontier Police had been guilty of irregu-
larities Cardew had done much to reform the force. He also
praised Cardew for nearly eliminating the slave traffic which the
chiefs still hankered after. Cardew was not liked because he treated
suggestions from others "as opposition to be arbitrarily and
definitely crushed", but his general policy was correct and Nathan
proposed to follow it. He saw no advantage in releasing Bai Bureh
who was not a great chief but it might be useful to release Nyagwa
—"a cruel brute but has learnt his lesson and would play a useful
role in his country wh. is disorganized under many subchiefs and
headmen".[195]

Chamberlain was most impressed by Nathan's letter and
thought parts of it would help the Colonial Office to compose its
conclusions on the Chalmers Report.[196] Practically all Nathan's
ideas were favourably received at the Colonial Office. There were,
however, some doubts about labour in lieu of the hut tax because
opinion in Britain would be upset by the idea of forced labour, and
Selborne objected to the tax being reduced.[197]

On 1 May Cardew presented a careful and apparently reasoned
point by point refutation of Chalmers which finally convinced
Chamberlain.[198] As Fyfe has pointed out, Cardew, like Chalmers,
did not hesitate to twist the evidence to suit his own interests, but
the great virtue of his reply was that it proclaimed a positive
policy; he looked to the development of the Protectorate by a
civilization and commerce whose worth he was sincerely convinced
of.[199]

Chamberlain no longer felt obliged to accept the Chalmers
Report—he told the Commons, "my position is that of a judge".[200]
Although he tried to avoid an outright repudiation of Chalmers,
to whose work he paid a tribute, Chamberlain came down strongly
in support of Cardew's policies in the conclusions that he sent
Nathan.[201] Although he refrained from making any judgement
on Cardew's allegations of Creole incitement the Secretary of

State exonerated Cardew and his officials from the charges made against them.[202] On slavery he dismissed Chalmers's conclusions and wrote:

> It seems clear that the serious political and social changes which were gradually and steadily being brought about by the extension of civilized influences into the interior, and especially those affecting slavery, by which the wealth and power of the chiefs were being diminished, had induced a wide-spread feeling of dissatisfaction and resentment, and so prepared the way for a general outbreak whenever there arose a reasonable pretext and common cause, such as was afforded by the imposition of the tax.[203]

Finally Chamberlain concluded that direct taxation, to be levied as a house tax, was necessary and that five shillings was a reasonable rate of tax.[204] He agreed with Cardew that each headman be given a commission of two and a half per cent for collecting the tax—as well as the five per cent already allowed to the Paramount Chiefs—because it was "desirable to enlist the chiefs more fully in support of the tax by making it worth their while to collect it". This not only greatly enriched the chiefs but also enhanced their status and was in effect a move towards a more conservative system of administration. As Lugard pointed out, in building up an effective system of native administration it was important to have tribal rulers collecting a direct tax and keeping some of it.[205]

In July Parts I and II of the Chalmers Report were tabled in the two Houses of Parliament, but there was some delay in printing and circulating copies.[206] Although Chamberlain promised to urge the printers to hurry so that the Papers could be circulated before the Colonial Office vote, apparently only Part I was ready in time.[207] During the debate the Secretary of State linked the collection of the hut tax with Britain's civilizing mission—especially with the suppression of slavery. He argued that Britain had to put down slave raiding in West Africa and this it could not do without occasional wars and bloodshed any more than one could make an omelette without breaking eggs. A direct tax had to be imposed to raise money for a frontier force and district officers whose task it was to spread the blessings of civilization, and:

I defy anyone to suggest any alternative to this direct taxation, if the money is to be found which is required in order to put down slavery.[208]

In 1901 Chamberlain used similar arguments to justify the agressive British policy which had led to the rising of the Ashanti in 1900. He maintained that they had rebelled because they disliked British interference with their barbarous customs of fetishism, human sacrifices, slave raiding and slavery.[209]

The Chalmers Report caused only a minor stir. Chalmers was dead, and few people continued to support his views after the Secretary of State had rejected them. Moreover, Chamberlain had cut the ground from under the feet of humanitarian critics by emphasizing British action against slavery and slave raiding as the underlying cause of the risings.[210] By autumn 1899 the much graver South African crisis was overshadowing the Sierra Leone risings, and West Africa in general. For the next quarter of a century there was comparatively little interest in West Africa and the British and Sierra Leone Governments were able to pursue their aims in the Sierra Leone Protectorate comparatively undisturbed.

First they set about restoring tranquillity and establishing mutual trust and confidence between the governors and the governed. The official verdict in 1898 made it clear that to succeed in this the governors would have to deal very tactfully with the governed and they would have to be particularly careful to avoid undue interference with customs and institutions like domestic slavery. It was felt that only after the consolidation of British power and influence would the governors be free to turn to their second aim of reshaping social, economic and political life in the Protectorate in ways more acceptable to British ideas of civilization and justice. This explains why the authorities handled slavery in the Protectorate so cautiously and why the institution survived so long.

NOTES

1. *C.R. II*, XXII, Petition of Chiefs, 15th October 1897, to the Legislative Council of Sierra Leone, against the Protectorate Ordinance.

2. *Ibid.*, 2234.
3. See above, p. 79.
4. N.A. Letter Books, No. 593, 15 November 1895, Parkes to Bai Simra; No. 80, 23 February 1896, Sanusi to Bai Sherbro; No. 160, 29 April 1896, Parkes to Bai Kompa.
5. *C.R. II*, 85. For more on Bai Kompa see below in this chapter.
6. *Ibid.*, 5458–73.
7. *Ibid.*, 3361–62, 3817–19, 6801; Fyfe, *A History*, p. 554.
8. Fyfe, *A History*, pp. 562–3.
9. *C.R. II*, 6790–6801, 6912–13, 7677–78, 7992.
10. *Ibid.*, 5189–91, 6802–3. I do not know his eventual fate.
11. *Ibid.*, 6002, 8136; Fyfe, *A History*, pp. 221, 554. See above, p. 109–10. Smart's name frequently crops up because of the great resentment aroused by the official favour he enjoyed and because of the part he and other collaborators played in aggravating the troubles in 1898.
12. *C.R. II*, 3062, 3078; Fyfe, *A History*, pp. 430, 575.
13. *C.R. II*, 119, 4140, 4161, 7910–11, 7914; Fyfe, *A History*, pp. 553, 573–4, 582. See above, Chapter III, Note 34.
14. *C.R. II*, 4217, 4223, 4231, 5096, 7912; Fyfe, *A History*, pp. 475, 484–5.
15. N.A. Letter Book, No. 277, Sanusi to Madam Yoko, 2 July 1896.
16. *Ibid.*, No. 164, 9 June 1897, Parkes to Madam Yoko.
17. *C.R. II*, XXVII, Letter, 10 November 1897, Madam Yoko to Secretary for Native Affairs, asking for assistance in collecting Hut Tax.
18. Fyfe, *A History*, p. 604; CO 267/517/34671, Haddon Smith to Crewe, 5 October 1909, refers to her suicide. The *Sierra Leone Weekly News*, 25 August 1906, refers to suspicions that she was poisoned.
19. *C.R. II*, 8557.
20. Chamberlain Papers, 9/5/3/10, Cardew to Chamberlain, 1 December 1896. In support of his preference for police officers Cardew told of an incident in which his only civilian District Commissioner had been involved. Arthur Hudson had been virtually imprisoned by natives angered by his liberation of a domestic slave. Cardew felt that a policeman would have dealt with the situation more effectively and would have avoided humiliation.
21. *C.R. II*, XXV, Letter, 15 November 1897, from various Chiefs to Sir F. Cardew—further representations against the Protectorate Ordinance.
22. *Ibid.*, 5163 and XII, Letter, 19 November 1896, Bai Kompa to Secretary Native Affairs.
23. *Ibid.*, VIII, 19 September 1896, Bai Samu, Bai Sherbro and Almami Hannah Modu to Sir F. Cardew.
24. *Ibid.*, 3277.
25. N.A. Letter Book of 1897 contains many examples of this reply to complaints from chiefs.

26. *C.R. II*, 6002; Fyfe, A History, pp. 221, 554; N.A. Letter Book, No. 74, Parkes to Bai Kompa, 1 March 1897; see above, p. 111.

27. N.A. Minute Paper, No. 265, 4 May 1896.

28. *C.R. II*, 4967–83, 4999–5005, 5312, 6001–2, 7428–31; Fyfe, *A History*, pp. 558–9, 568–9.

29. E. D. Morel, *Affairs of West Africa* (London 1968, 2nd ed.), p. 99. Morel cites Lugard, *Colonial Report, No. 346*, p. 11, 1 May 1901.

30. N.A. Letter Book, No. 21, Parkes to Caulker, 18 January 1897.

31. *Ibid.*, No. 68, 25 February 1897, Parkes to Caulker.

32. *C.R. II*, 2231–34; Fyfe, *A History*, p. 554.

33. Conf. N.A. Letter Book, No. 12, Parkes to H.E., 28 April 1898. Cave was obviously not the most tactful of men. In 1899 the Inspector General of the Frontier Police reported that Inspector Cave had "a most objectionable manner to those above him, and a domineering manner to those under him". See CO 267/445/7782, Cardew to CO, 8 March 1899.

34. N.A. Letter Book, No. 535, 21 December 1896 and No. 22, 19 January 1897, Parkes to all District Commissioners.

35. *C.R. II*, VII, Circular Letter, 21 October 1896, from Native Affairs Dept., explaining Protectorate Ordinance. Some chiefs never received this letter.

36. CO 267/426/21517, Cardew to CO, 28 September 1896, Prot. Estimates for 1897. Minutes by Mercer and Antrobus and draft reply.

37. *C.R. II*, X and XI, Letters, 20 October 1896 and 14 December 1897, from Chiefs to Secretary Native Affairs.

38. *Ibid.*, IX, Letter, 26 October 1896, Bey Simra to Sec. Nat. Affs., asking for further explanation about the Prot. Ordinance.

39. *Ibid.*, XIII, Letter, 3 November 1896, Madam Yoko to Sec. Native Affairs, as to Protectorate Ordinance.

40. *Ibid.*, XIV, Letter, 17 December 1896, Timini Chiefs to Capt. Sharpe.

41. *Ibid.*, XV, Letter, 18 December 1896, Chiefs of Sulima and Gallinas to Sir S. Lewis, C.M.G. (sic), asking him to put their petition against the Prot. Ord. before the Governor of Sierra Leone.

42. *Ibid.*, XVII and 1717–24, Petition, Timini Chiefs against Protectorate Ordinance, 28 June 1897.

43. See above, pp. 42–43, for the annexation of Koya.

44. *C.R. II*, 2476–77.

45. Hansard, *Parliamentary Debates*, 33, p. 916, 10 May 1895 and 50, pp. 372 and 650, 18 and 28 June 1897.

46. *Ibid.*, 53, p. 1355, 22 February 1898.

47. CO 147/121/1811, McCallum to CO, 20 December 1897.

48. *C.R. II*, XVIII and XIX, Letters, 5 July and 2 August 1897, from Chiefs to Secretary of Native Affairs.

49. Fyfe, *A History*, p. 551; CO 267/435/14849 Manchester Chamber

of Commerce to CO, 7 July 1897, minute by Antrobus, 12 July 1897.

50. CO 267/433/17303, Caulfeild to CO, 20 July 1897. It is odd that the Acting Governor took over three weeks to submit this petition.

51. N.A. Letter Book, No. 211, 14 September 1897, Parkes to Col. Sec., reporting interview with the chiefs.

52. *C.R. II*, XX, Letter, 15 September 1897, Parkes, replying to petition of Bai Kompa and other chiefs.

53. *Ibid.*, XXI, Letter, 18 September 1897, Bai Kompa and others to Sec. for Native Affairs.

54. C.P. Afr. (West), 533, Sierra Leone. Correspondence relating to the Administration of the Protectorate, CO to Cardew, 5 December 1896 and Cardew to CO, 31 December 1896.

55. CO 267/433/21774, Caulfeild to CO, 22 September 1897; CO 270/36, pp. 314–21.

56. CO 270/36, pp. 320–1, 2 September 1897.

57. *C.R. II*, 7026–27.

58. *Ibid.*, 2755.

59. *Sierra Leone Times*, 9 June 1894 and 15 June 1895.

60. *Ibid.*, July 1895, various articles; Fyfe, *A History*, pp. 532–4.

61. *Sierra Leone Times*, 4, 18 and 25 July 1896 and 28 August 1897.

62. *Sierra Leone Weekly News*, 23 June and 20 October 1894, 26 January and 26 October 1895.

63. *Ibid.*, 14 March 1896 and 23 January 1897. It suggested that the hut tax be replaced by a lower tax levied on each family compound.

64. *C.R. II*, XXII, Petition of Chiefs, 15 October 1897.

65. *Ibid.*, XXIV, Letter, 9 November 1897, from Chiefs to Sec. for Native Affairs, on arrival of Sir. F. Cardew.

66. *Ibid.*, 807.

67. *Ibid.*, XXIII, Text of an Address given by the Governor to certain Chiefs of the Karene District at Freetown, 15 November 1897.

68. *Ibid.*, 807.

69. *Ibid.*, 4469–70, for Pa Suba's complaint about Cardew's rudeness.

70. *Ibid.*, XXV, Letter, 15 November 1897.

71. Fyfe, *A History*, p. 553.

72. *C.R. II*, 2219–21.

73. *Ibid.*, XXVI, Letter, 20 November 1897, Sec. Native Affairs to Bai Suba (sic) and others, in reply to their letter of 15 November.

74. CO 267/434/27603, Cardew to CO, 8 December 1897.

75. Native Affairs Minute Paper, No. 101/7 February 1898, Acting D.C., Koinadugu, to Department of Native Affairs. Although Birch did not state the district was close to rebellion, he implied it.

76. *C.R. II*, 4460, 4463.

77. *Ibid.*, XXXIX, Report, 12 February 1898, Commissioner Sharpe, Karene District. Difficulties in Collecting Hut Tax—Arrest of Chiefs.

78. *C.R. I*, Chalmers, 77.

79. *C.R. II*, 3814. For the election see above, p. 110.
80. See above, p. 110.
81. *Op. cit.*, Note 76.
82. *C.R. I*, Chalmers, 87.
83. *Op. cit.*, Note 76.
84. La Ray Denzer, "Sierra Leone—Bai Bureh", *West African Resistance* (London 1971), M. Crowder (Ed.), p. 233.
85. *C.R. II*, XLII, Minute, 15 February 1898, Sir F. Cardew—Instructions for Major Tarbet and Twenty Men to proceed to Port Lokko to arrest Bai Bureh.
86. *Ibid.*, 7747–49.
87. *Ibid.*, 4954.
88. For more about the clash over Smart see above, pp. 110 and 113. Petitions signed by some or all of these three chiefs include *C.R. II*, XII, XVII, XXI and XXII.
89. *C.R. II*, XXIX, Circular Letter, 31 December 1898 (sic), D.C. Ronietta to Chiefs, asking payment of Hut Tax.
90. *Ibid.*, XXVIII, Letter, 2 January 1898, Bai Kompa to Parkes.
91. *Ibid.*, XXXI, Report, 10 January 1898, from Dr. Hood, Acting D.C. at Ronietta, indisposition to pay Hut Tax—disturbed state of district.
92. For the description of the events in Koya from January to April 1898 I have drawn heavily on the Chalmers Report, especially *C.R. I*, Chalmers 64–67, 95–101; *C.R. II*, 85–86, 117, 1239–60, 1889–93, 2345, 4966–5011, 5285–5402, 7824–40, 8369–86, XXXIV, LX, LXI, LXII and LXIII. See also Fyfe, *A History*, pp. 558–9, 568–9.
93. Both these influential chiefs were Temne. Bai Simra of Masimra (not to be confused with Bai Simra of Mayoppo) had repeatedly clashed with the Sierra Leone Government. His people had fought on the side of the Yoni in 1886, and Bai Simra had been imprisoned until he paid the Government a fine for his role in the Yoni War. After that relations between the chief and the Government had been strained. In 1891 he had only just avoided arrest by a speedy apology and by returning his plunder. There had been many other clashes between Bai Simra and the authorities. There were two different Bai Sherbros of Yoni. The arrested chief mentioned here was not the Bai Sherbro of Yoni on Sherbro Island, also known as Gbana Lewis. Gbana Lewis was the leader of the one-word Poro against Sherbro trade in 1897 and was imprisoned for his role in the Mende Rising; he died in Christiansborg in 1912. This Temne Bai Sherbro was of weaker stuff. On the way to prison he broke down and confessed to Moore that the chiefs had sworn an oath against paying the tax, but in the presence of the other chiefs he refused to repeat his confession. He was imprisoned in Freetown and presumably released when the trouble died down. See *C.R. I*, Chalmers, 113; *C.R. II*, 2324, 2969–73, 7754–57, 8582; Fyfe, *A History*, pp. 476, 490, 594–5.

94. Fula Mansa had been a prisoner of the British for seven years, but he had become one of Captain Moore's informers and was rather unreliable. It was he who had told Moore, apparently correctly, that Bai Sherbro of Yoni had sworn the Ronietta chiefs not to pay the hut tax. He was killed in action against the Mende town of Bunjema in May. See Fyfe, *A History*, pp. 559, 582.

95. Suri Kamara described himself as a farmer, but Sharpe said he was a sub-chief who had organized the blockade of the Rokel River with Sena Bundu and with the help of the Karene rebels, see *C.R. II*, 7411 and LXIII.

96. *C.R. I*, Chalmers, 101.

97. *C.R. II*, XI, *op. cit.*, Note 37. See p. 116.

98. *Ibid.*, XXXIII, Extract from Unofficial Report to Sir F. Cardew, 10 January 1898, of Commissioner Carr, as to Meeting of Chiefs at Mafwe.

99. *Ibid.*, XXXV, Extract from Opinion Book of Attorney-General, 18 January 1898.

100. *Ibid.*, XXXVI and XXXVII, Minutes from Sir F. Cardew and from Commissioner Carr, 21 and 29 January 1898.

101. Fyfe, *A History*, pp. 560 and 570.

102. *C.R. II*, 302–4, 333, 337.

103. *C.R. I*, Chalmers, 71–73.

104. *C.R. II*, XXXVIII, Letter, 5 January 1898, Dr. Arnold's report.

105. *C.R. II*, 8580. Cardew was quoting a letter to him from Carr, written on 11 April 1898.

106. *C.R. I*, Cardew, 31–32 and 46, for Cardew's not over enthusiastic defence of Carr's conduct.

107. Nathan MSS, Correspondence, 1896–1913, No. 248, Cardew to Nathan, 22 July 1899.

108. Attorney-General's Opinion Book, p. 237, 1900.

109. *C.R. I*, Chalmers, 110.

110. For details of the Mende Rising see *C.R. I and II*, and Fyfe, *A History*, pp. 570–7, 582–6.

111. *C.R. I*, Cardew App. L (1); *C.R. II*, 2044–45, 3000–2, 8582–83, *et al.* For more about this Bai Sherbro, see above, Note 93.

 For more about Fawundu, see *C.R. II*, 617, 1231–38, 5724–60. After protesting Fawundu was deposed because he had raised the question as to whether he was a British subject or not. In 1898 he was arrested in Freetown because of the influence he might have on the Mende there. When he was reinstated at the beginning of 1899 a Colonial Office official commented "I am not sure that we ought to have approved his deposition." See CO 267/445/2313, Cardew to CO, 6 January 1899, Minute by Wingfield.

112. *C.R. II*, 8583.

113. See above, pp. 88 and 94.

114. For the events in Panguma I have drawn on *C.R. I*, Cardew, App. B; *C.R. II*, 5013–19, 5128–29, 5681; Fyfe, *A History*, pp. 570,

585, 591. Chalmers in *C.R. I*, Chalmers, 127, pointed out the weakness of the official case against Nyagwa.

115. Hansard, *Parliamentary Debates*, 56, p. 645, 21 April 1898. Davitt, a Fenian who had been imprisoned for seditious activity, was greatly concerned with those whom he considered fellow victims of British oppression.

116. *Ibid.*, 57, p. 409, 5 May 1898.

117. *Ibid.*, 56, p. 958, 25 April 1898.

118. For details of the exemptions see above, p. 122.

119. Hansard, *Parliamentary Debates*, 57, pp. 699–715, 9 May 1898; CO 267/443/11049, House of Commons, 16 May 1898.

120. Yet, Humphrey thought the disturbances originated over the hut tax—a fact Chamberlain did not mention. See CMS G3 A1/o 56/1898, Humphrey, 19 March 1898.

121. Buxton had been Under-Secretary of State for the Colonies in the Liberal Government of 1892–95. He was the grandson of Sir Thomas Fowell Buxton who had taken over the leadership of the anti-slavery movement from Wilberforce and was himself closely connected with the Anti-Slavery Society. In 1931, as Earl Buxton, he pressed for a more vigorous anti-slavery policy.

122. *C.R. I*, p. 4, Royal Commission appointing Sir David Patrick Chalmers, Knight, to be Her Majesty's Commissioner to inquire..., 18 June 1898.

123. S. Gwynn, *The Life of Mary Kingsley* (London 1932), p. 177. He cites a letter from Mary Kingsley to Mr. Kemp, a Wesleyan missionary, 25 April 1898, see above, chapter II.

124. *Idem.* The Chamberlain Papers, 9/5/4/2–6, show they wrote to each other several times in 1898.

125. Morel Papers, F.8, Kingsley to Morel, no date given.

126. B. Porter, *Critics of Empire*, Chapter Eight, for a discussion of Kingsley, Morel and the Liverpool School. Morel wrote a pamphlet in 1899, *The Sierra Leone Hut-tax Disturbances.* He also expressed his views in the paper he started. See *West Africa*, 2 March, 20 April, 6 July, 9 November, 21 and 28 December 1901, 1 February, 19 and 26 April 1902.

127. *Manchester Guardian*, 15 April, 3, 6 and 7 May 1898.

128. Chamberlain Papers, 9/5/3/13, Hutton to Chamberlain, 6 May 1898. Chamberlain's comments were written on 7 May.

129. CO 267/450/9952, CO to Chambers of Commerce, invitation to meeting and notes of it, 3 May 1899; Fyfe, *A History*, p. 599.

130. The Bishop of Sierra Leone, John Taylor Smith, was a leading proponent of this view. He was closely identified with official policy. Mary Kingsley thought he was "the only person over there that the Governor will listen to"; see Chamberlain Papers, 9/5/4/5, Kingsley to Chamberlain, 8 May 1898. Chamberlain referred to the Bishop's view of Bai Bureh as a drunken slaver during a debate in the Commons, see above, p. 133.

131. R. Fox Bourne, "Sierra Leone Troubles", *Fortnightly Review*,

CCCLXXX, 1 August 1898, pp. 216–30. Fox Bourne obviously knew very little about Sir Francis Fleming whom he apparently confused with Sir Sandford Freeling who served in the Gold Coast in the 1870s.

132. Gwynn, *Mary Kingsley*, p. 211. He cites a letter from Kingsley to Morel, written in 1899.

133. CO 267/483/9094, Cardew, Tel. 25 April 1898, Minutes by Mercer, Cox and Selborne, 25–27 April 1898. H. B. Cox was the Law Officer at the Colonial Office. W. H. Mercer was Principal Clerk in the West Africa Department.

134. CO 267/438/10343, Cardew to CO, 10 May 1898, Minutes. R. L. Antrobus was Assistant Under-Secretary. Sir Edward Wingfield was Permanent Under-Secretary.

135. CO 267/438/13266, Cardew to CO, 28 May 1898, Minute.

136. Sir David Chalmers MSS, University of Edinburgh, No. 1, Notes made by Chalmers of his interview at the Colonial Office, before going to Sierra Leone, undated.

137. *Ibid.*, Nos. 2 and 3, Letters from Sir David to Miss Janet Chalmers, 3 and 10 July 1898.

138. *Ibid.*, No. 4, Sir David to Miss Janet Chalmers, 28 July 1898.

139. *Ibid.*, Nos. 5 and 6, as above, 5 and 19 September 1898.

140. *Ibid.*, No. 9, as above, 15 November 1898. C.R. II, LXXIV, (a), (b), (c), (d), and (e).

141. Sir David Chalmers MSS, *op. cit.*, Note 140.

142. *C.R. II*, 8550, 8553, 8587, 8613–5, 8617.

143. *Ibid.*, 8527–31.

144. *Ibid.*, 132–3, 158, 269–71, 280–2, 318, 3942–3, 5079–88; *C.R. I*, Apps. L (1), L (2).

145. *C.R. I*, O; *C.R. II*, 7763, 7841–3.

146. *C.R. I*, J; *C.R. II*, 787.

147. *C.R. II*, 536–42, 813–27. This is the argument Mary Kingsley used, see above, p. 134.

148. *Ibid.*, 1713–6, 1860–1, 1879, 1880, 1859–60, 1767–72.

149. *C.R. I*, K; *C.R. II*, 4106–12.

150. *C.R.II*, 4156–8, 4184.

151. *Ibid.*, 5222. This was the successor of the Fula Mansa who had led a force of "friendlies" and had been killed at Bunjema earlier in the year. See above, p. 127 and Note 94.

152. *Ibid.*, 5284.

153. *Ibid.*, 8157–8, 8171–2, 8179 and Note; C.M.S., G 3 A1/o, Nos. 58 and 74 of 1898, Letters from the Bishop to Rev. H. E. Fox and Mr. Baylis, 3 and 19 April 1898. See above, pp. 133 and 136.

154. *C.R. II*, 1364, 1369–70, 1462.

155. *Ibid.*, 2421–31, 2444–51, 2487. There are many others examples of similar missionary views, as in *C.R. I*, Cardew, Apps. F and G.

156. *Ibid.*, 7691–6.

157. *Ibid.*, 7990–3, 8001–5, 8011–4.

158. *Ibid.*, 4329–4401.

159. *Ibid.*, 5911. I have found no evidence to support or deny the theory that by imposing the hut tax the authorities hoped to stimulate the circulation of currency in the Protectorate. Two traders on a small scale, presumably British, supported Cardew, *Ibid.*, 2096–97, 2245–50.

160. *Ibid.*, 409–38. Similar views came from other expatriate merchants. *Ibid.*, 4671–98, 6396–6414, 7919–21, 7935–6.

161. E.g., the evidence of Frederick Dove, Mrs. Reader, Messrs. Morrison, Macaulay, Parkinson and Bobb, *Ibid.*, 1598, 1629–34; 2921; 2959–60; 3101–2; 3118.

162. *Ibid.*, 8187–8366.

163. E.g., the evidence of Limba Chiefs, Port Loko Chiefs, Bai Sherbro of Yoni, Pa Nembana of Koya, Karene District Chiefs, *Ibid.*, 2124–31; 2215–21, 2237; 2324; 2345; 4469–70.

164. CO 267/439/13904, Cardew to CO, Conf. 44, 4 June 1898.

165. CO 267/439/14074, Cardew to CO, Conf. 45, 7 June 1898.

166. CO 267/439/16859 and 18398, Cardew to CO, Confs. 52 and 59, 6 and 28 July 1898.

167. CO 267/444/16966, Blyden to CO, 28 July 1898.

168. CO 267/440/20390, Cardew to CO, Conf. 68, 23 August 1898. Fairtlough's and Sharpe's reports were also printed as Apps. L (1) and (2) in *C.R. I.*

169. CO 267/444/22812, A.P.S. to CO, 10 October 1898.

170. CO 267/440/24928, Cardew to CO, Conf. 81, 13 October 1898. Minutes by Chamberlain, 9 and 13 November 1898, by Selborne, 11 November 1898.

171. CO 267/444/27437, Chalmers to CO, 11 November 1898.

172. CO 267/444/27727, Chalmers to CO, 5 December 1898.

173. CO 267/450/1935, Chalmers to CO, 21 January 1899.

174. *C.R. I*, Chalmers, 33.

175. *Ibid.*, Chalmers, 29.

176. *Idem.*

177. *Ibid.*, Chalmers, 33.

178. *C.R. II*, 3410–16, 3466–7.

179. *Ibid.*, 4946–9.

180. *Ibid.*, 2705–7; Fyfe, *A History*, p. 549.

181. *C.R. I*, Chalmers, 125. It could be argued that Cardew's questions were loaded to get the required answers.

182. *Ibid.*, Chalmers, 192. He thought District Commissioners could be retained in an advisory capacity.

183. CO 267/450/1935, Chalmers to CO, 21 January 1899, Minutes.

184. *Idem.*

185. CO 267/450/3396, Chalmers to CO, February 1899, Minutes.

186. *Idem.*

187. *Idem.*

188. Chamberlain Papers, 9/5/3/4, Sir David Chalmers to Sir Edward Wingfield, 2 March 1899.

189. *Idem.*

190. *Ibid.*, 9/5/3/5, Chamberlain's comments on 9/5/3/4, 3 March 1899.

191. Major Nathan, later Sir Matthew, 1862–1939, was an officer in the Royal Engineers who had a distinguished career in the Colonial Service and in Britain. In February 1899 he met Mary Kingsley and they took a great liking to each other, see Gwynn, *Mary Kingsley*, pp. 216–55.

192. Nathan Papers, 273–4, SL, Notes of an Interview with Mr. Chamberlain, 6 March 1899.

193. *Idem.*

194. Chamberlain Papers, 9/5/3/15, Nathan to Chamberlain, 1 April 1899.

195. *Idem.* Nyagwa was discovered sending secret messages to his people and neither chief was released. See Fyfe, *A History*, p. 594.

196. *Idem*, Minute by Chamberlain, 21 April 1899.

197. *Ibid.*, 9/5/3/16, minutes on 9/5/3/15 by Mercer, Wingfield and Selborne, all on 22 April and by Chamberlain, 24 April.

198. *C.R. I*, Part II, Cardew to CO, 1 May 1899.

199. Fyfe, *A History*, pp. 597–8.

200. Hansard, *Parliamentary Debates*, 76, p. 120, 7 August 1899, 2nd Reading, Consolidated Fund (Appropriation) Bill.

201. *C.R. I*, Part III, Chamberlain to OAG, Sierra Leone, 7 July 1899. Tribute to Chalmers in para. 2.

202. *Ibid.*, Chamberlain 18–27, 31.

203. *Ibid.*, Chamberlain 29–30.

204. *Ibid.*, Chamberlain 53–63.

205. Lugard, *Dual Mandate*, Chap. XII, "Taxation", pp. 230–55.

206. Hansard, *Parliamentary Debates*, 74, 11 and 13 July 1899, pp. 428, 464, 665, 679.

207. *Ibid.*, 75, 24 July 1899, pp. 65–6; Fyfe, *A History*, p. 599, writes that Part II (the evidence presented to Chalmers) appeared after Parliament was prorogued. Certainly there was no reference to Part II in the debate. Lady Chalmers, "In Defence of Sir David Chalmers", *Nineteenth Century*, XLVII, pp. 485–97 (March 1900), wrote that Part I was presented to Parliament in August and Part II in September. In fact they were both tabled in July although there was some delay before the printed copies were circulated.

208. *Ibid.*, 76, pp. 122–3, 7 August 1899. While speaking Chamberlain was given news of Chalmer's death, which he announced to the House.

209. *Ibid.*, 91, pp. 353–4, 18 March 1901.

210. Lady Chalmers wrote a defence of her late husband, see above, Note 207. The mercantile interest continued to show some support for Chalmers's views, notably E. D. Morel in his periodical, *West Africa*, see above, Note 126.

CHAPTER V

Domestic Slavery in the Sierra Leone Protectorate during the Twentieth Century

After the disturbances of 1898 and the controversy over the Chalmers Report died down, the Sierra Leone Government was able to settle down quietly to its task of consolidating British power over the Protectorate. In doing so it had to face the problem of how a "civilizing" power should deal with institutions it found repugnant but which were important to the people being "civilized". This problem had been thoroughly aired in 1898 and 1899, and so it was somehow assumed that great progress had been made towards its solution.

This was certainly not true of the institution of slavery and other forms of servitude in the Protectorate. In fact, Chamberlain's final verdict on 1898 had made the problem of slavery even more awkward. He had stressed the British civilizing mission in the interior while pointing to resentment of British interference with slavery as the major cause of the troubles. So administrators had to "civilize" the Protectorate while allowing the continuation of slavery. They had to cope with the problems arising from the existence of slavery without being allowed the only possible solution—radical action against the institution. Because of 1898 they had to interfere with the political life of the Protectorate as little as possible.

Yet, at the same time they had to encourage economic development, and during the first two decades of the twentieth century the extension of British power had marked economic and social effects on the Protectorate. Urban centres developed, roads and railways were built and local administration was reorganized on more rational lines. Even though officials may have exaggerated

159

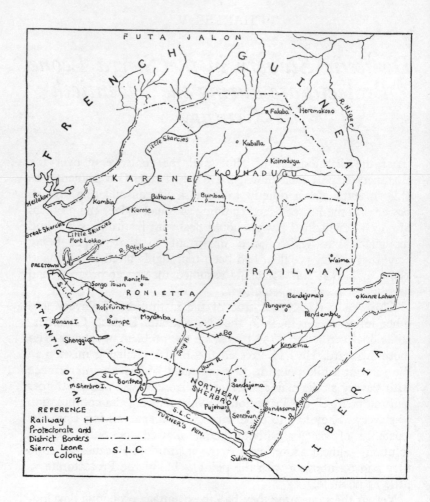

SIERRA LEONE IN 1912

the depth and scope of these changes they were undoubtedly very important and would have had a greater effect than they did on the lives of the people of the Protectorate if the Sierra Leone Government had not been so cautious. The conservative policies of the Government tended to mask the considerable impact of the social and economic changes affecting the Protectorate. Yet, official action could not stem the flood of economic and social change indefinitely. By 1920 the institution of slavery was under considerable pressure even though the effects of this were not yet being felt by the individual slaves in most of the country.

*   *   *

Despite substantial variations in both the prevalence of the institution and the conditions of slavery, it is possible to depict the life of a typical Protectorate slave during the first two decades of the twentieth century. There were variations not just from region to region but also from village to village and from master to master.[1] The slave had close contact with his master and was part of the social structure (unlike the Transatlantic plantation slave), and his fate depended more on local conditions than on the general social, political and economic climate of the Protectorate. The death of his master would mean at least as much to a slave as would very important changes in the government of the country. A slave could receive a rude shock if at the death of a lenient master he passed to an heir who was determined to enforce his rights over the slave.[2] A District Commissioner vividly described a case of this:

> A Timini captured in war 40 years before had been very happy and contented with his Mende master, a native trader in a fair way of business near Sumbuya, who had a great affection for him and had paid a dowry for four wives for him. On the master's death a younger brother succeeded to the estate and began to treat the aged domestic harshly, whereupon his relatives who had long known his whereabouts promptly redeemed him at his own request. He could have had himself redeemed years before but did not wish it.[3]

As in other parts of West Africa, personal relationships had much to do with how the slaves lived. Gradually the master/slave relationship became more familial and the stages toward freedom were reduced to the point where the third or fourth generations were virtually free—without having been formally redeemed. Many writers have described this gradual acquisition of freedom. J. C. Maxwell wrote that in time they formed a class indistinguishable from freemen, except that they had to render certain services to their nominal masters and could not go to another chiefdom with their property, and in time they became freemen without any formal redemption.[4]

Captain Stanley similarly described the status of children of slaves. It was customary for the second generation to be given farms, although the head of the household might demand some of their produce, and they sometimes married into the master's family and rose to positions of trust. "In the fourth generation such persons are practically indistinguishable from freemen."[5] In his book on the Mende, Professor Little similarly describes this rise in status.[6]

More often than not slaves were regarded as members of the family. Maxwell reported that among the Mende the term *ke ma lenga* was used for brothers, sisters and cousins, and it might also be used "by a man or woman speaking of his domestics, especially those born in the family".[7] Northcote Thomas, an anthropologist, wrote that among the Temne

> A house or domestic slave (oliso) was born in his master's house and could only be sold for a grave offence; they should be treated like sons and might get land from their masters which their children would inherit, unless they were sold for misbehaviour.[8]

Among the Susu a house slave could not be sold even if he was a thief.[9] Sir Samuel Lewis told Chalmers that "the patriarchal idea" attached slaves to their masters and that they were like free sons.[10] Colonel Warren thought the domestic slave was as often as not "an honoured member of the family".[11] Major Lyon wrote of Hara Siki, who had killed a leopard:

> It appeared that he was a slave, having been captured in the war when a mere child. He informed me, however, that he had no wish to be free, as he was the sole support of his master, now a very aged man, who had treated him like a son all his life and

whom he now regarded as being his father and entitled to all possible care.[12]

Local rulers, perhaps because they knew of the official distaste for the word "slave", often referred to their slaves as their children or their boys.[13]

After the ban on fresh enslavements in 1896 this quasi-familial relationship became more common because an increasing number of slaves were slaves of the house—in other words, born in the master's house. Slaves who had not been captured in war, purchased or enslaved for crime or debt were more likely to be treated with respect by other members of the household.

Although firm action by the authorities reduced the cases of enslavement to a very low number many continued to be temporarily enslaved by the practice of pawning. Most of the slave dealing cases dealt with by the courts were really cases of pawning.[14] It was sometimes hard to distinguish between pawning and enslavement, as Thomas discovered:

> At the same time it is recognized that a wastrel or troublesome person can be pawned to teach him manners: this can be done only with his consent, but as he can be fettered until he gives his consent, there is not much choice allowed him in the matter.[15]

The Susu were less harsh on pawns than the Temne—typically a pawn could pay off a debt of six pounds by working for his creditor for four years.[16] In the Protectorate it was more usual to regard the pawn's services as interest on his debt, which had to be repaid before the pawn could be released. A debtor would usually pledge himself or a member of his household, but not a wife, for a debt of two to four pounds—the same as the redemption fees for children and adults. A child could be pawned at the age of seven but a girl would normally be redeemed when she reached marriageable age.

Despite the general improvement in the lot of the slave there was still a great gulf between slave and free in 1920, and even when the slave enjoyed some of the privileges of belonging to the family he was still inferior to freemen. In the 1890s a Methodist missionary had noted the stigma of slavery among the Mende:

Of course, rice is the chosen food; cassada is the food of the poor and the slave. The freeborn will scarcely eat cassada if they can get rice, and to like cassada is taken as a sign of ill-breeding, it being regarded as a choice sneer for an enemy to tell him that "he eats cassada like a slave".[17]

Alldridge described how the freeborn greeted each other in the Sherbro in the same period and how

Slaves merely cringe up and place their two hands one on each side of their master's hand, and draw them back slowly without the fillip, while the head is bowed.[18]

Alldridge also wrote of the lowly status of Mende slaves of the house:

. . . . while children of "bought slaves", although enjoying certain advantages, were very apt to be looked down upon, and to be reminded and kindly in any warm discussion, that they were "born in the yard" and consequently inferior to the others.[19]

Even in 1924 the lot of many slaves had scarcely improved:

The slave is not a person; he cannot make a contract; he can have little interest in his work; his incentives are hunger and punishment, and a (half-atrophied) instinct to go on existing. His family life is precarious, depending on his master's requirements. Every 'good' he may enjoy is insecure. Mitigations in practice must not here obscure our view of his real position. At any time the master may consider his slave guilty of misbehaviour or disobedience and at once depress him to his theoretical condition of duties without rights. The slave becomes simply property; . . .[20]

The most significant fact in the lives of the slaves was that they were property. Not only the traditional authorities but also the British authorities in some ways accepted this. Even though the Protectorate Ordinance had forbidden the sale of slaves and had declared bequests of slaves null and void the Sierra Leone Government still accepted that slaves were heritable. On many occasions British officials settled disputes over the inheritance of slaves. In 1912 District Commissioner Fairtlough did not hesitate to tell the West African Lands Committee that slaves belonged to each family and that at the death of the head of the family would be shared out among the heirs like the rest of the estate; he added that a slave could be transferred to another owner when his or her master was still alive, perhaps as part of the dowry of the owner's daughter.[21] When the heritability of slaves was questioned in 1916 District Commissioner Stanley of North Sherbro thought that Assistant District Commissioners should be instructed that "slaves on the death of their owner may still pass to his heir, i.e. the person who becomes the head of the family to which they belong". The Attorney-General agreed, but made a clear distinction between a bequest of slaves, declared void by the Protectorate Ordinance, and the normal inheritance of slaves by customary law:

> A bequest is a disposition by will of property to some person who would otherwise not get that property, and is an artificial excrescence upon the customary law of inheritance. Therefore by the use of the word "bequest" I think the Ordinance excludes devolution by inheritance. Slaves thus pass to the heir.[22]

Among the Temne slaves were also heritable:

> A man might give a slave to his wife, and her children would inherit him; he would follow the wife to a new husband, provided she did not marry out of the family; a daughter might, however, inherit such a slave and would then be at liberty to take him to her husband's house. Another informant, however, thought that slaves were shared equally among the children, but would not remain with the wives after the husband's death.[23]

Since they were property, slaves could own nothing in theory and at redemption or emancipation lost everything. The Sierra Leone Government accepted this and at the time of abolition the Commissioner for the Southern Province made it perfectly clear that freed men would have no right to retain property or land they had enjoyed the use of while in servitude.[24] There were, however, exceptional circumstances under which a slave might have acquired property which was truly at his disposal. For example, a Fula master might have told his slave to plant some land with ginger and promised to reward his industry with a tenth share of the crop. If the slave sold his share of the ginger and bought a ring with the proceeds this ring in certain native law would be regarded as his property, although the burden of proof would rest with the ex-slave who sought to retain possession of it. Thomas thought that the slaves of the Temne were fortunate because their owners tended to regard themselves as trustees of their slaves' property on behalf of their slaves' children.[25]

These were the exceptions. As a rule slaves could not reap the benefits of their own energy and initiative. Their rewards depended on their masters' whims. If a slave set up as a trader his business would go to his master at his death, if not before. At the end of the First World War, Chief George of Mofwe told a British official that if his seven domestics had survived the East African campaign he would have taken the £35 each would have brought back, although he would have given £5 or £10 back according to his esteem for each man.[26] Slave holders continued to reap considerable benefits from their slaves until the institution was finally abolished. It was mere hypocrisy to argue, as one Creole trader did, that the masters were worse off than their slaves for whom they had to build houses, pay the hut tax and settle palavers, while the slaves never gave their masters a farthing; closer to the truth was the same man's description of the power of some Mende slave owners:

> The situation is this, a town is owned by only six or eight Chiefs, and of these Chiefs perhaps each has about six wives and ten slaves, and each slave may have two wives.[27]

In other words, each Chief had about thirty-six adults working for him. Most of the wives and slaves in the Protectorate belonged to men of considerable wealth, although there were some quite humble slaveholders with only one slave and even some slaves were said to have slaves of their own.[28] In some chiefdoms most adults might be slaveholders or slaves. Fenton described the work of the average Gallinas man as "going to his farm for a couple of days now and then during the farming season and seeing that his two or three reluctant slaves do something".[29] More usually slaves belonged to the higher ranks of traditional society—chiefs, sub-chiefs, headmen and perhaps successful traders. Slave ownership not only conferred economic benefits but also considerable social and political influence—at the expense of the slave.

Slaves were not even able to enjoy the normal rights of husbands, wives or parents. A slave "marriage" was insecure, especially when the man and the woman had different owners. They could be separated at any time because they were not married in the eyes of the customary law. They were merely living together with the consent of their masters, some of whom were so fearful of the growth of family feeling among their slaves that they would not let a slave woman have successive children by the same man.[30] Since the children belonged to the mother's owner, the slave parents could only enjoy limited parental rights over the children, whom the mother's owner claimed on the grounds that "Mine is the calf that is born of my cow".[31] At the age of seven children could be taken away by the mother's master and the girls could be given in marriage—sometimes just a disguised way of pawning the girl—without the consent of the slave parents.

On occasion being a slave meant peril to the person's life. Fairtlough was puzzled by a sudden rush to redeem old and sickly slaves until he discovered that from motives of economy their owners were donating them as Cannibal Society sacrifices.[32] Slaves were the last to receive food and shelter and were consequently mentally and physically stunted. Thomas noticed that among the Temne

> Slaves are, however, usually inferior to freeborn in physical development, and though the lot of the house slaves, who alone survive under present conditions, is doubtless better than that of ordinary slaves, they can hardly be considered as equals, mentally or physically, of the rest of the community.[33]

An American missionary thought that redeeming slaves would be of little use because

> As a general thing the slave children are of lower mentality and have no initiative of action because of the bad conditions under which they live. They are stunted in body and mind and few of them would be able to shift for themselves if released, . . .[34]

7—DS * *

Although a slave's life could be very hard most Protectorate slaves were reasonably secure during the first quarter of the twentieth century. They did have some advantages. First, since 1896 the law of the land had protected slaves from being sold, mutilated or killed. Second, the officials in the Protectorate nearly all disapproved of the institution of slavery, even if they were prepared to tolerate it, and the possibility of official intervention on behalf of slaves encouraged slaveholders to treat their slaves a little better than they might otherwise have done. Third, customary law often led to modifications of the institution of slavery, even if they were not enforceable in the customary courts.[35] A slave of the house could acquire the right to be protected from his master when necessary and pressure could be and was applied by customary courts to persuade slaveholders to treat their slaves justly. Some local usages gave the slaves added protection. For example, in the Vai Chiefdom of Soro, Governor Probyn came across a slave who had been stocked by his master without the permission of the local chief—as local custom required—and so the Governor instructed the local rulers to make sure this would not happen again.[36]

In order to counteract the attractions of the growing urban centres and the prospect of paid employment, masters had to treat their slaves more kindly than before. Slaves in many parts could run away to work on the railway or other public works, to work for a trading company or as a household servant, and even to enlist in the West African Frontier Force. These new opportunities did much to weaken domestic slavery.

More prosperous masters often settled trustworthy slaves in *faki*, or slave villages, and gave them land to clear and to cultivate. Under the supervision of slave headmen the *faki* sometimes became almost free, although the slaves had to send their owners some produce and children to work in their houses.[37] The slaves on the *faki* were becoming more like serfs.

The most effective protection of the slaves did not lie in the customs unearthed by British officials who were also amateur anthropologists, but in the fact that they were needed. They played a vital social and economic role in Protectorate society. The male slaves were needed to clear the ground for the women, both wives and slaves, to cultivate. Slaves collected palm kernels and extracted the palm oil. In areas far from rail and road they continued to carry produce and manufactured goods. Slaves built, maintained and repaired their masters' houses and they provided much of the labour on public and communal works. Generally slaves in the Protectorate had no special skill, although among the Yalunka the blacksmiths were slaves and the descendants of slaves.[38] They had to perform the heavy, the unskilled and the unpleasant work in the community; even though freemen sometimes also had to share in this work the heaviest burden fell on the slaves.

In some cases, particularly among the Mende, slaves shared this burden with wives who were little better than slaves. Captain Carr thought that in Bandajuma District a wife was really worse off than a slave.[39] The rows over the abduction or seduction of wives by government employees show that husbands thought of their wives as chattels.[40] The distinction between slavery and polygamy was blurred not just because slave women were often concubines or slave wives but also because the agriculture of the Protectorate depended equally on the labour of wives and slaves. A missionary with many years experience in the Protectorate noted this economic relationship between wives and slaves:

> And if a man had a large number of male slaves, then he must also have a large number of wives to attend to the ground the men prepared. The right proportion must be maintained. And if a man had a large number of wives, then he must also have a large number of male dependants to do the heavy work.[41]

*   *   *

There were two very important variables which affected both the numbers enslaved in the Protectorate and the conditions under which slaves lived. First was the nature of the culture of the societies in which the slaves lived and second was the magnitude of the impact of the British presence on these societies.

Only Captain Stanley made a systematic attempt to study slavery in the so-called tribes of Sierra Leone.[42] He estimated that about 15%—about 220,000 people—of the population of the Protectorate were slaves but it seems that his estimate was rather too low. He noted substantial differences in the percentages enslaved among the peoples of the Protectorate, ranging from 35%, 33% and 30% among the Mandingo, Susu and Vai down to only

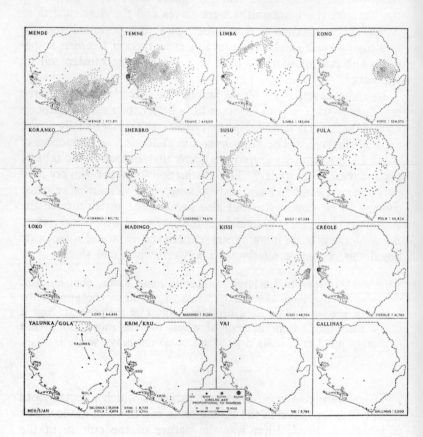

Ethnic Groups
(*Courtesy of University of London Press Ltd.*)

5% among the Loko, Kissi and Limba. The Mende percentage was close to the national average of 15% and the Temne figure was 20%. He distinguished between the people who had been successful in war and trade and had acquired the most slaves and those who had been their victims. In the former category were those with the high percentages of slaves—the Mandingo, Susu, Vai, Yalunka, Temne and Mende; in the latter he put those with the lowest percentages of slaves—the Gola, Krim, Koranko, Kono, Sherbro, Loko and Limba.[43]

Stanley's observations led him to certain conclusions as to how slaves fared in different societies. He was particularly struck by the aloof attitude of the Mandingo towards their slaves:

> Yet in no other tribe I am acquainted with does the fact that numbers of slaves are owned by practically every family of importance obtrude itself less, and this, despite the fact that from a social point of view, they regard their domestic slaves as distinctly inferior to themselves. The reason is that the Mandingo, especially when he is away from his own country, treats those in servitude under him with exceptional liberality and consideration.[44]

The Mandingo master, according to Stanley, saw that his slaves worked for themselves at least three days a week, that the young men married at a suitable age and that all had decent clothes to wear on Fridays and holidays. In some large towns the slaves lived separately in *Jong Kunde* or slave towns. In 1921 District Commissioner Sayers made similar remarks about the Fula who were believed to be harsh masters. He pointed out that few of their slaves sought redemption and

> In contrast to the other peoples of the Protectorate, and which is evidence of the fact that the status of slave is more clearly recognized with them, the Fulas keep their slaves as a rule in slave villages called "rounde", do not mix with them socially to any extent besides obliging them to adopt amongst other sumptuary distinctions, a peculiar method of hair dressing.[45]

Stanley thought the Krim treated their slaves with exceptional consideration, allowing them to rise to high positions and even marrying them. He remembered being greatly puzzled when hearing a case by the indifference of some so-called slaves towards redemption until he learnt from their Krim master that they were second and third generation slaves who had never been told that they were slaves. The Vai, too, were good masters, but not the Mende and the Temne who, although they attached less significance to social differences between slave and free, did not treat their slaves well.[46] Stanley seemed to believe that in a society with clearly defined social distinctions the upper classes were more aware of their obligations to the lower orders than were the upper classes in a more fluid social system. In certain cases he seemed to be applying the idea of *noblesse oblige* to the peoples of the Sierra Leone Protectorate.

The second significant variable affecting the prevalence and the conditions of slavery in the Protectorate was the social and economic impact of the British presence. This was greater near urban centres, adminstrative headquarters and public works— notably roads and the railway. Freetown had an especially great influence. Moving southeast from Freetown through the mainly Mende Southern Province about the year 1920 a traveller might notice a direct relationship between the percentage enslaved and the distance from Freetown. In Sembehun-Gbangbama, the District adjoining the Colony, the District Commissioner reported that less than 10% of the people were slaves.[47] The District Commisioner of Sumbuya, adjoining Sembehun-Gbangbama to the southeast, estimated that between a quarter and a half of his people were slaves.[48] In Pujehun and Mano River, the two most southeastern districts, the percentage of slaves was even higher. It reached a peak of 50% to 60% in the Vai Chiefdoms near the Liberian border and in these two districts cases involving slaves formed a large part of the work load of the District Commissioners.[49] This is confirmed by the Pujehun Native Affairs Record for 1919 and 1920. In 1919, 25 out of 90 cases concerned slaves (thirteen runaways, eight redemptions, one bequest and three others) and in 1920, 57 out of 220 cases involved slaves (37 runaways, 14 redemptions, four bequests, and two others).[50]

Proximity to centres of British influence was usually directly related to the way masters treated their slaves. Fenton wrote of Sembehun and Gbangbama:

The general condition of slaves here and in the Gbangbama District is good ... The slaves are not noticeable stigmatised: their owners work in the fields with them: they sometimes have money which their masters do not trouble to take from them: they are especially skillful in cutting palm kernels: they have an easy escape to the Colony if ill-treated.[51]

Despite the many other factors to be considered it is clear that the British presence in the Protectorate weakened the whole traditional system of economic and social organization—particularly the ties which bound the slave to his master.

The rapid development of urban centres offered the slave an alternative to a life of unpaid toil at subsistence level. Development was not confined to the Colony. New administrative centres upcountry and the railway line resulted in the rapid growth of of small towns in the interior. Bo, 136 miles east of Freetown by rail, grew fast in the early decades of this century. So did other towns like Blama, Makeni, Pendembu and other new centres near the railway in the rich oil palm territory. Colonel Warren attributed much of the progress in Ronietta District to the railway. When he had first come to the area Moyamba had been a hamlet of twenty houses inhabited by naked savages, but thirteen years later it was a town of two thousand people.[52] Alldridge was struck by the contrast between Pendembu in 1892—"mere collections of squalid native huts"—and in 1908—"a town with a fine open quadrangle containing some of the best native houses in the country". He also thought the wonderful changes in the Pendembu area were an "ever-recurring evidence that a powerful current of civilising influence is continually passing up from Freetown along the railway".[53]

One of the criteria Alldridge used to assess progress in the interior was the variety of trade goods available. He noted a wide variety at centres on or near the railway. Daru market seemed like Freetown's Kissy Road and at Baiima, the railway terminus more than two hundred miles from Freetown, he was pleased by the wide variety of goods, ranging from worsted caps to umbrellas and from cloves to sardines. Equally impressive was the extent to which currency was circulating in the Protectorate:

Perhaps the first thing to strike me was the arrival of what the natives call "Cop-por". In the conversation of my hammock boys with each other I frequently distinguished this word, indeed it seemed their main topic. It is the equivalent of our "cash". Now when I was here in the old days money, that is, coin, was practically unknown; so much so that there were times when my British coin would not pass in exchange for the domestic commodities I required, and when if my silver was received it was promptly melted down for ornaments; there was no local use for it as coin.[54]

The need to raise five shillings annually for the hut tax may have stimulated the circulation of currency, but even though at first the hut tax could have been paid in palm kernels or husked rice it was nearly all paid in cash. In the second year of the tax 97% of it, about £25,000, was collected in cash.[55] It was hoped that the tax would accustom the people to the use of currency, but this was not always successful, as a missionary noted in Yalunka country:

> We have had much difficulty in getting the natives to work for us, for as soon as their hut tax is paid they have no further need of money, and have no desire whatsoever to work either for payment in cash or goods,. . . .[56]

Although this may have been true of the remote Yalunka territory, in the more accessible parts of the Protectorate the old subsistence economy was changing rapidly as goods and currency circulated more widely. New "needs" were being discovered and many slaves must have longed to be free to earn money to buy the attractive new wares they saw. Slaveholders also must have begun to realize that there were other desirable forms of property besides slaves. In the nineteenth century the introduction of legitimate commerce to West Africa may have further encouraged slavery, but in the twentieth century in the Sierra Leone Protectorate it weakened the institution.[57] This was at least partly because by the twentieth century goods and coinage were much more widely available and because the British presence in the Protectorate was powerful enough to prevent any growth of slavery.

* * *

The Sierra Leone Government did not have to face the problem of an increase in slavery in the Protectorate during the twentieth century because the institution was being weakened by social and economic pressures. In fact the British and Sierra Leone Governments were more concerned to prevent too rapid changes and they made a series of political and administrative decisions which seemed to strengthen slavery in the Protectorate, or at least to maintain it. Laudably enough they sought to check the worst abuses of the institution, although they made little attempt to reduce the number of slaves. These measures, as Sir Benjamin Pine had pointed out half a century before in the Gold Coast, may well have tended "to smooth and varnish it (slavery) for its preservation".[58]

Although the continuation of slavery was clearly not the intention of the British and Sierra Leone Governments, it was the logical outcome of their policies, which were based on a combination of caution and pious hopes. The best way to avoid a storm in Britain about slavery seemed to the Colonial Office to play the problem down and even to make it believed that the problem no longer existed. Britain had been embarrassed by revelations of its officials collaborating with slave holders in the 1890s and the official verdict that the 1898 risings had been caused by action against slavery made it even more dangerous for British officials to tolerate slavery in the Sierra Leone Protectorate. The Liberal Government which had assumed office at the end of 1905 and routed the Conservatives in the 1906 election after campaigning on the Chinese Slavery issue was particularly sensitive to the possibility of being seen to permit the continuation of slavery.[59] Yet, slavery continued there until a storm of protest in 1927 forced Britain to emancipate the slaves. Until 1927 the Colonial Office managed to avoid it being generally known that slavery was still legal in a British protectorate. The officials in Whitehall did not scruple to censor the information that came from Sierra Leone. When Thomas presented his report on the Temne, Ellis wrote:

> I should also tell Mr. Thomas to omit the marked par. on the 1st page of the section on slavery. It will only give trouble to allow public reference to be made to slavery as an existing institution.[60]

Senior officials in the Sierra Leone Government also tended to deny the existence of the problem of slavery. When Colonial Secretary in Sierra Leone, Haddon Smith considered slavery virtually defunct and eleven years later, when he was Governor of the Bahamas, he told the West African Lands Committee that there was no slavery in the Sierra Leone Protectorate.[61] Governor Probyn minimised the problem. In 1906 he wrongly claimed that the children of slaves were born free and that the number of slaves was "relatively small" and a little later referred to the abolition of slavery as though it were a *fait accompli*.[62] This policy of playing down the problem was so successful that in 1910 John Harris, Secretary of the newly combined Anti-Slavery and Aborigines' Protection Society, paid tribute to the Sierra Leone Government:

> The fact that the Society has not, I believe, had occasion in recent years to address a single letter to the Colonial Office upon questions in Sierra Leone, is in itself an emphatic tribute to the perfectness of its administration.[63]

One reason for this may have been the weakness of the humanitarians at the time, described by Sir W. Brampton Gurdon in his Presidential Address to the Aborigines' Protection Society:

> He could not help feeling that there had been a falling off in humanitarian feeling since the time of Wilberforce and the abolition of slavery. He hoped soon to see a return of the old anti-slavery feeling.[64]

So the man on the spot was left to deal with the problems arising from the continuation of slavery in the Sierra Leone Protectorate. This was in line with the general policy of the Colonial Office under Chamberlain, which was reluctant to intervene directly in the affairs of individual colonies. Lord Onslow, Parliamentary Under-Secretary of State for the Colonies from 1900 to 1903, told the African Society:

> When I had the honour of taking a share in the Colonial Administration under Mr. Chamberlain, it was the settled policy of the Colonial Office that you ought never, except under very exceptional circumstances, to interfere with the decision and the policy of the man you had sent out to administer... So long as

we were kept informed of what was about to be done, the occasions on which the Colonial Office interfered were of the very rarest.[65]

This confidence in the man on the spot clearly did not extend to Governor Sir Leslie Probyn of Sierra Leone. Antrobus wrote, "I am anxious that Mr. Probyn is going out of his mind. He has written some odd things lately." Three years later Probyn was still in Freetown, now a knight, and the Colonial Office was still worried. Fiddian thought that except in dealing with native affairs Probyn's judgement was unsound and another official commented on "a condition of nervousness and want of balance bordering on temporary insanity".[66]

Although Whitehall and Freetown minimized the problem of slavery, it was very real to the officials in the Protectorate. In the years immediately after the 1898 wars the difficulties with the institution were seen as potential causes of disaffection, but by the 1920s they were regarded more as distasteful and burdensome problems which had to be dealt with. In 1904 a lieutenant reported to the War Office that:

> At present in certain parts of the Karina District there are "palavers" going on about Domestic Slavery. This is causing a certain amount of unrest among the owners who find it difficult to get their domestics to work. If any sweeping changes were made at any time in the near future in this matter it would be almost certain to bring on some kind of rising. It is in fact at the times of sudden changes of any kind, and, I believe, only then, that combined risings are to be expected.[67]

The traditional rulers were undoubtedly worried by the prospect of losing their slaves. The main worries of the newly constituted tribal assemblies in Karene were the difficulties in selling kola nuts and the exodus of their slaves.[68] In Sherbro District the District Commissioner noted that slaves were still a very important part of the wealth of the principal people.[69]

British officials who dealt with these principal people had to treat them with tact and caution. The Sierra Leone Government could not afford to forfeit their support by hasty action against slavery. Although fears of an insurrection had little foundation, there was a real danger that the chiefs of the Protectorate would refuse to co-operate with the Sierra Leone Government and this would lead to serious economic and administrative difficulties for the British officials. Britain supplied neither the men nor the money which would enable the Sierra Leone Government to govern and administer without the help of the chiefs. The administrative vacancies were not even filled until 1904.[70] The official policy was to exercise authority in the Protectorate through the native chiefs under government supervision.[71]

The Sierra Leone Government did more than just treat the traditional rulers with caution. It consolidated and strengthened the positon of most of them. With government backing and a good income from their stipends and their commissions, petty chieflings became men of power and influence. Alldridge observed in 1908:

> In these days paramount chiefs have a much greater recognized power and have much more to do with the Government than formerly.[72]

As they achieved power and influence chiefs increased their hold over their people and were more able to resist the challenges to slavery posed by economic and social development.

Since it could neither support nor oppose slavery the Sierra Leone Government made the obvious decision to do nothing. Officials tried to salve their consciences by doing as much as possible to alleviate the conditions of slavery but this does not seem to have had much effect. So they fell back on pious hopes and persuaded themselves that the institution of slavery would simply die away. Probyn summed this policy up:

> You are aware that although the Government has not abolished existing slavery in the Protectorate, the policy has been to stand aloof from the system: in other words, the power of the Government is never used to back up the system of slavery. The system of slavery is left to work itself out, and, in a decade or two, will probably cease to exist; ...[73]

As two decades later half the population of the remoter chiefdoms were still slaves, this policy clearly did not succeed.

This policy of aloofness was nothing but a sham. Implicitly and explicitly by legislative actions and administrative decisions the Sierra Leone Government not only tolerated but even strengthened slavery in the Protectorate. Although the Protectorate Ordinance of 1896 had weakened slavery, legislation during the first decade of the twentieth century—which formed the basis of Protectorate administration until the 1930s—tended to favour the master at the expense of the slave.

In addition to the need for chiefs as administrators the reasons for this policy were largely economic. To yield sufficient revenue for the expenses of administration the interior had to produce and export considerable agricultural wealth. Much of the agriculture was highly labour intensive. For example, many man hours were spent in the extraction of palm kernels. So for the Sierra Leone Government to pay its own way Protectorate labour had to satisfy certain requirements. First, it had to be cheap because Europe paid low prices for tropical produce. Both before and after the proclamation of the Protectorate labour costs were kept down by the system of slavery. If the producers had to pay for labour their costs and prices would be increased. Until a new answer to the problem of labour costs was found the Sierra Leone Government found it most convenient to tolerate the system of slavery. Second, labour had to be reasonably reliable and efficient. British officials did not think the people were naturally industrious. In fact, they were frequently shocked at their idleness. Governor King-Harman wrote of one of his visits to the Protectorate in 1901:

> From Mopalma I marched to Bandajuma in 2 days, passing through several small towns where the inhabitants appeared to be sufficiently provided with the necessities of life to allow them, for the most part, to loll in their hammocks all day, and to dance and sing all night.[74]

The Foreign Office agreed, but was less inclined to blame the people for this indolence:

> To continuous hard work of any kind the native evinces a strong antipathy, natural in itself, and doubtless fostered by centuries of insecurity of ownership and the degenerating effect of the prevalence of slavery.[75]

The Sierra Leone Government failed to work out any other system of making the people work hard to bring prosperity to the Protectorate and to the Colony which depended so greatly on it. For the time being it looked as though the only feasible way of organizing labour was the institution of slavery.

Third, there had to be sufficient labour to meet the demands of Protectorate agriculture. Although thinly populated, the Protectorate had sufficient labour under normal circumstances, but the British ended the import of additional labour by the slave trade at the same time as they began making extra demands for labour. The Protectorate had to find more labour to produce greater crops for exports and for public works initiated by the Government. These new demands disrupted the traditional economies and, as Nathan realized in 1899, would cause social problems too:

> The development of the resources of the Sierrra Leone Protectorate must be the salvation of the Colony in the future. The grave labour difficulties in the way of this development which have resulted from the unavoidable weakening of the influence of the native chiefs, from the exportation of labour and from other causes will have to be overcome.[76]

The most important priority was to develop the resources of the Protectorate and therefore the issue of slavery was shelved. Not until Britain had consolidated her power in the interior so that she no longer had to rely on the chiefs so much, did the Sierra Leone Government really want to face up to the issue of slavery. When that time came social and economic pressures had so weakened the institution that it was surprisingly easy to emancipate the slaves.

The reason for the shortage of labour in the Protectorate was simple. Life as a government labourer or in Freetown was pleasanter and more exciting than slavery in a remote village. The construction of the railway made very heavy, but not always steady, demands for labour until 1916. Unskilled labour worked on the main line from Freetown to Baiima which was completed in 1905, then on the tramline to Pendembu until 1908, and finally the branch line north to Makeni which was finished in 1916. In 1901 the Colonial Secretary reported that the number of labourers on the railway ranged from under a thousand in February to over five thousand in December. Towards the end of the year there had been ample labour, but from February to June work had been hindered by a shortage of labour.[77] This was presumably because early in the year the men returned to their villages to pay the hut tax and to clear their rice farms. This was the reason given by Governor Merewether in 1915 to account for the decline in the number of labourers on the railway from nearly nine thousand the previous November to just over three thousand in January.[78] The labourers were attracted by the prospect of ninepence to a shilling a day, described as "substantial wages" some years before by Governor Probyn, and many were reluctant to return to slave labour in their villages—Probyn commented that many were even reluctant to give unpaid labour on the roads.[79]

These roads and railways brought solid benefits to the chiefs. Besides increased trade and easier access to their villages and towns the chiefs laid their hands on the earnings of some of their slaves and, according to Governor Merewether, earned a commission for recruiting labour for public works.[80] Nevertheless, the chiefs were very worried about the exodus of their men to work on the railway and to Freetown:

> What the chiefs cannot understand is that their young men prefer leaving their villages for work on the railway and in Freetown; but, considering that they get a good wage for their labour, from 9d to 1s a day, they naturally prefer it to unpaid labour in their villages under their chiefs. This exodus from the villages to the railway works and the town is very noticeable, as the farms now seem to be worked solely by old men, women and children; but this will right itself before long, and those at present employed on the railway works will be compelled to return to their villages and help to work the land and develop the country.[81]

The demand for labour to build the railway was temporary, but the lure of the big city, Freetown, was more lasting. The influx into Freetown not only hindered Protectorate agriculture but also gave rise to social and economic problems in the city. Officials and Creoles had been concerned about this influx of unskilled and sometimes unemployable labour since the 1880s.[82] After the proclamation of the Protectorate the Government was apparently in a better position to stop slaves coming to Freetown. The Creole Press argued strongly for controls to keep able-bodied men working on the farms rather than idling in the Colony.[83] These Creole worries did not concern the Government as much as the problems arising from the disorganization of labour in the Protectorate, which was seen as the one great difficulty in the way of progress.[84] The need to safeguard the economy of the Protectorate had much to do with the formulation of three major ordinances early in the twentieth century.

The first of these, the Protectorate Ordinance of 1901, contained three important decisions on slavery and allied problems.[85] It did not implement Nathan's proposal that part of the hut tax could be paid by labour because Cardew had made out a strong case against the principle of forced labour, and Whitehall feared "a system of this kind is always liable to be misrepresented by well-meaning persons".[86] It omitted the clauses in the 1896 and 1897 Ordinances which had made it a criminal offence for a native person to adjudicate on the person of a slave, although such a judgement was still not recognized.[87]

Some attempt was made to solve the vexing problem of the abduction of women, wives and servants or slaves, from chiefly households. As Birch had discovered in 1898 passions ran high over this issue.[88] The problem was more difficult because so often these cases involved Government employees and Freetown was responsible to a certain extent. It was particularly embarrassing when a loyal chief complained. The abduction, or seduction, of one of Chief Nancy Tucker's girls in 1899 by Post Messenger Santiggi pointed to the urgency of the problem.[89] Dr. Hood decided that Santiggi should pay Nancy Tucker £3 for the girl, who would then become his wife by customary law. Parkes disagreed and pointed out that the less the Government had to do with transactions in which money was paid for an individual the better, as this might eventually be misconstrued. He suggested that anyone enticing or coaxing a servant away should be fined £3, to be wholly or partly awarded to the master or mistress for the loss of services sustained. Nathan felt that this problem made it much more difficult to administer the Protectorate. There was resentment at the number of women and girls leaving their owners. guardians, husbands and fathers for Government officials whose regular pay promised comparative luxury. The Mende resented this not from the moral point of view but because the girls were being taken away without the payment of the customary bride price of £3.[90] A legal officer suggested that Government employees should be sacked at once for taking away women and that in certain cases abduction should be a criminal offence.[91] Nathan considered both action and inaction dangerous, and he submitted the problem to London:

> If the Government insists on the girl being returned, it practically reconsigns her to domestic slavery. If, on the other hand, it insists on the abductor paying a fine equal to the market value of the girl, it goes very near to sanctioning the purchase of human beings. If, again, it takes no action in the matter, it will practically be sanctioning abduction and creating general discontent in the Protectorate.[92]

Nathan then went on to suggest that any native in Government service in the Protectorate should appear before the District Commissioner with the girl's parent, guardian, master or mistress who would be asked to consent to the "marriage"—otherwise the employee should be sacked. Cardew disagreed and wanted the problem to be left until his return to Freetown. He suggested that in the meantime parents should be able to take civil proceedings in seduction cases and criminal proceedings in abduction cases.[93] Chamberlain supported Cardew. Consequently Clause 92 of the 1901 Protectorate Ordinance covered civil proceedings by the injured husband, parent or other person for seduction and Clause 93 similarly covered cases of criminal intent.[94]

The next major ordinance, the Protectorate Courts Jurisdiction Ordinance of 1903, made no changes bearing directly on slavery, but it recognized customary law and thus strengthened the position of the slaveholding classes who administered customary law.[95] It defined more clearly the powers of courts in the Protectorate—official and customary—and one of its clauses later figured prominently in the controversy which led to the final emancipation of slaves. This provided for the application of native law and customs "not being repugnant to natural justice, equity and good conscience".

Labour shortages, abductions, desertions and other symptoms of the breakdown of traditional society continued to worry the Sierra Leone Government, which in 1905 drew up the third major ordinance. This was the Protectorate Native Law Ordinance of 1905. Governor Probyn's intentions were clear, he wrote in

1905 "I assume as an axiom that the tribal system by which a Chief is made responsible for law and order in his Chiefdom is to be maintained".[96] This ordinance attempted to safeguard the traditional system from the social and economic pressures which were weakening it. In so doing the Sierra Leone Government limited the liberty of the individual to such an extent that there is some truth in the accusation that the Protectorate Native Law Ordinance sanctioned a form of slavery.[97]

It regularized what had been previously a very informal system of communal forced labour. Although the expressed intention was to protect the people from exploitation, the result was a further increase in chiefly power at the expense of individual liberty, and the chiefs were quick to take advantage of their increased powers to call for communal labour. One possible advantage for the people was the provision for a cash commutation of labour obligations.[98] The Colonial Office initially opposed this but in 1906 it allowed Probyn to try it in one or two chiefdoms.[99] The experiment was reasonably successful, and the practice spread to other chiefdoms.

There were other limitations on individual freedom in the Protectorate Native Law Ordinance of 1905, including measures which were attempts to stop the depopulation of the Protectorate and the influx to urban areas. Clause 51 made it unlawful in the Protectorate to harbour a person who had left his chiefdom without obtaining the customary consent of his chief. Clause 52 provided for the punishment of those harbouring such people. Clause 53 obliged chiefs to repatriate those who had come to their chiefdoms after leaving their homes without the customary permission. Although it contained provisions for appealing to the District Commissioner against the refusal of permission to leave a chiefdom this ordinance made it more difficult for a person to leave his chiefdom for another chiefdom. Antrobus at the Colonial Office had no doubt that these restrictions were aimed at slaves.[100] Certainly slaves were unlikely to be granted permission to leave, and if they ran away to another part of the Protectorate they would be liable to be repatriated.

Probyn had been Secretary to the Southern Nigerian Government at the time of its House Rule Proclamation in 1901. This may explain certain similarities between the Sierra Leone legislation of 1905 and the Southern Nigerian Proclamation which officially recognized the House Rule system and even extended it to people who had never previously been organized in these Houses.[101] The House system had developed from the slave trading houses of the nineteenth century, and by giving it official recognition the Southern Nigerian Government was in effect legalizing an institution akin to slavery. The Southern Nigerian measures to stop the depopulation of the Protectorate and the influx into the cities were similar to Clauses 51, 52 and 53 in the Sierra Leone legislation four years later. Moreover, a recalcitrant House member could be fined £50 and sentenced to a year in prison. An employer who took on a House member without the approval of the head of his House was liable to the same penalties, and there was a similar punishment for the head of a House who neglected his duties. The considerations influencing Probyn in Sierra Leone in 1905 were very much the same as those in Nigeria. He wrote:

> If the tribal system is allowed to fall into decay it will be necessary to increase to an extent almost beyond the resources of the Protectorate the staff necessary for doing the work which is now done under the tribal system.[102]

In Sierra Leone two further ordinances in 1905 and 1908 made it yet more difficult for a runaway to remain at liberty. The Tribal Administration (Freetown) Ordinance enabled the headmen in Freetown to compel any natives who had left the Protectorate without leave to return to it and it included provisions for the punishment of those harbouring or assisting a runaway.[103] Probyn hoped that in conjunction with the Protectorate Native Law Ordinance this would have a healthy effect on the labour situation in the Protectorate, but its main result was to strengthen the hold of masters over their slaves.[104] In 1908 the Vagrancy Ordinance provided for the repatriation of natives who had spent three weeks in the Colony without employment or other means of subsistence.[105]

* * *

Another difficult problem which required legislation was that of the export of labour from Sierra Leone. This not only contributed to the depopulation of the Protectorate but it often sent

185

indentured labourers to work under conditions of near slavery. Many of the labourers had been slaves in the Protectorate. Much attention was focused on Fernando Po and other Spanish Colonies in the Gulf of Guinea and on the Congo Free State. In these places many workers lived and died under appalling conditions.

The problem was one of long standing. Since the 1880s labourers had been recruited from among those who had gone to Freetown from the interior.[106] At first the Sierra Leone Government had encouraged this export of labour by private contractors and even by officials. In 1889 Parkes himself, with the consent of the Governor, had at the request of the Belgian Government sent fifty old soldiers to the Congo. By 1890 A. T. Porter had emerged as the agent for shipping labour to the Congo. He was also shipping men to Fernando Po and, according to the United States Consul, he had even been approached by President Kruger of the South African Republic on the subject of Negro labour for the mines.[107] Complaints about the ill-treatment of the Congo labourers were made as early as 1890, but as there was no clear case against the Belgians no official protest was made. Shortly afterwards the Police Magistrate insisted that the labourers recruited in Freetown sign their agreements in his presence, but it is hard to see how this could have improved the situation. In effect the contracts were being officially approved even though the authorities had no way of ensuring that the conditions in the Congo would be as stipulated by the contract.

Cardew disapproved of the practice because of the conditions in the Congo and the depopulation of the Protectorate. In June 1894 he warned of the reports that labourers were made to act as soldiers and forbade them to leave the Colony without a written agreement stating the nature and the terms of employment, signed before the Police Magistrate of Freetown or a district commissioner.[108] In 1896 the Foreign Service Employment Ordinance restricted the recruiting of labourers for service abroad—it was to be allowed only with the approval of the Governor.[109] Despite his opposition to the general principle of exporting labour Cardew in 1896 allowed Porter to export 500 men to work on the Panama Canal.[110] It is hard to understand why Cardew gave this permission because he did not trust Porter and even sent detectives on board the SS *Castle Eden* to investigate conditions. When he reported the departure of the ship for Panama, Cardew deprecated the emigration of labour because the hinterland was being denuded of young men, and Freetown was being crowded with idle and criminal aborigines. Possibly he saw the departure of the *Castle Eden* as a golden opportunity to rid Freetown of 500 troublesome people. Chamberlain was angry:

> I am extremely dissatisfied with the Colonial Government in this matter. Write Strongly therefore. If they have any explanation we will consider it later but at present their case looks badly.[111]

Pooley also disapproved strongly of this decision. He pointed out that Porter had also shipped labour to the Congo Free State where many people had died and deplored the shipping of illiterate natives to Panama where conditions were hard. He enclosed copies of contracts with the Panama Canal and the Congo Railway Companies. They were similar. Labourers served for three years at £2 a month (£1.10.0 in the Congo) for nine hours a day, six days a week; free board and lodging and medical treatment were provided, and a sick labourer would be repatriated and return passages would be provided.[112]

Nevertheless, the export of labour with official approval continued. In 1898 it was reported that many still emigrated to labour in the Congo and elsewhere and that most labourers usually returned in two or three years.[113] In 1899 Nathan drew attention to the export of labour which had much to do with the grave labour difficulties of the Protectorate.[114]

The illegal export of labour continued well into the twentieth century. By 1903 the Governor felt able to report some success in stopping Protectorate men in Freetown from being enticed into French territory and sold:

> The victims in such cases are the innocent and unsophisticated natives of the Protectorate, who having in most cases run away from their chiefs, seek employment in Freetown and fall easy prey to those who under pretence of engaging them as labourers take them away in canoes and convey them out of the Colony.[115]

The problem was more difficult to solve in the Protectorate. When C. B. Wallis acted as District Commissioner of Sherbro he found the state of affairs there very unsatisfactory. In particular District Commissioner Alldridge had enraged the chiefs by his neglect of the problem of the illegal emigration of people from Sherbro to Liberia and on to the Congo Free State. Not one in twenty ever came back. At least a thousand "boys" were being enticed to Liberia annually in what was "nothing more or less than a gigantic and abominable traffic in human flesh".[116]

Even after the removal of Alldridge this illegal emigration remained a problem. In 1905 Probyn was worried about the export of labour to the Congo via Liberia from Bandajuma District as well as from Sherbro District.[117] The District Commissioner of Bandajuma confirmed reports from the British Consul in Monrovia that "boys" were being taken to Liberia, and agents were sent to investigate.[118]

In 1912 there was concern at the activities of the so-called Major Mackay Mackay, a plausible rogue who enjoyed official favour in Liberia and enticed labourers away from Sierra Leone to Liberia and then shipped them on to Fernando Po in German steamers.[119] In his report for 1913 the Consul-General in Liberia confirmed that there were men shipping Sierra Leone labourers to small depots in Liberia and forwarding them to Spanish and Portuguese islands in the Gulf of Guinea.[120] In 1915 it was alleged that two hundred Mende who had crossed into Liberia to avoid conscription as carriers for the British Army had been sent to Fernando Po by the firm of J. W. West.[121] Even in the 1920s this traffic continued. In 1921 the British Consul-General investigated the conditions under which labourers from Sierra Leone were working in Fernando Po:

> The general impression produced by my investigations so far is that the ignorance and helplessness of uncivilised natives from the interior bush of the Sierra Leone Protectorate are being abused and exploited by the unscrupulous individuals engaged in the business under conditions which are not at all far removed from slavery.[122]

Four years later the British Vice Consul at Fernando Po made a similar report. The labourers were brutally treated, their food and housing were poor, they received virtually no medical treatment and they were flogged to make them confess to crimes.[123]

Even if the Sierra Leone Government could argue that it could do no more to stop the illegal export of labour, it could not justify the continuing legal export of labour from Sierra Leone. In 1907 P. H. Davy, an unofficial member of the Legislative Council, protested against the recent engagement of labourers for service outside Sierra Leone, even though the last Governor had promised that this would stop. Davy found that the recent recruiting had caused a shortage of labour in Freetown and demands for higher wages.[124]

Probyn decided to extend the controls over the emigration of labour by making the 1896 Ordinance applicable to the Protectorate as well as to the Colony and in 1908 the Foreign Service Employment Ordinance was enacted to this effect.[125] In 1913 another ordinance was passed for the stricter regulation of the recruiting of labour for service outside Sierra Leone. The Acting Attorney-General, K. J. Beatty, explained the need for this new ordinance:

> The reason for this Bill is that it has come to notice that conditions approximating to slavery exist in certain islands to the South of British West Africa and that a certain number of native labourers of this and other West African Colonies are induced to go to these Islands and then find that they become indentured labourers with little hope of being able to return to their homes.[126]

It was hoped that this new ordinance would deal more effectively with the problem than the 1908 ordinance had. Two significant changes were that the person wishing to go abroad had to acquire in the presence of a magistrate the consent of his chief or tribal authority and that the contracts had to be for less than thirteen months. After this the problem became less urgent although Sierra Leone continued to supply labour for other countries. After the war labourers were sent to the Gold Coast mines—a practice that Acting Governor Maxwell deplored at a time when there was a shortage of labour in the Protectorate.[127] Yet, there seem to have been no more cases of the export of labour to the colonies in the Gulf of Guinea, where working conditions had given rise to so much concern.

* * *

Legislation alone could not solve the shortage of labour and the other economic and social problems of the Protectorate. The basic problem was that young people, especially slaves, would not remain at home as their parents had done before them. What the legislation of the early twentieth century did was to provide the framework for administrative action to halt the disruption of the traditional way of life. For some years after the proclamation of the Protectorate British administrators considered that this was their most important task. As the Annual Report for 1903 made clear, this meant that the administrators tended to favour the traditional authorities at the expense of the common people:

> Naturally they (the Chiefs) cannot have the same power over their people which they had in the old slave days, but their power is upheld in every way possible by the District Commissioners.[128]

Most administrators wanted to preserve the *status quo*, and in so doing they naturally favoured the established institutions—including domestic slavery.

Although the Protectorate Ordinance forbade legal decisions which recognized implicitly or explicitly the institution of slavery British officials continued to take administrative decisions affecting the institution. This meant that they were recognizing the institution, and by so doing they were helping to preserve it. Even officials like Addison, who clearly disliked slaveholders, found himself having to uphold their rights when he was an assistant District Commissioner.[129] In 1907 Addison rather high-handedly settled a dispute between the widow and the two sons of the late owner of twenty domestic slaves:

> Kottoo and Gendemah both lied and were insolent. They were not dutiful sons, so I gave verdict for the plaintiff, who was to get all domestics and various property from the defendants.

During a visit to part of the Sherbro District in 1909 Addison kept records of the twelve cases he heard. Two of the cases had nothing to do with slavery, two concerned runaway wives and the other eight were all slave cases—two disputes over the inheritance of slaves, three redemption cases, one attempt to regain runaway domestics and two attempts to make the defendant return slaves to the plaintiff.

The disputes about the inheritance of slaves often proved the most difficult. In 1906 the District Commissioner of Bandajuma called in three chiefs to judge a dispute of this nature and reported that the members of the family were satisfied with the decision.[130] In some cases British officials and assessor chiefs sat together. In a case involving 110 slaves the District Commissioner of Karene, the Acting District Commissioner of Bombali Sub-District and assessor chiefs awarded all the slaves to one claimant provided he paid the other claimant £70, a quarter of the slaves' value.[131]

Freetown did not usually challenge these decisions, but it was roused to action when Major Anderson, District Commissioner of Panguma, and his assistant, Mr. Greenway, made similar decisions on claims by the heirs and warriors of the late Chief Nyagwa of Panguma.[132] Twenty to thirty years before, Nyagwa had raided Kono country and taken many slaves, many of whom had escaped during the 1898 risings. After Nyagwa's death in exile in 1906 his warriors and his family tried to recover these Kono slaves and in some cases they approached Anderson or Greenway. Anderson was worried and wrote to Freetown in June 1907. He thought it was clear that these Kono slaves could be legally claimed but hoped the Attorney-General could find some legal way to avoid handing over the slaves to the claimants or that the Governor would make a special ruling in this case. Probyn thought Anderson had misjudged the situation because he should have refused any claims and he demanded explanations and details of cases already handled. After receiving Anderson's reply, Probyn rebuked him and pointed out that by Section 5 of the Protectorate Courts Jurisdiction Ordinance of 1903 no claim for or in respect of any slave could be entertained in Protectorate courts.[133] Anderson replied that he had intervened on behalf of the slaves and that the cases had not been court proceedings but investigations of native complaints made to the District Commissioner. In other words, his defence was that he had heard these cases in his administrative capacity and not his judicial capacity, and that he was justified in so doing. In this correspondence there is no evidence of any challenge to the legality of inheriting slaves.

*   *   *

Perhaps because the Nyagwa case focussed attention on the problem Freetown seriously considered providing redeemed slaves with certificates of redemption. The suggestion was apparently made in 1907 by Colonel Warren, District Commissioner of Koinadugu.[134] The Colonial Secretary and the Attorney-General approved, although the latter was worried lest the granting of redemption certificates be taken as evidence that the Government allowed slavery and gave a certificate to that effect.[135]

Payment of redemption was to be made to the master through the District Commissioner, who issued the certificate to the freed slaves. The certificates were signed by the District Commissioner and stated that, as a certain amount had been paid to redeem the person or persons listed, these persons were henceforward free, and not to be regarded as slaves by anyone.[136] In 1908 Probyn explained this procedure to the Kono Chiefs who wanted to free their people in captivity in Panguma and to protect runaways in their country from being taken away by Nyagwa's heirs. Probyn told them that although those who had been captured by Nyagwa and his warriors were free, their children who had been born in captivity and fed by their masters all their lives were not free, and these could not return home without redemption in the proper manner:

> All applications for redemption of each children (sic) should be made to the Konnoh Paramount Chief who will arrange the terms of redemption with the Paramount Chief of the master. When these terms are settled the matter must pass through the District Commissioner's Court, be registered by the District Commissioner and a certificate of Redemption to be given to the freed parties by the District Commissioner.[137]

The idea of redemption was not a new one. It had been an established practice long before the arrival of the British. Previously redemption had depended primarily on the will of the master, but after the establishment of the Protectorate the master was obliged to accept the redemption fee unless he could show that the redemption was not genuine. As early as 1894 Parkes proposed a form of redemption certificate to protect rescued and escaped slaves in the Colony.[138] He suggested that these people be given certificates of registration in the form of small squares of parchment when they reported to the Department of Native Affairs or to a District Commissioner. These squares could be

Domestic Slavery during the Twentieth Century

Copy

Redemption Certificate

Momo ~~Sir~~ Tibo

This is to certify that ~~the undernamed person~~ has this day been redeemed by Johnnie of Twasu in the Makpeli chiefdom on payment of £4 (four pounds sterling) to Shoaffa Guayande, and that the said Momo Tibo is henceforth a free man, and may not be regarded as a slave by any person.

At Bandajuma

Northern Sherbro District

this 14th day of August 1911   *C. T. Reaney*

District Commissioner

Received from Johnnie of Twasu in redemption of Momo Tibo the sum of £4 (four pounds sterling)

                                        his

                        Shoaffa X Sayaa Guayande

Witness   mark

Bandajuma

14th August 1911

(*All Courtesy of Rhodes House, Oxford*)

NORTHERN SHERBRO DISTRICT

This is to certify to all whom it may concern that Mapele who was a domestic of Boima Tamba of Gblama in the Gallinas Chiefdom of the Northern Sherbro District (East) has this day been redeemed by Monicu of Gblama aforesaid and that the said Mapele is now free and whosoever deprives the said Mapele of her liberty will do so at their peril. In witness whereof I have hereunto set my hand and seal this eleventh day of May 1911.----

(signed) E. Dudley Vergette

Asst. D. C.

Gendema

Gallinas Chiefdom

True copy

Dist. Commr.

22-8-11

Domestic Slavery during the Twentieth Century

Vandi of Potolo, Barri ChiefdomN.S.District has this day
redeemed from domestic servitude to Ahmadu Fulla of Pujehun
N.S.D the following persons:-

Mapanda ✓   (F full grown.)

Mini ✓   do .

Gilo ✓   do ,

Bundu ✓   do

Kitti ✓   (Girl about 8 years)

Jenny ✓   do 4 do

Tenni ✓   do 2 do

Morehai ✓ Boy do 11 do

Sando ✓ (Girl-Baby in arms)

As redemption mongyVandi has paid to Amadu Foulah the sum
of £21 (Twenty-One Pounds) .

The above named persons are now free and any one who
interferes with their liberty or attempt to restrain them
in any illegal manner does so at his peril.

Sgned H.C.Hodgson

A.D.C. -Pujehun 23/6/14

ned J.Bobb

    Interpreter.

easily worn round the neck or near the body and would be readily available to support claims for help from chiefs or police by ex-slaves if attempts were made to re-enslave them.

After the 1896 Ordinance gave official approval to redemption and before the decision to issue certificates of redemption officials in the Protectorate found themselves involved in very difficult redemption cases, which could have been simple if the freed slave had had a certificate of redemption. In one such case in 1905 the Koinadugu District Commissioner could take no action because there was no proof of a runaway domestic's claim that he had already been redeemed for one bull and four country cloths.[139] Wherever possible British officials tried to satisfy both the owner by awarding him the redemption fee and the slave by giving him a chance of redemption.[140]

The redemption certificates did give the redeemed slaves greater security but they did not succeed in stopping sham redemptions—cases in which redemptions served to disguise the transfer of slaves from one master to another. Rather optimistically Colonel Warren thought this problem had been solved by 1915:

> There was formerly a tendency to regard Redemption as a fresh sale of domestics sanctioned by the Government, but it may confidently be stated that now a redeemed domestic fully appreciates that he can if he wishes to obtain his freedom.[141]

Other officials did not share this unfounded optimism, and in 1918 it was necessary to order that:

> The District Commissioner should satisfy himself that the person paying redemption fee is a relative of the redeemed person, as otherwise it very often happens that the payment made is not regarded afterwards as a redemption fee, and as often as not the person who should have been redeemed finds himself in slavery to a new master.[142]

As late as 1924 the Governor informed London that unless the working of the redemption clause was very carefully supervised by the political officers it was liable to be used as a disguise for the transfer of slaves.[143]

Nor did the introduction of certificates lead to great numbers of redemptions. Records before the introduction of the provincial system in May 1920 are patchy, but in the first two and a half years after that there were 1,950 official redemptions—an average of 800 a year out of a slave population of a quarter of a million.[144] Stanley added that this low figure was the result of allowing only a relative or the slave himself to pay the redemption fee. He was, however, aware that if this restriction were lifted there would be a great increase in sham redemptions. Stanley and many others were inclined to agree with Colonel Warren's opinion that the slaves led pleasant enough lives.[145] Some went even further and suspected slaves who sought redemption of wanting it for the wrong reasons:

> Thirty-nine domestics were redeemed from servitude during the year. It would be interesting to follow the subsequent careers of some of these people. Some I have observed to take out Hawker Licenses—forsaking the soil at the first opportunity—while others join the riff-raff in Freetown and the trading villages along the Railway and Rivers.[146]

Yet, the following year the same official, H. C. Hodgson, seemed to take quite a different view. He commented that redemption was invariably most bitterly opposed by the master, and

> That a slave recently hanged himself sooner than return to his master shows what sort of relations exist between owner and "domestics" in some cases.[147]

The Provincial Commissioner, Captain Stanley, brushed aside Hodgson's concern—"Too much importance should not, in my opinion, be attached to an incident of this kind." In the earlier report Hodgson was echoing the official line that people in the Protectorate must stay on the farms; in the second he was more genuinely expressing his shock at the reality of slavery.

Those who did not toe the official line often found themselves in difficulties, as in the case of Addison. When he was assistant District Commissioner in Karene some chiefs complained that he had been freeing slaves.[148] Freetown instructed Colonel Warren to enquire and to report.

In addition to official reluctance in many cases, there was an even more serious obstacle to be overcome by slaves seeking redemption. In the first instance they had to approach the traditional authorities, who were the slave-owning classes and inclined to protect the interests of their class. It was not easy for a slave to gain access to a British official against the wishes of his master and his headman. In some cases chiefs saw redemptions as sources of extra income. In the Railway District in 1917 Paramount Chief Boima Dowie was deposed for various reasons, including:

> He obtained redemption money for a slave whom he did not redeem though he kept the money. In connection with the redemption of another slave (which he acquired for nothing) he levied £27 in "expenses" and from £16 to £30 in "fines".[149]

It was difficult enough for the slave to raise £4 per adult without having to pay "extras" of this sort.

The most important factors deciding the numbers redeemed were economic. Redemptions were high just after the First World War and before the depression of 1922. As Governor Wilkinson pointed out, a number of domestics returned from service in East Africa with large sums of money and some took the opportunity to redeem themselves, but others did not.[150] If, like Chief George of Mofwe, the slaveholders considered themselves the owners of all their slaves' money, it is hard to see how the returning carriers could have redeemed themselves and their families.[151] In some cases, whatever Wilkinson thought, these people had no option but to return to a life of slavery, if their masters so wished. A traveller in the Protectorate reported:

> I had a long talk with Major de Miremont on the very bad slavery conditions in this Colony. It came up over the dislike of men who had served as soldiers to going back to slavery. A Sergeant or Sergeant-Major, a man of position while serving, might be required on discharge to go back as slave to his old master and work in the farm or do other menial work required of him.[152]

Nor could ex-servicemen, in one district at least, avoid returning to slavery by not going home. Captain Stanley assured the North Sherbro Chiefs that the carriers would be sent back to their own villages with their pay and that they would not be allowed to scatter round the Protectorate or stay in Freetown where they could waste their wages. He told the Colonial Secretary that the returning carriers should be paid off in Pujehun, headquarters of North Sherbro District, not in Freetown.[153]

In the times of prosperity soon after the war, the poorer classes had more money and redemptions rose. H. G. Frere wrote in his Report on Port Loko for 1920:

> 11. 312 persons obtained their freedom by redemption during this year. This large number tends to show the wealth in the hands of the poorer classes of the community.
> 12. In 1917, 76 persons were redeemed and in 1919, 130, so the increase this year is very marked. The majority of these people have opportunity to make farms for themselves and have time to work for their own benefit in other ways. There is no cost for labour amongst them, where as they have received a great (sic) increased price for their produce.[154]

By 1922 the boom had faded, and Frere reported:

> One hundred and one slaves were redeemed during the year, as against 312 in 1920 and 132 in 1921. This falling off is, I think, accounted for by the bad trade year; the domestics getting such small prices for their produce that they have not been able to afford redemption.[155]

Despite some variations from time to time and from place to place few slaves could raise their redemption fees, and during the twentieth century the redemption rate was so low as to have virtually no effect on the numbers enslaved.

*   *   *

The best hope for freedom was still escape to the Colony or another part of the Protectorate—despite the legislation of 1905 and 1908. The problem of runaways continued to bedevil relations between the Sierra Leone Government and the traditional authorities until slaves were finally emancipated. There are no statistics on the numbers of runaways in the twentieth century, and it is not clear how easy it was for a slave to escape. District records indicate that a fair number of slaves did run away, and in the absence of other ways to obtain freedom it is fair to assume that many slaves did escape from their masters. This supposition is supported by the composition of the population of the Colony. The 1921 Census

199

showed that over half its population, then over eighty thousand, had come from the Protectorate.[156] Many of these must have been runaway slaves.

Captain Stanley thought there were few runaways because the institution was not unpleasant. He argued that it was easy enough for a slave to escape to Freetown or French territory from the Northern Province, but

> ... notwithstanding these numerous opportunities of forsaking their masters, the number of attempts to run away in proportion to the number of persons in servitude is absolutely infinitesimal, and this despite the fact that there is no doubt that such few adult persons as seriously do attempt to leave their masters succeed in doing so.[157]

The *Sierra Leone Weekly News* approved, and argued that the slaves were practically free. It warned the critics of slavery— "academic reformers"—that hasty action might endanger the productive capacity of the Protectorate and cause a flood of vagrants into Freetown. The following year the paper again asserted that there was nothing objectionable in slavery.[158]

Yet, the exodus of slaves from the Protectorate continued to bother the Government, which usually did little about the problem. It sometimes resorted to the Protectorate Native Law Ordinance of 1905 and the Vagrants Ordinance of 1908, but it could not return slaves to their masters' chiefdoms without risking a major row, if this became known in Britain. When Government employees were concerned, Freetown felt it had some obligation to act. The difficulty was to establish whether the wives or slaves of the chiefs who had joined the Government employees had done so voluntarily or as the result of enticement. In 1911 the Karene Chiefs were complaining bitterly that the soldiers of the West African Regiment were taking their wives and slaves away from them. The District Commissioner was fairly sympathetic:

> At the time of writing, one very influential Paramount Chief has been compelled to leave his town and build a new town near Batkanu, solely on account of the West African soldiers running away with his wives and domestics.[159]

The Acting Governor was less inclined to sympathize with the chiefs, many of whom had numerous wives who were neglected, but he acknowledged

> ... the seriousness of this matter and recognize that it is only fair, just and conducive to peace that, having regard to native custom, the Chiefs and people should be protected in regard to their wives, and their minds relieved of all anxiety as to the safety of their "possessions", whether soldiers of the West African Regiment are quartered in their country or otherwise.[160]

The chiefs were equally perturbed about their slaves who ran away and enlisted in the army or the police. In Nigeria Lugard tried to solve the problem by ordering that the recruiting officers should try to find out first whether the recruit was a slave or not. Although it was not possible to discharge an enlisted man because he was claimed as a slave, it was reasonable to refuse to enlist a slave. Every recruit should be warned that if he was proved to be a fugitive slave he would have to pay for his redemption—Lugard suggested £5.[161] In 1916 Governor Wilkinson of Sierra Leone referred the problem of a master claiming three runaway slaves who had enlisted in the West African Frontier Force to the Colonial Office, which suggested that he adopt a procedure similar to that of Lugard.[162] As Wilkinson pointed out in this very important despatch, the problem of runaway slaves kept recurring in one way or another and would continue to do so as long as slavery was tolerated in the Protectorate. So he made some tentative suggestions to pave the way for the extinction of slavery.[163]

*　　*　　*

Another problem which continued to vex the Sierra Leone Government as long as slavery was tolerated was that of slave dealing in one form or another. This was not just a matter of the sale or bartering of slaves, which was being stopped, but also of various practices analogous to slave dealing. Some argued that these practices were nothing more or less than slave dealing, while others held that they were merely traditional customs which benefited all concerned.

Cardew had achieved great success against organized slave dealing late in the nineteenth century and most of the cases in the twentieth century involved private transfers of a slave or two from one person to another. Yet, there is evidence of a more substantial slave traffic across the Liberian and French borders.

Karene District had the most cases of slave dealing. This may have been because it was easy to take slaves across the border to French territory or even because, as Mr. Page suggested, there were many Susu in the district and they were notorious slave dealers.[164] Even in Karene the District Commissioner's Court did not hear a great number of slave dealing cases. In 1902 out of the 124 cases heard there were twenty-one which resulted in convictions for slave dealing and in 1906 there were only three such convictions—which were really cases of pledging.[165] During the years 1914 to 1917, out of the more than a thousand cases heard by the District Commissioner of Karene only 27 resulted in convictions for slave dealing or pledging.[166]

Despite these reassuring statistics the Sierra Leone Government was worried about the slave traffic. Although nobody directly admitted it, officials felt that many slave dealing cases went undetected—especially in the remoter parts of the Protectorate. Dr. Maxwell reported that in Karene in 1902, the year when there were twenty-one convictions for slave dealing, there were many offences of the nature of slave dealing that were never reported.[167] When Warren was touring Koinadugu he spoke to the people about slave dealing and reported to Freetown:

> I am sorry to say there still exists a lot of slave dealing along the Eastern border, this being no doubt due to the ready market across the Frontier.[168]

Yet, neither in 1903 nor in 1905 were there any convictions for slave dealing in Koinadugu.[169] Either Warren was exaggerating the problem or, as seems more likely, the authorities were bringing very few slave traffickers to justice. The cases which came to the attention of the Government represented only the tip of the iceberg.

Evidence from French territory north of Karene and Koinadugu gives a far gloomier picture of the situation in these two districts. In 1908 Georges Deherme, who had toured French Colonies in various parts of the world, published a book on French West Africa. He reported that Sierra Leone was a never-ending source of slaves and that there were incessant slave raids just south of the

Melakori River—the border between French territory and Sierra Leone.[170] He alleged that anyone in this part of British territory who was not strong enough to stop another from capturing him would soon be sold as a slave in French territory. Also he wrote that there were slave markets in Sierra Leone, where the Fulas went to buy slaves in exchange for cattle. He quoted the administrator of the French district of Melakori, who wrote in 1904 that the whole frontier was occupied by slave raiders who sold captives from French territory in British territory and captives from British territory in French territory.

When the Sierra Leone Government did acknowledge the problem of the slave traffic across its frontiers, it tended to shift the blame on to its neighbours. Criticisms of the French became comparatively rare very early in the twentieth century. In 1905, however, both Judge Hudson and District Commissioner Warren blamed the authorities in French Guinea for the slave traffic near the borders, although Warren had heard that the French were getting stricter and so therefore he hoped to end the traffic soon.[171]

The British continued to blame the Liberians for the slave traffic across their mutual borders for many years more. They had some justification for so doing. As the Foreign Office pointed out, slavery and the slave traffic continued in Liberia because the Liberian Government was powerless in the interior, and it even permitted these evils in the coastal strip it did control effectively.[172]

Obviously the Liberian situation made it more difficult to control slave dealing in the southeastern parts of the Protectorate which bordered on Liberia. Close to the frontier the situation was very confused and, it was deemed necessary to separate five chiefdoms from Pujehun District to form a new District in June 1922 —the Mano River District. The Provincial Commissioner reported that the administration of the new district was in good working order but

> ... two or three years must elapse before we can see the deeper effects of closer adminstration on this frontier which, owing to its propinquity to a state whose people's views on "domestic servitude" are more conservative, and yet show more latitude than our own, will still present problems and possibilities of importance.[173]

One of the problems was that during border raids and wars captives were carried off to Liberia as slaves. A certain Betty who was captured during a "Foni War" was doubly unfortunate, after escaping from slavery in Liberia she fell into the hands of a man in the Protectorate who maltreated her.[174] A second problem was that Protectorate slaveholders were tempted to sell their slaves in Liberia. One master tried to make a double profit out of a slave he had sold in Liberia, the slave had escaped back to the Protectorate and was seized by his master again.[175] Another case involved a woman who ran away when her master planned to sell her in Liberia; she ran away but the master caught her and beat her to death.[176]

A third and a more serious problem was that some people from the Protectorate had joined with some Liberians to organize quite an extensive slave traffic from Liberia to the Protectorate. In 1912 Major Newstead, Officer Commanding the West African Frontier Force, charged that J. Abayomi Cole had bought about fifty Bandi slaves from a Liberian official called Cooper and a Bandi chief called Mambu, and that he had taken them to Kangahun in Ronietta District.[177] Investigations showed that Cole had brought a number of boys across the frontier, ostensibly to teach them agricultural work and to send them to school. The Governor decided that no steps could be taken against Cole because he would argue that he was educating the boys and because it would be difficult to prove he had taken the boys without parental consent. In November the District Commissioner reported that he had one of the boys who had escaped from Cole. The boy had told him that they had been sent to Cole on the understanding that they would be educated. He said they had been escorted from Liberia to Baiima by a Mende interpreter and two Liberian soldiers who had changed into civilian clothes near Baiima.[178]

The next year Major Cowie, a Commissioner delimiting the Anglo-Liberian boundary, made three serious charges which were based on information he had received from Mr. Twe, a Liberian District Commissioner.[179] One charge was that a Liberian official, Dr. Cole, was introducing slaves into the Protectorate:

> Mr. Twe told me that Momo Fo (Massaquoi) stayed at Baiima to help Cole; that the slaves were sent to Baiima and Pendembu; that the chiefs of those two places aided in the traffic by providing

houses in which to lock up the slaves pending their removal by train or otherwise; that Momo Fo had taken 120 and sent them to his farm in the Gallinas district of this Protectorate; that a large proportion of the slaves were women and children.[180]

Official investigations were made but no evidence was found to support this charge.

Major Cowie's second charge was that:

> Mr. Twe told me he had met certain Sierra Leone officials and that they had handed over to him some of these slaves, that others had been refused to him on the plea that they were domestics, and others because their owners declared they had bought them as wives.

The District Commissioner of Railway District, Dr. Maxwell, believed that he was the official referred to in the second charge, which arose from a meeting he had had with Mr. Twe in September 1912. Mr. Twe had said he was anxious to restore confidence in Bandi territory and to persuade Bandi refugees to return home. He asked for help in getting the refugees back, that Bagba be allowed to return and that Bandi people who had been taken to the Protectorate as slaves be returned.[181] Maxwell told Protectorate chiefs to let Bandi people go back to Liberia if they wished, he informed Bagba of the Liberian Commissioner's wish and he had warned Protectorate chiefs that the Bandi could not be brought into the Protectorate as slaves. He had told Mr. Twe that he would take action if he was given evidence of Bandi people being enslaved. Some of them had returned to Liberia but others were unwilling to go, "which is not surprising even if they were slaves; at all events they had peace and reasonable security in British territory".

Maxwell thought the Major's third charge that the Protectorate was "a big open market for slaves and that over 2,000 have been recently brought over" an exaggeration. He did admit that there were slave dealing cases and that important Bandi men had brought their slaves with them from Liberia. Although the Sierra Leone Government did not produce any real evidence of slave dealing in their not very enthusiastic investigations, it is clear that the problem of the slave traffic in the southeast and across the Liberian border was a serious one.

*   *   *

In addition to the cases of blatant slave dealing, there were numerous transactions in all parts of the Protectorate based on the economic value of an individual but which could be defended as traditional customs rather than attacked as forms of slave dealing. It was sometimes very difficult to draw the line between slave dealing and other sorts of transactions which were legal. Pledging was the commonest of these and many of the slave dealing cases which came before British officials were really cases of pledging. The Colonial Secretary, Haddon Smith, pointed out that many of the 28 cases of slave dealing in the Karene District in 1903 were "merely cases of pledging which is hardly in a Native's eyes a crime".[182] The District Commissioner of Karene reported that in 1914 the commonest form of slave dealing was pledging.[183] H. G. Warren, when he was District Commissioner of Karene, doubted whether pledging really was a crime:

> There is, however, a form of "servitude" in the Protectorate which is often hardly within the meaning of the law. Every child of sufficient age takes his or her part in the work on the farms or in the house, and it constantly happens that a child is "lent" by one family to another for some reason. It may be that the repayment of a loan cannot be managed at the time, and the services of the child are given, not in settlement of the debt, but as a guarantee of good faith, and possibly in the place of the exorbitant interest on overdue debts which is generally charged. The feelings of parents and children cannot be judged from our standpoint, and so long as the child is well treated and is willing thus to accommodate his parents, it can hardly be made a case under the provisions of the Ordinance.[184]

The only District Commissioner to challenge this extraordinary apologia was J. Craven. He pointed out that "a guarantee of good faith" was practically the same thing as a pledge and he refused to accept Warren's statement that the people concerned lacked natural family feelings—on the contrary, both mother and child suffered greatly when the child was handed over to a creditor. Yet, the Governor, the Colonial Secretary and other District Commissioners approved of Warren's instructions, parts of which were incorporated into the *General Orders of the Colony of Sierra Leone* in 1918. Order 485, for example, closely followed the passage just quoted, but without the reference to the lack of family feeling.[185] Warren and other conservationists were really playing with words in an attempt to justify their unwillingness and possibly their inability to deal with pledging. They tried to show that the practice was harmless and omitted to mention that the services of the pawn were equivalent to the payment of interest on the debt and that the pawn had no option but to go to the creditor.

Another form of transaction not unlike slave dealing was wardship. Typically this was a bargain between a Protectorate family and a Creole in the Colony. The child was sent to the Colony to learn civilized ways and to have the chance of going to school, but in practice these wards were often treated as unpaid domestic drudges. In 1916 the Commissioner of Police, Major Heslip, reported that African officials were obtaining children from the Protectorate and sending them to Freetown, on the pretence of giving them an education. The Major wanted this practice stopped. Consequently the Executive Council ordered that in future government officials should obtain the consent of district commissioners before sending or bringing any child of tribal origin to Freetown.[186] This did not stop the practice. Chief Abraham Tucker complained in 1919 that "the type of education to which you refer is often a cloke (sic) for abuses, and further, that the mother of the girl desires her return", when he was trying to get a ward back from Freetown.[187]

A more dramatic case of this type concerned a boy called David in Freetown. It came to the attention of Robert Young, Chairman of the House of Commons Ways and Means Committee. Young wrote to Lord Arnold, Under-Secretary of State, about the practice of taking boys and girls from the Protectorate to Freetown, where they were kept in a state of virtual slavery, and he alleged that hundreds were involved.[188] The Governor investigated and sent the Colonial Office a detailed account of the case of David.[189] David was living with a Mrs. Rollings, who admitted that she had not yet sent David to school. A neighbour, Mrs. Barrow, had taken David into her home because she thought Mrs. Rollings had been ill-treating him. Mrs. Rollings sued Mrs. Barrow for enticing David away from her. The Chief Justice treated the case as one arising from the ordinary relationship of master and servant and awarded £10 damages to the plaintiff. The Governor thought ¼d. damages would have been more appropriate and thought child protection laws were needed. The Provincial Commissioners agreed that the wardship system was virtually slavery and that it was on the increase, and the Governor thought it had a direct bearing on the wider question of domestic slavery.[190]

Also related to the wider question of domestic slavery was the problem of forced labour. A man in the Protectorate had to give fifteen days a year to the Government and fifteen to the traditional authorities—unpaid in both cases.[191] The labour for the Government was mainly on roads, bridges and public buildings and could be justified as a form of taxation.[192] Without it the Sierra Leone Government might have had to raise taxes or face serious financial difficulties. In 1916, for example, the Roads Department alone received £19,400 worth of unpaid labour.[193]

The question of forced, unpaid labour for the customary authorities was more complex because it was based on rather vague customs in some cases and because it was not always easy to distinguish between labour for the benefit of the community and labour for the personal benefit of the local chief. The local rulers had certain obligations to house and to feed destitutes, important visitors and their own subjects who had come a long way to visit them. It was not unreasonable to expect the villagers to help maintain farms and buildings for this purpose. In many cases chiefs demanded labour on their own farms, possibly with the argument that they were too busy with chiefdom affairs to look after their own farms properly, and although Maxwell argued that this labour would be given as a favour it is hard to see how a villager could refuse.[194]

In 1906 Probyn had introduced the option of cash commutation for communal labour obligations and this practice had spread gradually.[195] Normally the chief, in exchange for a shilling a hut and some rice, agreed to pay the wages of the chiefdom clerk and the fees of his son or sons at Bo Schol, and not to make any extra levies.[196]

Despite attempts at regulation the system of unpaid labour for the Government, the chiefs and for others continued to cause problems. In Southern Nigeria the question was discussed after the murder of Assistant District Commissioner Crewe-Read in 1906, possibly because of undue demands for forced labour.[197] In 1909 the Aborigines' Protection Society was still concerned about forced labour in Southern Nigeria, especially the system whereby chiefs were made responsible for supplying labour, which was "one which may easily lend itself to grave abuse, being indeed in the nature of slavery".[198] In Sierra Leone some chiefs saw in the system of unpaid labour yet another opportunity to exploit their subjects. An official request for labour was usually accompanied by a present which, according to Captain Stanley, was large enough for something to be paid to the men who did the work; yet, the Governor was probably right in thinking that the present stayed with the chiefs.[199]

Chiefs also made money my supplying labour to firms in their chiefdoms. Especially after the 1914–1918 War when firms still paid the pre-war wage of a shilling a day, the chiefs must have been needed to coerce their people to work for these firms. Some merchants assumed that chiefs were obliged to ensure a supply of cheap labour. In 1919 the agent for the African Association and J. B. Tucker complained to the Acting District Commissioner that the new chief at Pujehun was not co-operating in supplying labour. Shuffrey replied most unsympathetically. He pointed out that the firms did not pay enough and that the men could earn more by agricultural work in the palm belt than by carrying loads for the firms.[200]

Shuffrey's reply shows the beginning of a new official attitude to the people of the Protectorate. Although by 1919 over twenty years of British rule had made little apparent difference to the lives of the people of the Protectorate, the British presence had resulted in economic and social pressures which could not be successfully resisted much longer. Society had been changing for over two decades and the First World War had accelerated this process. In particular the developmental policy was becoming unworkable and officials were reversing their attitude towards slavery in the post-war years. Slavery was fated, and the story of the post-war decade in the Protectorate hinges largely on the successful attempts to destroy slavery and its associated institutions.

NOTES

1. The Mende and the Temne together made up more than 60% of the population of the Protectorate so I have concentrated on slavery among them rather than among the other fifteen peoples who constituted the remaining 40%.

2. Bo Archives, C.S.P. Conf. 22/1924, D.C. Sembehun (Fenton) to the Commissioner, Southern Province, 26 January 1924. J. S. Fenton served many years in the Protectorate and eventually became Chief Commissioner for the Protectorate. He wrote the very useful *Outline of Native Law in Sierra Leone*, first published in 1932.

3. Bo Archives, D. C. Sumbuya (A. H. Stocks) to C.S.P., Conf. 24 January 1924.

4. CO 267/503/16672, Probyn to CO, 25 April 1908, encloses Part I of Maxwell's Report on Native Laws and Customs in Sierra Leone, see p. 30. Maxwell, a District Commissioner and an able amateur anthropologist, later became Colonial Secretary in the Gold Coast and then Governor of Northern Rhodesia.

5. *Cmd. 3020 Sierra Leone, Correspondence relating to Domestic Slavery in the Sierra Leone Protectorate, 1928.* Enclosure 5 in Despatch No. 3, Minute by Captain Stanley, 9 October 1923, para. 6. This correspondence is referred to as *Cmd. 3020* in subsequent notes. Stanley had years of experience in The Gambia and in Sierra Leone where he became Commissioner for the Northern Province and sometimes acted as Colonial Secretary.

6. Little, *The Mende*, pp. 38–9.

7. CO 267/538/2154, Govr. Merewether to CO, 9 January 1912, transmits Memorandum by Dr. Maxwell. Further enquiries have failed to show that *ke ma lenga* is or was an accepted term.

8. N. W. Thomas, *Anthropological Report on Sierra Leone. Part I, Law and Custom of the Temne and Other Tribes* (London 1916), p. 158.

9. *Ibid.*, p. 161.

10. *C.R. II*, 2742.

11. CO 267/565/19113, Merewether to CO, 9 April 1915, transmits Railway District Report for 1914 by Colonel H. G. Warren, see para. 51.

12. CO 267/610/43608, Govr. Slater to CO, 13 September 1925, transmits Annual Report Northern Province 1924, Enclosure, Karene District Report by Major Lyon, see p. 14.

13. E.g., in giving evidence to Chalmers, Madam Yoko and Momo Grama, both Mende, spoke of their slaves as their children. See *C.R. II*, 4108–13, 4146, 4209.

14. E.g. CO 267/484/22187 and 267/494/24057, Circuit Judge's Reports, 1 June 1906 and 12 June 1907.

15. Thomas, *Anthropological Report*, p. 167.

16. *Ibid.*, p. 170.

17. W. Vivian, "The Mendi Country", *The Journal of the Manchester Geographical Society*, XII, 1 (January 1896), p. 15.

18. Alldridge, *The Sherbro*, pp. 62–3.

19. Ibid., *A Transformed Colony*, p. 212.

20. Fenton, *op. cit.*, Note 2. These conclusions were based on his experiences in the predominantly Mende Southern Province.

21. CO Print, April 1916. West African Lands Committee: Committee on the Tenure of Land in West African Colonies and Protectorates. Evidence of Major Fairtlough, 15 November 1912, 6316–9.
22. Pujehun Archives, Out Letter Book II, N. Sherbro, 1916–17, p. 43, No. 13/1917, D.C. to Col. Sec., 15 January 1916. The letter should have been dated 1917. The Attorney-General agreed, see *Cmd. 3020*, p. 15.
23. Thomas, *Anthropological Report*, pp. 160–1.
24. Bo Archives, C.S.P. Conf. 4/3, 78/28/1927, to all D.C.'s in the Province, 8 October 1927.
25. Thomas, *Anthropological Report*, p. 160.
26. Stocks, *op. cit.*, Note 3.
27. *C.R. II*, 2984–90. Evidence about the Mafwe area of Mende country given by Mr. Macaulay, J.P.
28. CO Print, *op. cit.*, Note 21. Report by Dr. Maxwell, para. 18. He thought this practice was more conspicuous among the more advanced tribes—the Mandingo and better class Temne. Thomas, *Anthropological Report*, p. 159, wrote that sometimes a slave could purchase another slave to take his place.
29. Fenton, *op. cit.*, Note 2.
30. Stocks, *op. cit.*, Note 3.
31. *Idem.*
32. CO 267/560/42361. Merewether to CO, 16 October 1914, transmits N. Sherbro District Report, 1913. Human parts were used to make "medicine" for initiates but I would have thought that healthy victims would have been preferred because of the belief that initiates gained the victims' attributes.
33. Thomas, *Anthropological Report*, p. 158.
34. U.B.C. Microfilm 116, H. H. Thomas to Mrs. J. Hal Smith, 12 November 1917. This referred to slaves at Mofuss, apparently somewhere near Shenge.
35. Fenton, *op. cit.*, Note 2.
36. CO 267/483/20975, Probyn to CO, 28 May 1906.
37. Fenton, *op. cit.*, Note 2. Thomas, *Anthropological Report*, p. 158, states that after two years a slave of the Temne might go to a slave village. Conversations I had in Pujehun confirm the opinions of these writers. *Faki* was apparently a Mende term for a slave village —it was commonly used by British officials.
38. W. T. Thomas, "Industrial Pursuits of the Yalunka People", *Sierra Leone Studies*, o.s., No. 1 (June 1918), pp. 39–43.
39. *C.R. II*, 269–71.
40. This problem of runaway wives will be discussed below.
41. K. H. Crosby, "Polygamy in Mende Country", *Africa*, X, No. 3 (July 1937), pp. 249–64.
42. Stanley, *op. cit.*, Note 5. At least no other attempt is available in the official records, or in the private papers I have seen.
43. See R. H. Finnegan, *Survey of the Limba People of Northern Sierra Leone* (London 1965), pp. 16 and 40, for the same theory

that the Limba had few slaves because they had been the victims of the slave raiders. In 1927 Stanley decided that he had to revise his estimates of those in slavery upwards. See Bo Archives, C.N.P., C289/10, Letter No. C295/10, to H.C.S., 12.8.27, para. 13.

44. Stanley, *op. cit.*, Note 5.
45. CO 267/591/35024, Govr. Wilkinson to CO, 22 June 1921, transmits Report Northern Province 1920, including App. C, Annual Report Koinadugu District by E. F. Sayers, 25 January 1921.
46. Stanley, *op. cit.*, Note 5. Numerically the Mandingo, Fula, Vai and Krim slaves were relatively insignificant—3,046, 900, 7,362 and 2,347 compared to 83,651 Mende and 62,283 Temne slaves in Stanley's rather too low estimates.
47. Fenton, *op. cit.*, Note 2. To the south-west of the District was Sherbro Island (administrative capital Bonthe), which was also part of the Colony and attracted runaway slaves.
48. Stocks, *op. cit.*, Note 3.
49. Fenton, *op. cit.*, Note 2.
50. Pujehun Archives, Native Affairs Record, II, 1919–20. I could trace no other similar volumes. It is strange that the number of cases in 1920 should have been so much greater than in 1919. This may have been because a backlog of cases accumulated during the 1914–1918 War, when district officers were away on military service.
51. Fenton, *op. cit.*, Note 2.
52. CO 267/521/7412, Probyn to CO, 24 February 1910, transmits D.C.'s reports for Ronietta 1909.
53. T. J. Alldridge, *A Transformed Colony*, pp. 175, 177. The construction of the railway meant heavy demands for labour which could disrupt local economies.
54. *Ibid.*, pp. 159, 165–7, 186.
55. *Colonial Reports Annual 299 (1899)*, Cd. 354–5, p. 46.
56. *C.M.S. Annual Letters*, 1904, p. 418, from Mr. H. Bowers, at Falaba, 2 December 1904.
57. The effects of legitimate commerce on slavery in West Africa during the nineteenth century have been discussed in Chapter II.
58. CO 96/41, Conf., Govr. Pine to CO, 1 October 1857, cited in Metcalfe, *Great Britain and Ghana*, pp. 264–7. Pine's criticism seems equally applicable to twentieth-century Sierra Leone.
59. The "Chinese slaves" were the indentured labourers being sent to the Transvaal goldmines.
60. CO 267/569/51374, Thomas to CO, 5 November 1915, minute by Ellis.
61. *Cd. 788-31 (1902) Colonial Reports Annual for 1901, 361*; CO Print, *op. cit.*, Note 21, 6046.
62. CO 267/483/9097, Probyn to CO, 1 March 1906; CO 267/488/40153, Probyn to CO, 19 October 1906.

63. CO 267/528/28702, A.S. and A.P.S. Conf. to CO, 14 September 1910.
64. *The Times*, 23 March 1906. This weakness prompted the amalgamation of the two societies in 1909. Not till after the First World War did "the old anti-slavery feeling" revive.
65. Speech by the 4th Earl of Onslow, 8 March 1907, *African Affairs: Journal of the African Society*, VI (1907–8), pp. 304–5.
66. R. Hyam, *Elgin and Churchill at the Colonial Office* (London 1968), p. 479. Hyam cites CO 267/496/34704 and 267/525/33402. Probyn had previously had a distinguished career as a legal officer in the Caribbean, and from 1901 to 1904 as Secretary to the Government of Southern Nigeria. From 1904 to 1910 he was Governor of Sierra Leone, and—despite doubts as to his mental balance—was promoted to the Governorships of Barbados and then of Jamaica.
67. CO 267/474/15854, War Office to CO, Conf. 3 May 1904, forwards report on Karina District by Lieutenant Hart.
68. CO 267/501/1994, Probyn to CO, 1 January 1908, transmits report of proceedings of native local assemblies in Karene.
69. CO 267/501/8463, Probyn to CO, 15 February 1908, enclosing a report by Mr. Page.
70. Fyfe, *A History*, p. 607.
71. FO Historical Section, *Peace Handbook*, XV, No. 92, Sierra Leone, p. 13.
72. Alldridge, *A Transformed Colony*, p. 176. This would not have been true of chiefs like Suluku of Bumban, Nyagwa of Panguma and the Alkalis of Port Loko. Their chiefdoms were large and they had great ability. They would have been powerful figures without British support. In fact, the extension of British power weakened them.
73. CO 267/484/20975, Probyn to CO, 28 May 1906, encloses his instructions to D.C.s.
74. *Cd. 1097, Accounts and Papers, 1902*, LXVI, "Sierra Leone Report by Governor Sir Charles King-Harman, K.C.M.G., on his visits to the Protectorate", No. 1, 26 February 1901.
75. Foreign Office Historical Section, *Peace Handbooks*, XV, No. 90, "British West Africa General", p. 6. The idea that slavery promoted indolence was one of the reasons for the decision to abolish slavery more quickly. This is discussed further in Chapter VI.
76. CO 267/447/20183, Nathan to CO, 11 July 1899, para. 30.
77. *Cd. 788–31, op. cit.*, Note 61, pp. 33–4.
78. CO 267/565/19112, Merewether to CO, 9 April 1915. Merewether had held various posts in the Straits Settlement between 1880 and 1902, he was Lieutenant-Governor of Malta from 1902 to 1911 and Governor of Sierra Leone from 1911 to 1915, then he was Governor of the Leeward Islands from 1915 to 1921. It seems he did very little when Governor of Sierra Leone.
79. CO 267/478/25194, Probyn to CO, 1 July 1905.

80. CO Print, *op. cit.*, Note 21, Merewether's evidence, 2028-33. When he gave his evidence in July 1912 he had been Governor for over a year but he did not know the date of the Protectorate and thought there were thirty to forty Paramount Chiefs when in fact there were about two hundred.

81. *Cd. 2238-1 (1905) Colonial Report Annual No. 423*, Sierra Leone, 1903, p. 28.

82. See above, p. 71.

83. See *Sierra Leone Weekly News*, 5 July 1902 and 9 April 1904; *Sierra Leone Times*, 26 March and 9 April 1904. The latter was, as always, more outspoken. On 26 March 1904 it referred to domestic slaves in Freetown enjoying liberty by vile loitering at ease and "bringing nothing by their filthy habits, deciding to do nothing but plunder by night and loafing by day".

84. CO 267/488/40153, Probyn to CO, 19 October 1906, para 4.

85. No. 33 of 1901, for text see CO 269/6.

86. CO 267/454/34446, Cardew to CO, 6 October 1900, and minute by Cox. For Nathan's proposal, see above, p. 147.

87. See above, p. 198.

88. See above, p. 123.

89. N.A.M.P., 322/20 July 1899, Ag. D.C. Ronietta to Governor.

90. Attorney General's Opinion Book, N.A.M.P. 322/1899, pp. 396–400, minutes by Parkes, 28 July and 2 August 1899, and by Nathan, 7 August 1899.

91. *Idem*, minutes by P. Crampton Smyly, 10 August and 27 November 1899.

92. CO 267/447/22898, Nathan to CO, 14 August 1899.

93. CO 267/451/24427, Cardew to CO, 11 September 1899.

94. CO 267/454/34446, *op. cit.*, Note 86. The "other person" might well have been an owner.

95. Ordinance No. 6 of 1903, CO 271/10 for text—*Sierra Leone Gazette*, No. 775, 3 July 1903. Part of Clause 6 is cited.

96. CO 267/481/30414, London Chamber of Commerce to CO, 23 August 1905, memo. by Probyn, 27 November 1905.

97. This accusation was made by E. Baillaud, *La Politique indigène de l'Angleterre en Afrique Occidentale* (Paris 1912), pp. 76-7.

98. CO 267/477/16954, Probyn to CO, 4 May 1905, submits Protectorate Native Law Ordinance; for printed text see CO 269/6.

99. *Idem*; CO 267/483/9097, Probyn to CO, 1 March 1906.

100. CO 267/475/1999, Probyn to CO, 3 January 1905. Next to a section in which Probyn was explaining the prohibition of people from leaving their chiefdoms Antrobus made the marginal comment—"i.e. They were slaves?"

101. J. C. Anene, *Southern Nigeria*, pp. 306-8.

102. *Ibid.*, p. 250. Anene cites CO 520/9, Probyn to CO, Conf. 15 September 1901.

103. Ordinance No. 19 of 1905; text in CO 269/6.

104. *Cd. 2684-57 (1906). Colonial Reports Annual, No. 511*, Sierra Leone 1905, Probyn's covering letter, para. 4.
105. Ordinance No. 17 of 1908; text in CO 269/7.
106. For this paragraph on the early story of the export of labour I have drawn heavily on Fyfe, *A History*, pp. 504–5 and 546–7; and on Parkes's report on the recruitment of men for the Congo—N.A. Letter Book, No. 99, 26 March 1897, Parkes to Governor.
107. Despatches from U.S. Consuls to State Department on microfilm in Fourah Bay College Library. Microfilm 101, Robert Pooley, U.S. Consul in Sierra Leone, to Assistant Secretary of State, Conf. 25 February 1897.
108. *C. 7944-12 (1896) Colonial Reports. Annual No. 160*, Sierra Leone 1894, p. 12.
109. *C. 8650-6 (1897) Colonial Reports. Annual No. 208*, Sierra Leone 1896, p. 8. For text of Ordinance No. 19 of 1896 see CO 269/5.
110. M.P. 81/3 October 1896, Cardew's query whether Porter was authorized by the Panama Canal and Congo Railway Companies to engage labourers; M.P. 115/6 November 1896, Supt. Civil Police to Col. Sec, on complaint against Mr. Porter of ill-treatment of men on board the S.S. *Castle Eden.*
111. CO 267/427/25930, Cardew to CO, 2 December 1896.
112. Pooley, *op. cit.*, Note 107.
113. *C. 9498-7 (1899) Colonial Reports. Annual No. 273*, Sierra Leone 1898, p. 27.
114. CO 267/447/20183, Nathan to CO, 11 July 1899, para. 30.
115. CO 267/469/39285, King-Harman to CO, 8 October 1903.
116. CO 267/472/14840, King-Harman to CO, 8 April 1904, forwards report on Sherbro District by Acting D.C.
117. CO 267/476/8489, Probyn to CO, 2 March 1905.
118. Bo Archives, Bandajuma Conf. Letter Book, p. 77. Conf. M.P. 66/1905, various dates in 1905. The agents were apparently ex-Court Messengers who posed as recruits.
119. CO 267/542/28553, Acting Govr. Haddon Smith to CO, 22 August 1912.
120. CO 267/562/19472, FO to CO, 27 May 1914, transmits Liberian Consul-General's Annual Report 1913, p. 5.
121. Bo Archives, M.P. 28/15, Manager of the Bank of British West Africa to Col. Sec., 29 January 1915. This throws doubt on the official view that the Mende and other Protectorate people were eager volunteers for service as carriers in the First World War. See below, Chapter VI.
122. CO 267/594/35983, FO to CO, 16 July 1921, encloses letter from H.M. Consul-General, 26 May 1921.
123. CO 267/612/39197, FO to CO, 26 August 1925, transmits copy of despatch from British Vice-Consul at Fernando Po.
124. CO 270/43, Minutes Legislative Council, 11 April 1907. Davy's specific complaint was about the recent despatch of 130 men to work on the British Consulate in Monrovia and on Liberian roads.

See CO 271/13, S.L. Royal Gazette, 1907, for official authorizations for sending this labour to Liberia.

125. Attorney-General's Opinion Book, pp. 209–10, minute by Probyn, 1 August 1907. The 1896 Ordinance was No. 19 of 1896, see above, p. 186.

126. CO 270/52, Minutes Legislative Council, 29 August 1913. This was the Native Labour (Foreign Service) Ordinance, No. 25 of 1913. For text see CO 269/8.

127. CO 271/29, Sierra Leone Gazette, contains various examples of authorization to Gold Coast Mining Companies. See CO 267/593/63846, Maxwell to CO, 15 December 1921.

128. *Cd. 2238-1, op. cit.*, Note 81.

129. S.L.A., Shaingay D.C.'s Letter Book, January 1906—October 1909, pp. 42–3, 12 February 1907 and 206–15, 19 September 1909. For more about Addison see below, p. 197 and Note 148.

130. Bo Archives, Bandajuma Conf. Letter Book, p. 76, M.P.C. S/1106, D.C. to Col. Sec., 13 March 1906.

131. S.L.A., Port Loko Decree Book, pp. 131–2, N.A. 40/1916 and B 52/1916. Decision made on 13 December 1916. Many similar decisions have been recorded in District records.

132. S.L.A., M.P. 2623/23 June 1907.

133. This was a re-enactment of Clause 81 of the 1896 Protectorate Ordinance.

134. *Cmd. 3020, op. cit.*, Note 5, p. 9, Slater to CO, 20 June 1924.

135. Attorney-General's Opinion Book, 1907–1909, pp. 168–9, minutes on M.P. 4015/1907 by Attorney-General and Colonial Secretary, 8 and 10 October 1907. I could not trace M.P. 4015/1907 in the Sierra Leone Archives.

136. *Cmd. 3020*, Enc No. 1 in No. 3 is a specimen redemption certificate. See also pp. 193–5 for some examples of redemption certificates.

137. S.L.A., Bandajuma Decree Book, 1905–1908, p. 138, Extract from Konnoh Decree Book.

138. S.L.A., Records of Commissioner Chiefs, September 1894—March 1901, Parkes, 19 September 1894, N.A. 443/1894, As to Rescued and Escaped Slaves.

139. S.L.A., Koinadugu Decree Book, 1904–1927, p. 25.

140. E.G.'s, *Ibid.*, pp. 6, 7, 8, 10 and 17, *et. al.*

141. CO 267/565/19113, Merewether to CO, 9 April 1915, transmits Railway District Report 1914, para. 51.

142. *General Orders of the Colony of Sierra Leone*, (1918), No. 484. This sometimes posed a very difficult problem for the District Commissioner, as in the Banja Case, which is discussed in Chapter VI.

143. *Cmd. 3020, op. cit.*, Note 5, p. 31, No. 3, Slater to CO, 20 June 1924.

144. *Ibid.*, Enclosure N. 5, minute by Captain Stanley.

145. Warren, *op. cit.*, Note 141.

146. CO 267/591/35024, Governor Wilkinson to CO, transmits Report Northern Province 1920, App. B, Annual Report Karene District by H.C. Hodgson, para. 11.

147. CO 267/596/26292, Slater to CO, 16 May 1922, transmits Annual Report Northern Province 1921. Stanley's comment was in para. 15 of the Report. Hodgson's comment was in Section VI of the enclosed report for Port Loko District.

148. Attorney-General's Opinion Book, August 1912–October 1913, p. 377, L.M. 152/1913, 8 May 1913. I could not trace the Minute Paper and do not know the outcome of Warren's enquiry. Mr. Hollins, who served in Sierra Leone from 1910 to 1935, told me that Addison was very much the odd man out in the administration. Addison was sometimes very dictatorial, but seems to have favoured the less fortunate—see above, p. 190. After Addison was prematurely retired in 1923 he sent the Colonial Office a strong attack on the Sierra Leone Government—particularly because it tolerated slavery. This will be discussed in Chapter VI.

149. CO 267/574/8793, Wilkinson to CO, 29 January 1917.

150. CO 267/588/57116, Wilkinson to CO, 28 October 1920.

151. See above, p. 166.

152. F. W. H. Migeod, *A View of Sierra Leone* (London 1926), pp. 123–4. Migeod visited Sierra Leone in 1924–25. Major de Miremont was the Commanding Officer at Daru, the Headquarters of the West African Frontier Force.

153. Pujehun Archives, Out Letter Book II, N. Sherbro, p. 178, No. 6/1917, 11 February 1917, D.C. North Sherbro to Col. Sec.

154. CO 267/591/35024, Wilkinson to CO, 22 June 1921, transmits Report Northern Province 1920, App. D, Annual Report Port Loko District by H. G. Frere.

155. CO 270/51, Annual Report Northern Province 1922, App. C, Annual Report Port Loko District by H. G. Frere.

156. T. N. Goddard, *The Handbook of Sierra Leone* (London 1925), pp. 49–50, for a discussion of the 1921 Census.

157. CO 267/596/26292, *op. cit.*, Note 147, Stanley, para. 15.

158. *Sierra Leone Weekly News*, 30 September 1922 and 3 March 1923.

159. CO 267/540/17042, Haddon Smith to CO, 17 May 1912, transmits Report Karene District 1911 by Colonel Warren.

160. CO 267/541/22985, Haddon Smith to CO, 9 July 1912.

161. Lugard, *Memoranda* (1906), No. 6, Slavery Questions, para. 35.

162. CO 267/572/42984, Wilkinson to CO, 23 August 1916. The CO suggested £4 for the redemption of the soldier—the maximum redemption provided for by the Protectorate Ordinance.

163. *Idem.* This very important despatch will be considered again in Chapter VI, which deals with the abolition of slavery.

164. CO 267/478/21669, Probyn to CO, 5 June 1905, Enc. 3, Circuit Judge's Report. Judge Hudson argued that there was more slave dealing in Karene and Koinadugu because of their nearness to

French Guinea. Also CO 267/476/10417, Probyn to CO, 13 March 1905, forwards Annual Report Bandajuma 1904.

165. CO 267/467/16288, King-Harman to CO, 16 April 1903, transmits Annual Report Karene 1902; CO 267/493/13116, Haddon Smith to CO, transmits Annual Report Karene 1906.

166. CO 267/565/22813, CO 267/570/23387, CO 267/574/22575 and CO 267/577/29256, Annual Reports Karene, 1914 to 1917.

167. Annual Report Karene, *op. cit.*, Note 165.

168. CO 267/475/3642, Probyn to CO, 18 Jan. 1905, forwards letter from Warren, 3 January 1905, para. 5.

169. CO 267/473/26118, Ag. Govr. to CO, 9 July 1904, transmits Report on Blue Book 1903, pp. 46–50; CO 267/483/11775, Probyn to CO, 12 March 1905, transmits Report Koinadugu 1905 by Warren.

170. G. Deherme, *L'Afrique Occidentale française. Action politique, action économique, action sociale* (Paris 1908), p. 379.

171. *Op. cit.*, Notes 164 and 168.

172. CO 267/606/60015, FO to CO, 23 December 1924, transmits draft of letter which it is proposed to address to Sir F. Lugard. This allegation was repeated more than once by the Foreign Office and its Consular Representatives in Liberia. See also CO 267/562/19472, FO to CO, 27 May 1914, transmits Liberia Consul-General's Report 1913, containing the allegation that in the interior of Liberia fighting, slave raiding and cannibalism were "events of every-day occurrence".

173. CO 270/51, Annual Report Southern Province, 1922.

174. Pujehun Archives, N. Sherbro Decree Book II, 1906–1911, p. 71, 28 December 1907.

175. Pujehun Archives, Native Affairs Record II, 1919–1920, M.P. 103/1920, 1 May 1920.

176. *Ibid.*, M.P. 84/1919, 9 December 1919.

177. Bo Archives, Bandajuma Conf. Letter Book, C 184/1912, Conf. M.P., O.C./W.A.F.F. to Col. Sec., 20 September 1912.

178. *Idem.* Minute, Bowden to Col. Sec., 27 November 1912. Baiima is well into the Protectorate and the Liberian soldiers must have marched into the Protectorate still in uniform.

179. *Ibid.*, M.P. C 195/1913, from the Secretariat, 11 September 1913, Slavery in the Sierra Leone Protectorate, Kanre Lahun area.

180. Momo Fo had been Chief Momolu Massaquoi of Gallinas until his deposition in 1906 for oppression and other offences, including misappropriation of slaves whose ownership was being disputed by the family of their deceased owner. See CO 267/484/13652, Probyn to CO, 3 April 1906.

181. The Bandi territory had been devastated by Liberian officials and soldiers and many Bandi had fled to the Protectorate. Presumably Bagba was one of their leaders.

182. CO 267/473/26118, Ag. Govr. Graves to CO, 9 July 1904, transmits Reports on Blue Book 1903 by Haddon Smith. The Colonial

Office criticized this report for its length, its bad taste, its poor grammar and its allusion to contentious matters. Haddon Smith wrote about slave dealing across the French border and this section was omitted from the printed version.

183. CO 267/565/22813, Merewether to CO, 28 April 1915, transmits Karene Report 1914 by Hooker, para. 16.

184. S.L.A., M.P., D.C. Karene 121/21 October 1916, Notes and instructions prepared by D.C. Karene for officers in charge of sub-districts and also various minutes. Warren was a strong conservationist. These notes also stressed the importance of the chiefs in native affairs.

185. *General Orders of the Colony of Sierra Leone* (1918), pp. 119–20, Order 485. The Nigerian Government was also condoning pawning human beings for debt; in the Oyo Province in 1924, for example. See CO 267/606/60015, FO to CO, 23 December 1924, minute by Mr. Harding, 18 February 1925.

186. CO 270/48, Minutes Executive Council, 8 January 1917.

187. Pujehun Archives, N. Sherbro Out Letter Book, III, 1917–19, p. 80, No. 133/1919, Acting D.C. (P. Shuffrey), N. Sherbro, to Commissioner of Police, Freetown, 26 February 1919. Shuffrey was quoting the Chief and asking for the return of the girl.

188. CO 267/606/12398, Young to Arnold, 11 March 1924.

189. CO 267/604/24774, Slater to CO, 13 May 1924.

190. Yet, wardship outlived slavery for many years. This will be discussed in Chapter VI.

191. Pujehun Archives, N. Sherbro Conf. Letter Book, 1916–27, p. 48, Conf. 22/1925, Acting D.C. Gbangbama to Commissioner, Southern Province, 15 January 1925.

192. Slater held that free labour was a form of direct tax; see CO 267/604/32038, Slater to CO, 21 June 1924, para. 32.

193. CO 267/620/X4464/27, Slater to CO, 4 July 1927; CO 267/574/17212, Wilkinson to CO, 14 March 1917. Slater thought it would be impractical to abolish unpaid forced labour. See also Chapter VI.

194. CO 267/495/28249, Probyn to CO, 26 July 1907, transmits report by Dr. Maxwell, 13 November 1906.

195. See above, p. 184.

196. S.L.A., Pendembu District Decree Book, 1906–1927, pp. 118–26, for several examples of commutation agreements.

197. CO 267/574/17212, Wilkinson to CO, 14 March 1917, minute by Fiddian, 23 June 1917.

198. *Idem*, Fiddian quoting the letter from the A.P.S.

199. *Ibid.*, Wilkinson's despatch, paras. 10–11.

200. Pujehun Archives, N. Sherbro Out Letter Book III, 1917–19, p. 169, No. 226/1919, Acting D.C. (Shuffrey) to Col. Sec., 29 April 1919, forwards complaints; also S.L.A., M.P. D.C./N.S. 22/29 April 1919.

CHAPTER VI

The Abolition of Slavery and its Aftermath

By the outbreak of the First World War the system of indirect administration in the Sierra Leone Protectorate was acquiring an air of permanency. Freetown left the conduct of local affairs almost entirely in the hands of the traditional rulers. The logical consequence of this policy of non-interference was that Freetown tacitly accepted the social, political and economic organization of the peoples of the Protectorate, including domestic slavery. Only when traditional rulers abused their position too flagrantly did the Government feel compelled to interfere.[1]

Yet, this air of permanency was deceptive. Even in the remotest areas the impact of the British presence was beginning to change the traditional way of life. Ordinary people were becoming aware of the alternatives to their old way of life, and they were growing conscious of their personal rights and status as individuals rather than as members of a group. As Bowden wrote in 1913:

> Men and women who were formerly merged in the family of a powerful relative are beginning to realize that they have an individuality of their own and are beginning to demand rights and to resent wrongs, which formerly they were all unconscious of.[2]

Despite legislative and administrative attempts to preserve the *status quo* the war clearly tipped the balance on the side of change. It was almost a catalyst, bringing the forces of change to the surface.

The war had tangible effects on the Protectorate, especially the disruption of trade and the recruitment of carriers for service with the armed forces. Before 1914 the Protectorate depended heavily on the German market for its produce, about two-thirds of which were palm kernels. In 1908 57% of the produce of Sierra Leone went to Germany, compared to 20% to Britain; in 1913 about half Sierra Leone's exports went to Germany.[3] The war closed the German market to Sierra Leone and her exports fell sharply from £1,490,288 in 1913 to £1,041,907 in 1914 and to £942,868 in 1915.[4] In 1917 the value of exports began to rise again and reached a peak in the short sharp boom just after the war. By 1921 the value was falling again and continued low throughout the 1920s and even in the 1930s. Despite the inflation during the war the value of exports in 1922 was lower than it had been in 1912.[5] The falling railway revenue dramatically illustrates the decline in exports. It fell from £78,263 in 1913 to £43,096 in 1914 and down to £38,378 in 1915.[6] The need to raise extra revenue led the Governor to impose an export duty on palm kernels, palm nuts and kola nuts—a step which further damaged the export of produce. In 1918 the influenza epidemic led to a shortage of labour and inflation caused great distress and discontent which was reflected in the anti-Syrian food riots in 1919. The war and its aftermath seriously affected the economy of Sierra Leone.

The war also challenged the existing social order. Large numbers of slaves were recruited as carriers. It has been estimated that three-quarters of the French colonial contingents were slaves or ex-slaves, and probably most of the Sierra Leone carriers were also slaves.[7] About 8,000 carriers from Sierra Leone served in the East African and Camerouns campaigns.[8] The slaves were treated like their free colleagues, given a shilling a day, and they could return home with a substantial sum of money. Many of them were Mende, whom officials thought were eager to serve, but a substantial number of Mende crossed into Liberia to avoid military service.[9]

Service as a carrier did not necessarily facilitate redemption after the war. Captain Stanley told the chiefs and carriers that the carriers would be sent home with their pay at the end of the war. He was well aware that most carriers were slaves and that he was sending them back to a life of slavery after the war. He justified his policy on the grounds that

> ... so long as the Chiefs are called upon by the Government to assist in recruiting, the carriers are not strictly volunteers. It

may, in fact, be said that the greater portion of these men may agree to serve as carriers simply because they are under tribal discipline and any arrangement, therefore, which would tend to remove them from tribal discipline on their return would not only be highly unpopular with the Chiefs and Headman, but would render recruiting in the future more difficult and uncertain as without the co-operation of the Chiefs little can be done in this matter.[10]

In North Sherbro both sides clearly understood that the chiefs were lending their slaves to the Government for the duration of the war. Nevertheless, after the war some carriers refused to go home to a life of slavery, others only returned home to redeem themselves and others had no option but to return to slavery, which seemed even more irksome after their war experience.[11]

The arrival of a new Governor was also very important in the encouragement of a fresh approach to the problems of slavery and forced labour. Richard Wilkinson arrived in Freetown early in 1916. He had served in the Far East for twenty-seven years as Inspector of Schools, Land Revenue Collector, Postmaster General and Colonial Secretary. He had had no experience of Africa and was not thought highly of at the Colonial Office. His appointment was a puzzling one, even in wartime. He was the only Governor of the Colony and Protectorate who was not knighted and after his term in Sierra Leone no other post was found for him, although he was only 55 and apparently in good health. One official who served in Sierra Leone referred to Wilkinson as "a Governor of imagination who had been none too well treated by the Colonial Office of the day".[12]

Perhaps it was his imagination that led him to criticise what he found in Sierra Leone. In 1917 he complained of the mal-administration of the Protectorate, and he raised the questions of "dashes" to Government officers, forced labour and forced levies of produce.[13] A few months earlier his attention had been drawn to slavery by the claim of a chief to three runaway slaves who had joined the West African Frontier Force, and he had written a despatch to Colonial Office which had led Whitehall to consider the whole problem seriously.[14] He wrote that it would be imprac-tical to compensate aggrieved chiefs for their runaway slaves because of the likelihood of collusive and fraudulent claims. No

European officer had been able to give him even a rough estimate of the numbers of slaves and, as the status of slave descended to the children of slave women, he saw little hope of the institution dying out. He therefore suggested that an immediate attempt be made to obtain a rough estimate of the prevalence of slavery in the Protectorate. After the war an Assistant District Commissioner should be assigned to each of the proposed provinces to draw up a slave register which should then be made the final record of slave holding at a certain date. Subsequently the slaves could be gradually emancipated by freeing the younger women first and by offering remunerative work to enable male slaves to buy their freedom.

To its surprise the Colonial Office found that this problem had received little attention in Sierra Leone, even though the institution of slavery had been abolished in the rest of British West Africa except for the Northern Territories of the Gold Coast and Ashanti.[15] Because of the war the Colonial Office stressed the need for caution, and one official even feared a repetition of the 1898 rebellions:

> It would be very undesirable to have a rebellion in S. Leone just now which would be a probable result of any attempt to interfere with this institution.[16]

His colleagues were not quite so alarmist, but the Secretary of State's instructions to Wilkinson were explicit:

> As regards the general question of slavery I am of opinion that, however informal may be the enquiries and investigations which you suggest, it is practically certain that the chiefs will come to know of them, and that they will probably consider that the Gov't is contemplating some drastic modification of the tribal system with the result that there will be unrest and possible disturbance, and this at a time when a considerable portion of the West African Frontier Force will have been sent to East Africa.[17]

Wilkinson was told to take no action until after the war, and then only in consultation with the Secretary of State. This despatch is important because for the first time since 1894 a Governor of Sierra Leone pressed for firm action against slavery, and although it urged delay, the Colonial Office accepted that slavery would have to be dealt with.

During the war the Anti-Slavery and Aborigines' Protection Society began taking a fresh interest in slavery in Sierra Leone. This was at least partly due to the foundation of its subsidiary body—the Sierra Leone Auxiliary—by Creoles in 1912.[18] Even though the Sierra Leone Auxiliary often seemed more concerned with problems that had little connection with slavery and the Protectorate, it did state its opposition to domestic slavery.[19] Moreover, it kept the parent society in touch with events in Sierra Leone. When the Anti-Slavery Society received a complaint in 1918 about the recognition of slavery and official assistance in the recovery of runaway slaves, it referred the matter to the Sierra Leone Auxiliary which passed a resolution urging the parent society to use its influence for the abolition of domestic slavery in Sierra Leone.[20]

One important case that concerned the Sierra Leone Auxiliary was the Banja Case. This was a dispute over redemption, an issue which gave rise to many problems. The case is also important because it forced the issue of slavery on the attention of the Governments in Freetown and in London. The Banja Case began in the middle of 1917 when Banja and her eight children, who had been living with a Mrs. Fibian Williams for a year, were claimed as slaves by Madam Kunna.[21] The claim was upheld by the District Commissioner of North Sherbro. Mrs. Williams then tried to redeem Banja and her family for £30. Stanley, the District Commissioner, refused because Mrs. Williams had enticed the slaves away from Madam Kunna. Furthermore, although Banja's situation had been known for years, Mrs. Williams had only claimed relationship with the slaves and tried to redeem them when she was compelled to return them to Madam Kunna—a woman well on in years, married to the slave who was father and grandfather of Banja and her children and who had always treated the slaves well. Mrs. Williams's father, a Creole trader and Justice of the Peace called Cooper Williams, protested to Captain Stanley about the refusal of redemption, but he received no satisfaction. Stanley repeated his reasons for refusing redemption and added:

> Personally I always try to effect as many redemptions as possible, but the matter is one which for political reasons has to be handled

with tact and cases naturally arise where the District Commissioner has to exercise his discretion.[22]

Stanley was certainly not following the provisions for redemption laid down in the Protectorate Ordinance if that was really his attitude. Cooper Williams thought of appealing to the Governor and Stanley asked Freetown for advice.[23] The Solicitor General was vague. He thought that the redeemer should have some sort of legitimate interest in the person of the slave but pointed out that it was as difficult for the District Commissioner to prove that the redeemer had no interest as it was for the redeemer to prove that he had. He concluded that Stanley could act within his own lights until some court stopped him, and so Stanley saw no reason for altering his decision.[24]

Cooper Williams then wrote to the Anti-Slavery Society which approached the Colonial Office.[25] In his report Wilkinson replied that District Commissioners only refused redemption when attempts were being made to transfer slaves to a new master or to procure women for immoral purposes. Stanley had refused redemption in this case because the slaves had been working as domestics for Mrs. Williams and one of the women had been used for immoral purposes.[26] This case confirmed the Governor's view that, now the war was over, the problems of slavery and forced labour should be settled and, though many of his officers minimised the evils of slavery and favoured inaction, he recommended that slaves be registered as a preliminary step to emancipation. Slavery could not last for ever, and if the Government did not act it would have abolition forced on it sooner or later. Officials at Whitehall seemed to favour inaction. Ellis wrote:

... I am of opinion that the matter should still be postponed. The Gov'r has not impressed me with any confidence of his ability to deal with a difficult and delicate matter like this. In all matters he is very impatient of advice from officers with experience of W. African conditions.

Grindle and Fiddes were worried about possible repercussions if the Colonial Office rejected the proposal to get on with the abolition of domestic slavery. Fiddes wrote:

The thing has been labelled "slavery", & the Anti Slavery etc. Society will be only too glad to hold us up as accomplices of a community of Legrees.

So the Colonial Office told the Society that the Banja Case was not one of genuine redemption and Lord Milner, the Secretary of State, instructed Wilkinson to come to London as soon as possible to discuss the problem.[27] When the Society protested again, the Colonial Office reiterated its conviction that justice had been done in the Banja Case and added that the Secretary of State was going to discuss slavery with Wilkinson; at this discussion Wilkinson satisfied Lord Milner that there was a good case for "a voluntary and unhurried registration of slaves".[28] The Society then obtained permission to speak to Wilkinson, who managed to persuade representatives of the Society that he wanted to end domestic slavery when it was feasible to do so.[29]

A year later, however, Wilkinson's abolitionist zeal appeared to have cooled. When Lord Milner asked what progress had been made in registering slaves, all the Governor had to report was that when principal men at Port Loko had complained about difficulties in recovering their domestics, mainly women who had been enticed away, he had suggested that the registration of slaves might solve their problem.[30] He added that many carriers who had returned from East Africa had not redeemed themselves and therefore the life of a slave could not be too hard. When he had the staff he proposed to second a political officer to register the domestics—a task which would have to be handled with infinite tact and care. The Colonial Office merely noted his reply without comment.

Although Wilkinson's enthusiasm for abolition had dwindled, there were others in Sierra Leone, officials and private individuals, who began to press for stronger measures against slavery. There was growing concern about slow economic progress in Sierra Leone, and the argument that slavery hindered the economic development of the country was heard with increasing frequency. In 1920 a newspaper correspondent attributed the shortage of rice to the exodus from the Protectorate to Freetown. Those in the city did not return to the Protectorate just because they were lazy but because they were too frightened to return to a life of slavery in Mende territory, where "however strong and rich a slave may be, he cannot redeem himself"—true if the master insisted on his customary rights to the slave's property.[31] In 1921 the same newspaper reported that people were fleeing the Protectorate to escape the oppression of the chiefs and headmen.[32]

Acting Governor Maxwell, whose views were respected at the Colonial Office, was also worried about economic stagnation. He thought that to end it

> The first and important measure to be taken is the abolition of domestic slavery. At first sight this is a political question; it is also, however, a most important economic one, and properly handled the results would be far-reaching and beneficial.[33]

Maxwell's specific arguments against slavery were that slave labour was wasteful labour, slaves had no security of property, that many slaves ran away to swell the ranks of thieves and rogues in the Colony, and that because manual labour was slave's work freeborn people were unwilling to demean themselves by doing manual labour. He opposed Wilkinson's proposed slave register which would take several years to compile and would therefore delay further action. Churchill guardedly agreed that more vigorous measures for the abolition of slavery might be practicable and suggested that the problem be left for the new Governor.[34] Meanwhile Maxwell wrote to Ellis to suggest the outright abolition of domestic slavery:

> (I may be) snubbed for presuming as an acting officer to suggest such a serious administrative change as the abolition of domestic slavery. It is wanted if we are going to make much improvement in the Protectorate.[35]

*   *   *

When the new Governor, Ransford Slater, arrived early in 1922 he found a considerable body of official and unofficial opinion pressing for the abolition of slavery because the institution was hindering progress.[36] The depression in trade and the generally difficult financial situation in Sierra Leone which developed towards the end of 1921 gave added strength to the arguments for abolition. Domestic slavery was obviously a suitable target for attack and perhaps a convenient scapegoat for the failures of the businessmen and the Government of Sierra Leone. Maxwell's argument that slavery hindered social and economic progress was often repeated in the early 1920s—a marked contrast to the argument two decades earlier that the preservation of the institution was the only way to avoid social and economic chaos. The report for the Southern Province in 1921 provoked another controversy about slavery by blaming the economic stagnation of Sierra Leone on the merchants' lack of enterprise and initiative.[37] The Liverpool Chamber of Commerce retaliated by attacking the state of affairs in the Protectorate where the people were not allowed to keep what they earned, and it urged that steps be taken to stop chiefs from robbing and exploiting their people.[38] As Major Lyon made clear in his report on Karene District in 1924, slavery was the means by which chiefs robbed and exploited their people. Lyon thought trade suffered because accumulating wealth could be dangerous for an ordinary person. One danger was that a rich native was a mark for litigation, for example:

> A third, C, will claim that the wealthy man's great-great-grandmother, having been a slave of C's great-great-grandmother, and never having been redeemed, the wealthy man and all that is his rightly belongs to C.[39]

In 1923, after hearing that he was being prematurely retired, District Commissioner Addison told the Colonial Office that Sierra Leone was doomed unless minerals were found, because no country where slavery was tolerated and perpetuated could prosper. Unless slavery was ended, the destruction of forests halted, and agriculture was improved, he could see little hope.[40] Later that year the Colonial Office was very disturbed by reports on the prospects of rice cultivation in Sierra Leone by Mr. Pillai, an expert sent from India to report on rice in Sierra Leone.[41] Pillai saw the institution of domestic slavery as the main cause of the labour difficulties which hindered the cultivation of rice. The Commissioner of Lands and Forests agreed that rice production in the Southern Province could not be substantially increased unless the slaves were freed, and he made various proposals which depended on the abolition of slavery.

Governor Slater made enquiries and discovered that the

political officers would like slavery abolished if it could be done equitably, but he pointed out that the chiefs and even the editor of the *Sierra Leone Weekly News* would defend the institution.[42] Although he had not yet got to grips with the problem, he suggested a declaration of freedom for all children born in the Protectorate after a certain date. In November 1922 he spoke of his worries about domestic slavery:

> I have already seen enough, however, to convince me that the present system needs investigation as to whether it is not one of the local conditions which hinder rather than help Sierra Leone on its road to prosperity, and I have grave doubts whether any enduring progress can be made while the system remains in force.[43]

The Governor also called for figures of the redemptions since the division of the Protectorate into Provinces and asked Captain Stanley for his views and recommendations on slavery.[44]

Captain Stanley stressed the mildness of domestic slavery and hesitated to suggest firm action against it.[45] He suggested legislation to provide for the end of slavery—an ordinance declaring all persons born after the commencement of the ordinance free and the emancipation of all slaves when their masters died. Slater circulated Stanley's minute and other papers to the Provincial Commissioners and asked them to study slavery carefully in preparation for a discussion at a conference of Provincial Commissioners to be held in April 1924.[46]

* * *

While the officials in Sierra Leone were making their preparations international and humanitarian pressures against slavery were building up. One of the effect of the First World war was a revival of the humanitarian and abolitionist ethic—part of the conviction that something must be done to make the world a better place for all its people. On moral grounds there was a growing campaign for strong action against the slave trade, slavery and other forms of social oppression. The Treaty of St. Germain-en-Laye in 1919 bound its signatories to "endeavour to secure the complete suppression of slavery in all its forms and of the slave trade by land and sea".[47]

The mandated territories were an obvious field for anti-slavery activity. In 1921 the Anti-Slavery Society wrote to the League of Nations raising the question of domestic slavery in what had been German East Africa and asking for the manumission of all slaves at a given date.[48] The next year Tanganyika Territory Ordinance No. 13 of 1922 was passed—"An Ordinance to Abolish Involuntary Servitude in the Territory"—which laid down that no person could be kept as a slave against his will nor be dispossessed of property because he was or had been a slave. Slaves, however, could stay with their masters if they wished.[49] Presumably the letter of the Anti-Slavery Society the year before had some bearing on the decision to end slavery in this mandated territory; certainly it confirmed the Society's conviction that slavery could be stopped by international action, especially with the help of the League of Nations.

In September 1922 Sir Arthur Steel Maitland, representing New Zealand, raised the question of slavery which he thought the League of Nations, "as being a trustee of humanity", ought to tackle, and he proposed a motion:

> The Assembly resolves to refer to the appropriate Committee the question of the recrudescence of slavery in Africa in order that it may consider and propose the best methods for combating the evil.[50]

Later that month the appropriate Committee, the Sixth Committee, gained the Assembly's approval for the inclusion of the slavery question in the agenda of the fourth assembly and for a request to the Council for the information it had received on slavery.[51]

A few days later the Council instructed the Secretary-General "to request the Governments of the Members of the League to supply the Council with any information on the existing situation which they may possess and which they may see fit to communicate to it".[52] France and Belgium sent detailed and lengthy replies but Britain, which apparently did not see fit to communicate much information, merely reported that there was nothing to justify any apprehension of a recrudescence of slavery in the territories for which she was responsible.

In September 1923 the Fourth Assembly of the League of

Nations requested a League Commission on slavery, apparently partly because of pressure from the Anti-Slavery Society. Mr. Wood, the British representative, supported this move "in complete ignorance of the attitude of His Majesty's Government in such matters", according to an official at the Colonial Office. This implies that the British stance against slavery was at least partly the result of Mr. Wood's failure or unwillingness to understand the official policy.[53] The Temporary Slavery Commission first met at Geneva in July 1924. Its members were nominated by the Secretary-General and represented the six imperial powers—France, Portugal, Belgium, Britain, Italy and the Netherlands; they were joined by a representative from the International Labour Organization and later by a representative from Haiti.[54] Lugard, who had not been known for his abolitionist zeal, was chosen to represent Britain. Although he had opposed slavery in principle, his policy in Nigeria had been to keep slaves in the service of the local "gentry". For fear of offending them, he had ordered:

> Residents will therefore do their best to discourage wholesale assertion of "freedom" by such persons, pointing out to them, when occasion arises, the liberality, and from some points of view in present circumstances, the advantages of the form of labour contract under which they serve.[55]

Ten years late Lugard did not take quite such a rosy view of the conditions of domestic slaves and the "labour contract" under which they worked; during his term as Governor-General of Nigeria, Ordinance No. 35 of 1916 was passed to abolish slavery throughout the country.[56]

At its first session the Temporary Slavery Commission was mainly concerned with establishing the scope of its operations. These were to embrace the enslaving of persons, slave raiding, the slave trade, slave dealing by exchange, sale, gift or inheritance, slavery and serfdom; in addition it was to deal with practices restricting personal liberty, such as the acquisition of girls by purchase disguised as payment of dowry, adoption with a view to enslavement, and pledging. It was to consider measures to end these practices and also to look at systems of compulsory labour, public and private, paid and unpaid.[57]

231

Meanwhile the Secretary-General, in accordance with a resolution of the Assembly in December 1923, made a second attempt to collect information about slavery. The Imperial powers were asked two similar questions:

1. What means, legislative, administrative or other, have been applied in the territory of Great Britain or in its Colonies, Protectorates, and mandated territories, to secure the suppression of slavery?
2. What have been the results of the application of these measures? Has slavery thereby been automatically and completely suppressed, or is it gradually dying out? What are the economic and social results of the measures taken, for the former masters, for the slaves, for the Government, and for the development of the territory involved? Is it intended to supplement the measures already taken by any further Governmental action?[58]

It was three months before these queries were forwarded to the Governor of Sierra Leone, but they did arrive in time to influence the Provincial Commissioners' Conference in April 1924.[59]

Because the Secretary-General wanted replies by the beginning of June the Governor only had the time for a brief reply in which he outlined legislation affecting slavery and slave dealing. Despite the suppression of slave dealing he thought a mild form of domestic slavery existed to a considerable extent and was only gradually dying out. He was vague about the economic and social results of the measures taken against slavery although he had been considering the subject for the past two years. He hoped that the Provincial Commissioners' Conference would lead to proposals for further official action against slavery.[60]

*   *   *

At the same time as international and humanitarian pressures were persuading the Colonial Office to think seriously about abolishing slavery in the Sierra Leone Protectorate, officials in Sierra Leone were growing impatient with the policy of inaction over the problem. Moral considerations were being invoked and slavery was seen as an obstacle to the development of the Protectorate. Perhaps most important of all from the point of view of the local officials was the fact that slavery presented the administration with many problems. Slater wrote:

... if only for the reason that a large part of their time is wasted over the innumerable "palavers" that arise therefrom ... a District Commissioner's work necessarily consists largely of settling tedious disputes, many of them of a trifling character, but the tedium must often border on exasperation when the officer has to bolster up a system which is totally repugnant to one of his most cherished traditions.[61]

Slavery cases did cause a lot of work for the District Commissioners—especially disputes over runaway slaves and the inheritance and redemption of slaves.[62] Most officials agreed with Slater, except Captain Stanley, Commissioner for the Northern Province and Acting Colonial Secretary in 1924. Stanley's views were more conservationist than those of his colleagues. A. E. Tuboku Metzger, a Creole unofficial member of the Legislative Council and a former ex-assistant District Commissioner, confirmed Slater's view when he told the Council that:

From my own experience, if this Bill becomes law it will relieve District Commissioners when touring the districts from the unpleasant duties of listening to and adjudicating complaints about domestics which used to detain one for hours in one place where he had no desire to remain long.[63]

At the conference the three Provincial Commissioners—Bowden in the Central Province, Ross in the South and Hooker who had been acting in the North for most of the previous two years —agreed that for a variety of reasons action should be taken against slavery.[64] It led to social and economic evils and caused administrative problems. They opposed compensation for slave owners. They were worried about the import of slaves from Liberia and recommended that slaves introduced from Liberia and other foreign territory should be freed. They favoured a clean-cut abolition of slavery but failed to agree on the date of abolition—Bowden felt that there had already been too much delay and suggested the beginning of 1925, but Ross and Hooker wanted adequate time for the Government, the masters and the slaves to prepare for the change and favoured the beginning of 1929.

The Governor favoured neither plan. He thought the recommendations "drastic" and considered other courses open to the

Government. He dismissed the present policy of leaving slavery to die a natural death, which would take fifty years or so. He did not think it fair to the political officers to leave the law as it was at the same time as instructing them to take no cognizance whatever, either in their judicial or executive capacity, of complaints involving the recognition of the status of slavery. He thought abolition with compensation to slave holders would not be expedient and pointed out that the Government had neither a legal nor a moral obligation to pay compensation.

He thought four possible courses were open to the Government. First, to alter the law by explicitly declaring that slavery should receive no legal recognition and declaring that after the date of the Abolition Ordinance all children born in the country and all persons brought into the country should be free; this was the policy followed in Nigeria in 1901. Second, to declare that slavery must not receive legal recognition and that all children born after the Ordinance are free—this course, which had been followed in The Gambia, was favoured by Captain Stanley. Third, absolute emancipation some time after the Abolition Ordinance— the policy favoured by Ross and Hooker. Fourth, absolute and immediate emancipation, which had been the policy in the Gold Coast in 1874 and which Bowden now favoured.

To the Governor's satisfaction, the Executive Council unanimously favoured the second plan, which he now proposed to the Colonial Office. His only doubt was whether it would be possible to ensure that the freed slaves had some cultivable land. In addition he proposed that from the beginning of 1925 all persons brought into the Protectorate from Liberia or other foreign territory should be, *ipso facto*, free.[65]

The Colonial Office liked Slater's despatch but felt his proposals did not go far enough to secure abolition.[66] Even Ellis, hitherto wary of attempts to end slavery, thought that further action was necessary not merely because of the urgings of the Provincial Commissioners but also because of the interest of the League of Nations. The League had recently sent a questionnaire on slavery which the Colonial Office had been unable to answer satisfactorily regarding Sierra Leone, although the French, probably falsely, claimed complete abolition in their dominions. Slater's suggestions would mean that it would take forty to fifty years for slavery to die out, "and it may well be thought that this is too long to wait" especially as the fear of any upset to the Protectorate's economy appeared ill-founded. Read also favoured more vigorous steps, something on the lines of the abolition in Tanganyika in 1922, and he suggested that Slater be called to London "with a view to evolving a more drastic plan of campaign".

The minute by Ellis shows that the interest of the League had much to do with the new policy of the Colonial Office, which had previously curbed the abolitionist zeal of Governors like Cardew and Wilkinson but was now trying to persuade Slater to adopt a more radical anti-slavery policy. Since British representatives were so deeply involved with the formulation of the League's anti-slavery policy, it would be doubly embarrassing if it were generally known that the British Government was prepared to tolerate domestic slavery in the Sierra Leone Protectorate, possibly for another fifty years. A British representative, Steel Maitland, had raised the question of slavery in 1922 and this had led to the formation of the Temporary Slavery Commission, of which Lord Lugard was an important member—in fact, Lugard was one of the principal authors of the Commission's first report of the extent of slavery and of its various recommendations.[67] At the suggestion of Lord Cecil, Chancellor of the Duchy of Lancaster, the Foreign Office used the Commission's report as the basis of its draft International Convention on the Slave Trade, Slavery and Similar Conditions; Lord Cecil presented the draft to the League and it was finally adopted by the Assembly in September 1926.[68]

The more immediate problem of slavery in the Sierra Leone Protectorate was discussed in August 1924 at the conference at the Colonial Office, when Slater was told that abolition of slavery must come more quickly.[69] Slater was worried about unrest among the chiefs and difficulties in the campaign to improve agriculture if slavery was attacked too vigorously, but he agreed to the Colonial Office proposals, although he reserved the right to reconsider the proposals after consulting with his senior officers. The proposed Bill would provide for the complete abolition of slavery by a clause similar to Clause 2 in the Tanganyika Abolition Ordinance—"After the commencement of the Ordinance no person in the Territory shall detain any person against his will in his service as a slave". There was no question of compensating slave owners. The Colonial Office thought that if these proposals went through they would have to omit the provision for declaring persons born after a certain date free because this would imply that others could not gain their freedom; nor could the payment of redemption fees be demanded because this effectively recognized the status of slavery. Lord Arnold made these points in an official despatch to Slater and added that if detaining a person as a slave was made unlawful then a clause providing for the punishment of those so doing was needed.[70]

Attention was then focused on the problem of forced or compulsory labour in the Protectorate and the problem of slavery appeared to be a little less urgent. The day after writing his long despatch on slavery, Slater wrote to the Colonial Office about compulsory labour for the Government and pointed out that this was regulated by law. Ross had objected to compulsory labour because it was unpaid and gave the labourers no money to spend to boost trade, because it interfered with agriculture and encouraged young men to leave the Protectorate for the Colony where there was no compulsory labour, and because the chiefs tended to call up too much labour and use the balance for their personal advantage. The Governor disagreed with Ross's proposals to pay for all labour although he realized that if slavery were abolished further steps would have to be taken to introduce direct payment for labour and possibly the cash commutation of labour obligations to the Government.

Read thought the abolition of compulsory unpaid labour should be accelerated but Lord Arnold thought that consideration of this problem should be postponed until the admittedly interdependent problem of slavery had been settled. When the Colonial Office, incorrectly as it happened, thought the problem of slavery had been settled by the 1926 legislation it again wrote to Slater about the abolition of compulsory labour early in 1927. As a result of straitened financial circumstances and because he was in his fifth year of office, Slater was unwilling to end unpaid labour.[71] Yet, he knew the League opposed this. The Temporary Slavery Commission Report of July 1925 had, as Slater pointed out in 1927, approved of compulsory labour only if it were paid labour on public works.[72] Although in 1926 the Secretary of State telegraphed permission to approach the chiefs about raising the House Tax to 10/- and to explain that the extra money would be spent on communal labour, the tax remained at 5/- and forced unpaid labour continued for many years.[73] The only concession Slater could make, because of financial difficulties, was to pay 6d. a day for forced labour on Government buildings from the beginning of 1928. He could not afford to pay those building and maintaining roads. The Colonial Office accepted Slater's decision with reluctance because it was contrary to the League's recommendations.[74] The Forced Labour Ordinance of 1932 confirmed the rights of Paramount Chiefs to exact unpaid forced labour for a wide variety of communal works, although there was a tendency to commute such obligations with payments of money. These obligations continued until the Cox Report in 1956 recommended that the rights of chiefs and Government to forced labour be abrogated because they were partly responsible for the recent riots in Sierra Leone.[75]

The central issue was domestic slavery, but for some time after Arnold's despatch of September 1924 events tended to favour the conservationists rather than the abolitionists. The officials in Sierra Leone were focusing their attention on the problems abolition would bring rather than on the welfare of the slaves. One problem was the property which the slaves had had while in servitude. Colonel Mair, the Officer Commanding the Troops, was surprised to find that the Sierra Leone proposals did not include a clause similar to Section 4 of the Tanganyika Abolition Ordinance, which had made it illegal to dispossess a freed slave of the property he had acquired by his own industry. Even Bowden, the most abolitionist of Slater's senior officers, opposed protecting the slave's property as contrary to native law—a strange argument when the Government was planning a much more serious infringement of customary law—the abolition of domestic slavery.[76]

In March 1925 Slater reported that five out of his six top officials opposed abolition on the Tanganyika model. He therefore was making new proposals, which were in fact very like those he had favoured before. The Sierra Leone Bill would have three clauses—first, slaves to be freed on the deaths of their masters, second, all persons born or brought into the Protectorate after a certain date to be free, and third, from 1 January 1930 the legal status of slavery should be abolished.[77]

Moreover, the Colonial Office was less inclined to press for a speedy abolition of slavery after it saw the Report of the Temporary Slavery Commission in July 1925. The report did not mention Sierra Leone and stated:

> The legality of the status is not recognized in any Christian State (Mother Country, Colonial Dependencies, and Mandated Territories) except Abyssinia.[78]

Amery was happy to accept Slater's recommendations except for the clause abolishing the legal status of slavery, which in view of the Commission's Report was unnecessary and should therefore be omitted. It also seems likely that Amery disliked this clause which might draw attention to the fact that the British Government was not convinced that the legal status of slavery did not exist in the Sierra Leone Protectorate.

Slater could then communicate these proposals to the Sierra Leone Legislative Council at the beginning of the 1925–1926 session.[79] Mainly in the pages of the *Sierra Leone Weekly News* many important Creoles expressed their opposition to these proposals. One distinguished conservationist was A. J. Shorunkeh-Sawyerr, a successful Creole lawyer who had been a member of the Legislative Council for many years and who had been awarded a C.B.E. Back in 1885 he had detested the "rum and gin civilization" being imposed on the Sierra Leone hinterland, and he was clearly still doubtful about the benefits of civilization in the Protectorate forty years later.[80] He complained that Slater had not indicated any intention of paying compensation to the slaveholders and that to refuse compensation would be unjust and would cause trouble.[81] The following week the editor of the paper supported compensation and warned that abolition would damage the productive capacity of the masters and would lead to a dangerous influx into Freetown.[82] Then Shorunkeh-Sawyerr returned to the attack; he again argued for compensation and said that nothing had been done to prepare the people of the Protectorate for abolition.[83]

Later the paper asked why the Assemblies of Chiefs had not been consulted and it expressed pity for the deprived masters and the helpless freed slaves.[84] In January 1926 C. D. Hotobah During criticized the proposed abolition without proper investigation, consultation or compensation and went on to call domestic slavery "a time honoured institution"—a curious phrase for one of the founders of the Sierra Leone Auxiliary of the Anti-Slavery and Aborigines' Protection Society to use.[85] In the same month the *Sierra Leone Weekly News* warned the Government to "make haste slowly" on abolition.[86] In March 1926 the paper published an open letter from Shorunkeh-Sawyerr to the Paramount Chiefs in the Legislative Council, in which he urged them to oppose the proposed abolition because they had not been consulted and would not be compensated.[87]

When he introduced the second reading of the Slavery Bill, the Attorney-General was careful to show that it was not a clean-cut abolition but a measure to hasten the end of slavery.[88] Existing slave owners were not being deprived of their slaves, and so there was no need for compensation. Compensation had not been paid in other British West African Protectorates. Protectorate slavery was more like serfdom than real slavery, and there would be no hardship for those already owning slaves. This last argument against compensation figured prominently in the explanations of the proposed legislation to the chiefs who, as Ross reported, were "much impressed with the salient fact, that no living owner was to be deprived of domestics now living during his, the owner's life-time".[89]

The Rural Member, Tuboku Metzger, seconded the Bill, but the other two unofficial Creole members tried to delay it. The First Urban Member, E. S. Beoku Betts, proposed that the Bill be referred to a Select Committee to consider the matter of compensation and that in the meantime the Assemblies of Chiefs be consulted.[90] When the Governor expressed surprise that the people of Freetown, a city which owed its origins to the abolition of slavery, did not oppose domestic slavery Beoku Betts sought to justify his policy by arguing that Protectorate slavery was not really slavery at all. It was part of the people's customs that some should have to work for others, no case of injustice had come from the system in recent years and so there was no reason to interfere with it. Dr. Bankole Bright, the Second Urban Member, seconded Beoku Betts' amendment. He was on slightly stronger grounds when he challenged the legal right of the Government to abolish slavery in the Protectorate, which had been acquired under the Foreign Jurisdiction Act. Moreover, the Government had promised to respect the domestic life and customary laws of the Protectorate people.[91] There are two apparent reasons for this

Creole attack on abolition. First, Freetown feared an even greater influx of people from the Protectorate if slaves were freed of their customary restraints. Second, Creoles resented the cavalier way in which the Government had treated them and their opinions since the proclamation of the Protectorate, and in their defence of slavery there may have been some stirrings of African nationalism —an attempt to protect the African way of life from British interference.

Paramount Chiefs Bai Kompa and Bai Comber, the two unofficial members from the Protectorate who were present at the debate, supported the Government but pleaded for justice for the slave owners and for compensation. Bai Comber went so far as to complain that Creole settlers in the Central Province had misrepresented the Bill to the people there. Betts' amendment was defeated and the second reading of the Bill was then passed unanimously.

There was little debate in the third reading but Tuboku Metzger pointed out that children would be free while their parents remained slaves and he was worried about slave owners distributing their slaves to their children before their death. The Governor agreed with Tuboku Metzger to a certain extent and reassured him that the latter would be punished as slave dealers, but he stressed that complete abolition was not practical.[92] Bai Comber said that intermarriage was ending slavery; in 1924 he had taken his two slave wives to be redeemed before the District Commisioner so that their children would be free and able to inherit his property. Little more of interest was said. The Bill passed its third reading and received the Governor's assent on 2 April, 1926. It was known as Ordinance No. 9 of 1926—The Protectorate (No. 2) (Amendment) Ordinance, 1926.[93]

The Sierra Leone Government could now inform the Colonial Office that it was conforming to Article 2(b) of the draft International Convention on the Slave Trade, Slavery and Similar Conditions, which was being prepared by the Foreign Office. It could accede to the clause in question:

> To bring about progressively and as soon as possible the disappearance of slavery in every form, notably in the case of domestic slavery and similar conditions.[94]

As a result of the new Ordinance the Colonial Secretary had to send fresh instructions to the Provincial Commissioners.[95] In future they and their district commissioners were to stop helping slave owners recover runaway slaves because it was now illegal for Government officers, even in their executive capacity, to recognize the legal status of slavery. It should, however, be explained that there was nothing illegal in holding domestic slaves. There would be no objection to any official explaining the position to a master or a domestic, but you will "no doubt, in your discretion, endeavour to secure that there is as little economic disturbance as possible when masters die". Finally, if any slaves gained their freedom through the provisions of the new ordinance they should be given certificates of redemption without charge, if they applied for them.

The Colonial Office was pleased that the problem of domestic slavery had been so easily settled and even before the 1926 Ordinance was passed the Anti-Slavery Society resolved to send the Governor of Sierra Leone a letter of appreciation.[96] The *Sierra Leone Weekly News* thought the 1926 Ordinance had abolished "the last vestige of slavery in the Colony and the Protectorate" but did not find that this was much cause for satisfaction because no compensation had been paid.[97] It also feared difficulties for the rice industry because the ex-slaves who had worked on the plantations were now free to join "the rush of the lower classes in the Protectorate to the Colony".

*   *   *

Yet, those more directly connected with the Protectorate knew that such satisfaction was unfounded. The 1926 Ordinance had not finally abolished slavery, and it had failed to solve two of the most tiresome problems which faced British officials—cases of redemptions and runaway slaves. Clause 3—"No claim for or in respect of any slave shall be entertained by any of the Courts of the Protectorate"—could make it even more difficult for British officers in the Protectorate to deal with these problems.

After receiving the instructions of 10 April the District Commissioner of Karene, E. F. Sayers, pointed out that the legal status of slavery in the Protectorate was still implicitly recognized. With remarkable foresight he argued that a master exercising his customary rights over a slave of reasonable chastisement for misconduct or restraint to stop him running away could not be sued by the slave for such assault because Ordinance No. 6 of 1903 recognized native custom not repugnant to natural justice. He wanted to know therefore if the District Commissioner could regard such chastisement or forcible restraint as assault.[98] The Attorney-General admitted that Sayers had made a valid point and that he had forgotten the distinction between claims in respect of the person of any slave and claims in respect of any slave when he was piloting the Bill through the Council. Since the Ordinance of 1926 ruled out the latter, the action for assault contemplated by Sayers would not lie.[99]

This correspondence was circulated in the Protectorate but Mr. Hodgson, then on leave, did not see it.[100] In 1927 Mr. Hodgson, then District Commissioner of Kenema, was in some confusion about redemption.[101] He interpreted the Ordinance as meaning that no court in the Protectorate could make a slave return to his master and therefore the slave could not be made to pay redemption fees. In one chiefdom in his district over a hundred slaves had left their masters, and he had given those whose masters had tried to get them back certificates of freedom without charge in order to prevent any assaults or breaches of the peace. Among these was a woman called Gbese who had obtained such certificates of redemption for herself and her children from Hodgson in Kenema. She had then returned to Pujehun District where her children were enslaved and had approached the District Commissioner there with her certificate and had asked him to ensure the release of her children. Fenton in Pujehun decided he could take no action under Clause 3 of the 1926 Ordinance which outlawed claims for or in respect of the person of a slave.[102] This led to some correspondence between the two District Commissioners and the case was referred to the Provincial Commissioners of the Central and Southern Provinces. By the time Hooker, the Commissioner for the Central Province, came to consider this case, the issue of the rights of slaves to leave their masters freely was at stake in a case being judged by the Full Court of Appeal in Freetown. So Hooker instructed his District Commissioners to avoid similar cases until the Court reached a decision.[103]

The particular point at issue in the case before the Full Court was whether a slave could take action against his master who recaptured him and resumed ownership over him against the will of the slave. The larger question at issue was whether the status of a slave as such was recognized by the law of Sierra Leone. The cases in which these points were raised were those of Rex v. Salla Silla and Rex v. M'fa Nonko and others. The defendants were charged with assault and conspiracy to assault on runaway slaves whom they were trying to recapture when the assault was committed.[104] The background to these cases is rather obscure but the *Manchester Guardian* was probably right in thinking them a deliberate attempt to test the laws on slavery in Sierra Leone.[105] A Mandingo sub-chief (the newspaper was probably referring to M'fa Nonko), although not a slaveholder, was opposed to abolition, and he approached several chiefs and told them that they were entitled to recapture runaway slaves. He then helped some to do so. The local District Commissioner, Sayers, brought proceedings in two cases and the defendants were convicted and fined in the Circuit Court. They then appealed against their conviction to the Full Court of Appeal, which was sitting in Freetown in June and July 1927.

On 1 July 1927 the Full Court delivered its verdict on the cases of Rex v. Salla Silla and Rex v. M'fa Nonko and others, which had been combined for the purpose of appeal. By a majority of two to one it quashed the convictions in the Circuit Court and acquitted the appellants of the charges of assault and conspiracy. The two judges reached their verdict on the grounds that the appellants had been using reasonable force to regain possession of their property. It was clear to them that the legal provisions for the cash redemption of slaves meant that the status of slaves as chattels was recognized in the Protectorate.[106] Judge Petrides dissented and held that the appellants had been properly convicted in the Circuit Court. Even if the legislature had negligently allowed an anomaly it was not for a court of justice to do another wrong and "also to blind its eyes and approve of assault". In the words of Ordinance No. 6 of 1903 he argued that the recapture of runaway slaves was "repugnant to natural justice, equity and good conscience".[107]

Captain Stanley, back in the Northern Province again, wrote a comprehensive account of the events leading up to the appeal. His sympathies were clearly with the slave owners and he drew attention to the "very special and exceptional circumstances which led to the action of sub-chief M'fa Nonko and other masters in attempting to recover their slaves by force".[108] He thought the difficulties had arisen from misunderstandings about the 1926 Ordinance. At least two of his officers had over-estimated its scope and had issued redemption certificates gratis to certain slaves who had asserted their freedom; also a general rumour had got about that all slaves had been freed. Some slaves had stayed with their masters and had told them that under the new laws they were free and no man could make them work. So Stanley informed his district commissioners that the native authorities could compel slaves who refused to work—and did not run away—to work, and they could punish natives inciting the slaves not to work.[109] Yet, friction between master and slave continued and in November 1926 Stanley had to mediate between masters and recalcitrant slaves. After he explained the law the slaves agreed to return to work provided that they were not punished for their strike.[110]

There was further trouble in the Karene and Bombali Districts. Limba and Loko slaves were running away from their Mandingo masters in Biriwa Chiefdom and settling with their own people in the neighbouring Sella Limba and Sanda Loko Chiefdoms. The Mandingo masters from Biriwa were crossing into the neighbouring chiefdoms to try to recapture their escaped slaves. Stanley told the disputing parties—sub-Chief M'fa Nonko of Biriwa and Paramount Chief Bai Samura of Sanda Loko—that he would prevent fugitive slaves from finding shelter in chiefdoms next to the chiefdom from which they had fled.[111] This was a completely unjustifiable restriction of the right of the slave to run away from his master, but a few months later the District Commissioner of Karene, Sayers, issued decrees to this effect.[112] In March 1927, after further disturbances caused by Mandingo attempts to recapture runaway slaves, Sayers decreed that no runaway slaves should be allowed to settle in the Sanda Loko and Sella Limba Chiefdoms if they had escaped from bordering chiefdoms; those who had already done so would have to leave Sanda Loko and Sella Limba Chiefdoms by 1 May, 1927. It was this problem that led to the proceedings against M'fa Nonko, Salla Silla, and others, but it is not clear whether the assaults by the defendants were committed before or after the decrees by Sayers. It is probable that the assaults prompted Sayers to issue the decrees.

* * *

Naturally the Full Court's decision that a slave owner could use reasonable force to recapture his runaway slave caused a considerable stir in Britain and elsewhere. Yet, unofficial reaction in Sierra Leone was strangely muted. The *Sierra Leone Weekly News* did not even comment until 17 September, 1927—two and a half months after the judgement. It reprinted an article from the *Daily Telegraph* which had expressed surprise that a slave could be lawfully recaptured and argued that British courts must not appear to sanction slavery. The Freetown paper blamed the Government for the situation, which would have been avoided by taking the advice it had given to compensate the slave owners—in view of the circumstances it thought the Full Court judgement had been inevitable.[113]

Nor was the Sierra Leone Government eager to act. It was slow to consider the implications of the Full Court judgement and acted only after the Colonial Office instructed the Acting Governor to abolish slavery as soon as possible. Luke, the Acting Governor, was obviously not willing to take decisive action pending the arrival of the new Governor, and he was by no means a convinced abolitionist. He later referred to slavery in the Sierra Leone Protectorate as "one of the least oppressive forms of servitude in the history of human labour".[114]

In Britain there was shock and dismay at the realization that slavery still existed in the Empire. Luke described the unofficial reaction in Britain as a

... tremendous agitation in sections of the British Press, an agitation stimulated in part by humanitarians whose hearts tended to rule their heads, in part by those who found here a useful source of notoriety.[115]

Just before the autumn recess a Liberal Member of Parliament asked about the decision and wanted to know what steps the Government would take to make slavery in all its forms illegal. The Acting Secretary of State informed the Commons that the text of the judgement had not arrived yet but that if there was a fault in Ordinance 9 of 1926 an amendment would be considered.[116] The Government was fortunate in having the autumn recess to deal with a very embarrassing problem. By the time Parliament reassembled in November slavery had been completely abolished and the Government could answer any questions confidently.

Yet, it was not until late August that the Full Court judgement was drawn to the attention to the general public. It was then that Sir John Simon wrote to *The Times* criticizing a law allowing slavery in a British dependency and pointing out how unfortunate it would be if the West African Chiefs should conclude that the British Government backed them as slaveholders. He ended with a veiled threat:

> The Colonial Office is doubtless considering what action should be taken, especially as the League of Nations is receiving reports at Geneva next month with a view to the final suppression of the remains of slavery throughout the world.[117]

The next day the *Manchester Guardian* published the text of the judgement and summed up the humanitarian arguments; it warned that Britain would be embarrassed at Geneva, and it pointed out similarities between the Mansfield Judgement of 1772, which had freed all slaves on English soil, and the Sierra Leone judgement. Both cases had arisen from the forcible recapture of runaway slaves, but the result of the latter had been to strengthen the institution of slavery.[118]

Sir John Simon and the *Manchester Guardian* knew that the British Government was unusually sensitive about slavery at a time when it was playing a prominent role in the League of Nations campaign against slavery and related institutions. The last thing the Colonial Office wanted was the embarrassment of having the issue of slavery in the Sierra Leone Protectorate raised at Geneva. So the Colonial Office was very susceptible to humanitarian pressures, and it tried to secure the support of John Harris, Secretary of the Anti-Slavery Society. Harris asked for an interview with Mr. Ormsby-Gore, who was out of town, and then he asked to see the full text of the judgement before his departure for Geneva.[119] After this was printed the Colonial Office assured him that steps would be taken, and Harris promised that at Geneva he would try to get some of the foreign delegates to draw attention to the difficulties the Liberian situation caused in the Sierra Leone Protectorate.[120] When Harris wrote to *The Times* urging the abolition of slavery the Colonial Office concluded that Harris was running with the fox and hunting with the hounds and except for a curt acknowledgement of Harris's letter of 3 September about his proposed visit to Geneva the correspondence between Harris and the Colonial Office ended.[121]

When the question of slavery in the Sierra Leone Protectorate came before the Sixth Committee of the League Assembly on 13 September the British representative, Hilton Young, explained that the Full Court judgement had come as a disagreeable shock to the British Government and that the hiatus in the law was being remedied as quickly as possible. The *Manchester Guardian* was relieved that Britain had not been caused greater embarrassment and commented that this was really an awkward incident, which had been satisfactorily explained at Geneva.[122]

The fact remained that speedy action had to be taken to avoid criticism in the future at Geneva and at Westminster after the autumn recess. The Colonial Office's worries about Parliamentary criticism were clearly expressed by Fiddian after the successful abolition of slavery—"We are now armed cap à pie against any criticism which may come our way when Parliament meets".[123] Some of those directly concerned with Sierra Leone still opposed abolition and argued that if the slaves had to be emancipated compensation should be paid to the slave owners. Two members of the Sierra Leone Legislative Council who happened to be in Britain took advantage of the unusual interest in Sierra Leone to air their views. The Bishop of Sierra Leone at first defended the good intentions of Governor Slater, who had been working to end slavery since his assumption of office in 1922.[124] The Bishop's next comments to the Press were rather more embarrassing for the British and Sierra Leone Governments.[125] He told *The Observer* that Britain did not have sovereign rights over the Protectorate and should not ride roughshod over the African and his customs. Unless the Imperial Government was prepared to compensate the slave owners he could see no immediate way to free the Protectorate slaves. Bankole Bright, an Urban Member, also spoke to the Press in Britain.[126] He repeated his arguments for the compensation of slaves owners. He estimated that about one hundred thousand slaves would have to be redeemed and suggested that this could be done in four years for £200,000. When the Legislative Council debated final abolition the other two unofficial members also had reservations about speedy abolition and both Beoku Betts and Tuboku Metzger supported compensation, even though the latter had taken quite a different stand on compensation in 1926.[127]

Other groups who opposed immediate abolition without compensation were easily handled. The Paramount Chiefs, who were not consulted, were obviously unhappy at losing their slaves so soon and without compensation, especially as they had been recently promised that no living slave owners would be deprived of their slaves. They did, however, accept the situation with resignation, if not with enthusiasm. Luke warned the Paramount Chiefs in the Legislative Council that there could be no compensation and so during the debate they did not support the Creole members arguing for compensation. As a result, the debate on final abolition went smoothly because Beoku Betts and Tuboku Metzger were isolated and, to Luke's great relief, the Bishop who could have caused trouble from good intentions and Bankole Bright who could have caused trouble from bad intentions were both in Britain.[128] After final abolition Ormsby-Gore commended "the loyal and public-spirited attitude adopted by the Paramount Chiefs in the council towards a measure which was admittedly in conflict with their personal interests".[129]

At least two of the Provincial Commissioners also opposed a clean-cut abolition. Captain Stanley would be embarrassed by this because, in accordance with Ordinance No. 9 of 1926, he had repeatedly assured the chiefs that the Government had no intention of depriving living slaveholders of their slaves.[130] Hooker thought that as

> ... the clean-cut was not in fact carried out no change should now be made in the law for the reason that it would be looked upon by the chiefs and people generally as a breach of faith on the part of the Government.[131]

Nevertheless, the Colonial Office was in command and it wanted speedy abolition. There was no question of leaving the problem to the men on the spot. Although the Colonial Office had been concerned about the dangers of abolition since the proclamation of the Protectorate, its doubts had suddenly evaporated. It could be argued that the gradualist and developmental approach had modified and weakened slavery to such an extent that it was now ready for a quick and painless death, but the Colonial Office had still strongly opposed immediate abolition as late as 1919. This was at least partly due to the myth created by Chamberlain and his officials in 1899. The belief that the 1898 risings had been caused by British action against slavery died hard.

Whatever its previous hesitations, the Colonial Office in 1927 acted against slavery with speed and decision. On 27 July it telegraphed Sierra Leone for a full copy of the Full Court judgement.[132] It then informed Luke that the judgement had given rise to much comment in Britain and ordered him to draft a new ordinance.[133] Luke began framing a new ordinance and asked whether it should be considered when the Legislative Council met again in November or whether a special session was necessary; the Colonial Office favoured a special early sitting of the Council to abolish slavery.[134] In a series of telegrams details of the proposed ordinance were worked out. The Colonial Office insisted that Ordinance No. 9 of 1926 be repealed and that the abolition should be from the beginning of 1928, not from the beginning of 1929 as most of the Provincial Commissioners preferred.[135] Quickly and easily the Bill became law on 22 September —Ordinance No. 24 of 1927—"Legal Status of Slavery (Abolition) Ordinance, 1927".[136]

* * *

The passing of the Ordinance was rather an anti-climax in Britain and in Sierra Leone. Its most immediate effect was to relieve the British Government of an awkward problem and to enable it to resume its abolitionist stance at home and abroad without the risk of being accused of hypocrisy. In 1928 and 1929 Britain kept the League of Nations informed about measures against slavery in its other dependencies as well as about the effects of abolition in the Sierra Leone Protectorate.[137] Moreover, it may well have been the fear of further embarrassments that prompted Britain to guard against the repetition of the Sierra Leone case in other dependencies by passing a series of ordinances in 1930 affirming or reaffirming that slavery did not exist.[138]

In Britain, too, there was little embarrassment. When Parliament reconvened in November the final abolition of slavery in the Protectorate had become law. Lord Buxton asked a four-part question in the Lords but, as he assured the Parliamentary Under-Secretary of State for Dominion Affairs, he was seeking information and not criticizing.[139] He wanted to know what arrangements had been made to tell the slaves about their impending freedom, what measures would be taken to stop slave owners depositing their slaves across the Liberian border, what assistance would be given to freed slaves unable to look after themselves and what arrangements had been made to give the freed slaves land and forest rights. Lord Lovat replied that the administrative officers would tell the people about the emancipation of slaves, that action would be taken to stop slaves being taken to Liberia before emancipation and that the administrative officers would follow up the last two matters with the closest attention.[140]

There were other Parliamentary questions on Sierra Leone slavery and these were usually answered in general terms to the satisfaction of the questioners, who did not appear to know much about the matter anyway. One question did cause the Colonial Office some concern. This arose from a report in *The Times* on the effect of emancipation at the beginning of 1928.[141] The writer pointed out that by law no man could leave his chiefdom without the customary permission of the Paramount Chief who required a small fee for this permission, and this was beyond the means of the newly-freed slaves. A question about this was asked in the Commons on 20 February and the Governor was asked for a report.[142] Governor Byrne admitted that a chief might try to keep a slave in his chiefdom with him or the slave's former master, but in that case the ex-slave would probably run away to another chiefdom and if the other chief returned him he could appeal to the Sierra Leone Government—anyway, the Sierra Leone Government was watching the situation carefully.[143]

Otherwise there was little interest in Britain in the events in Sierra Leone. The *Daily Mail* did send out a correspondent to observe the Legislative Council debates on final abolition in September 1927, but he found little to say except to criticize the Creoles for their indifference and in some cases their hostility to abolition.[144] He thought this shocking in people who were descended from freed slaves.

The Freetown Press continued to lament abolition and to argue for compensation. The *Sierra Leone Weekly News* foresaw grave social and economic difficulties—especially a flood of freed slaves coming to Freetown and a shortage of land for the freed slaves.[145] One effect of abolition that the Creoles did not foresee was the damage to their reputation. The petulant opposition of some Creole leaders to abolition encouraged the belief that the Creoles of Freetown were unreliable, untrustworthy and ungrateful.

On the other hand the chiefs co-operated in the abolition of slavery, and there was very little disruption when emancipation came into effect at the beginning of 1928. Officials compared the behaviour of the chiefs very favourably with that of the Creoles. There were some minor incidents at the beginning of 1928, but there was no economic and social disruption. Some wives tried to leave their husbands on the grounds that they were not wives but slaves. Some ex-slaves defied chiefly authority. Others refused to work on the farms in 1928, but the hungry season taught them a sharp lesson and next season more farms were cultivated. In one chiefdom 50 out of 4,189 houses were reported empty after the departure of former slaves.[146] The general effects of emancipation were well summarised by the Commissioner for the Central Province:

> The abolition of the legal status of slavery throughout the Protectorate came into force on the first of the year and was received with a calm bordering on indifference.[147]

This "calm bordering on indifference" was largely due to the fact that little change actually took place. Although the Abolition Ordinance was a legal landmark and important in the history of Sierra Leone and even in the history of the British Empire, it had little immediate effect on the everyday lives of the people of the Protectorate and on the powers of the chiefly slave-owning classes. Domestic slavery was too closely integrated with the traditional way of life to be uprooted at a stroke by a British law. Even if the name of slave was no longer acceptable those who had been slaves continued to lead very much the same sort of lives as they had done before emancipation. The change was superficial for many slaves. More than a quarter of a century later Roy Lewis quoted a Vei chief—"No, we don't have slaves now—we have cousins".[148]

After emancipation most slaves carried on as before. They "sat down" with their former masters as clients or "cousins" and continued to work for them without pay but for the use of a piece of land on which they supported themselves and their families. The District Commissioner of Sembehun estimated that about 90% of the ex-slaves remained where they were, and this seems typical of the Protectorate as a whole.[149] They had little choice. Not only were they bound by economic ties to their ex-masters but also by political and family ties. Their former masters still had to be given respect as the heads of the households and the powers of the traditional authorities made it difficult for freed men and women to leave the scene of their enslavement. Social, economic and political factors all combined to keep most of the former slaves in the same places. In many parts of the Protectorate it is still remembered who were slaves and whose parents were slaves. Near Pepel those of servile origin are obliged to perform the more menial tasks, like butchering the sacrifices, for the Secret Societies.[150] There are still separate villages or parts of towns for those of slave origins. Near Makeni, for example, there is a separate village for those of Limba descent who had originally come to the area as slaves.[151]

Practices not unlike slavery continued for many years after abolition. In 1953 a student discovered that nearly half the children at school in Freetown were wards and that many of them were living in conditions very close to slavery.[152] In 1944 the Anti-Slavery Society was concerned about the alleged pledging of a girl in Sierra Leone.[153]

The most convincing evidence of the continuation of slavery or practices like it comes from the Cox Report on the disturbances in Sierra Leone from November 1955 to March 1956. It found that the abolition of 1927 "did not improve the material well-being of the ex-domestic slaves and their dependants, who in many cases yet remained beholden to their former Chiefs or owners".[154] Many testified that they were having to work as slaves for the chiefs.[155] The Commission of Inquiry found that much of the discontent was aggravated

   ... by the relics of slavery which in its domestic form was abolished only in 1927 when thousands of men, women and children were deprived of 'home' and the means of sustenance; they had freedom but nothing else and many returned to the houses and farms of their former proprietors there to give free labour from time to time in return for the use of the lands they occupy and the shelter they receive. These people exchanged legal serfdom for economic serfdom but now with the social revolution, taxpaying and the ballot box they have become discontented with their lot.[156]

The Cox Report makes it clear that it was not British laws but social, economic and political change that determined the fate of domestic slavery in the Sierra Leone Protectorate. Just as the Government failed to preserve the institution by its legislation early in the century so did it fail to destroy it by the legislation of 1926 and 1927.

*   *   *

Despite all the controversy aroused by the issue, the abolition of domestic slavery had a comparatively small effect on the Protectorate of Sierra Leone. Since the middle of the nineteenth century those concerned with West Africa had tended to magnify the problem of domestic slavery unduly. Much of the controversy about the institution was ill-informed and prejudiced. At times domestic slavery was not so much the source of controversy as the convenient battle ground for the proponents of the different ethical criteria for Britain to follow in West Africa.

In the early days of the British presence in West Africa the existence of domestic slavery was used by the two opposing schools of thought to justify their conclusions. The abolitionists thought that radical action should be taken to free the people from their chains of barbaric institutions and superstition. The conservationists argued that the existence of domestic slavery showed how different West African society was from British society and that therefore it was foolhardy and wrong to interfere unnecessarily with the internal affairs of the people of that region. At the time of the 1898 risings in Sierra Leone both abolitionists and conservationists argued that the existence of domestic slavery justified their two opposing policies of more and of less intervention in the Sierra Leone Protectorate. During the first two decades of the twentieth century the developmentalist ethic triumphed in official circles. Again the existence of slavery was used to justify economic intervention combined with the minimum of

253

interference with the social and political organizations of the West Africans in Northern Nigeria, the Sierra Leone Protectorate and elsewhere.

During the economic difficulties of the 1920s those who favoured more active intervention in the Sierra Leone Protectorate blamed the hard times on domestic slavery. The conservationists thought it would be doubly rash to make a major social change at a time of economic difficulties.

The advocates of the three main schools of thought all seemed to be responding to empirical considerations. In fact they were largely using the facts as they saw them to justify their preconceived attitudes towards Africa and its problems. This is why abolition had relatively little impact when it came to various parts of West Africa. The abolitionists who had seen slavery as an important obstacle to progress were surprised and disappointed to find that after abolition life went on much as before. The conservationists lost their battle to preserve the status quo as far as possible and their predictions of social, economic and political disruption after abolition were not fulfilled. Clearly West African society could be changed without disaster. The developmentalists were also proved wrong. As the example of the Sierra Leone Protectorate shows, social and political progress did not automatically follow economic development.

This is not to deny the historical importance of the existence of domestic slavery in British West Africa during the nineteenth and twentieth centuries and the effects it had on British policy. These were significant even if few understood or tried to understand the true nature of the institution. A study of domestic slavery throws light on the development of British attitudes and policy to West Africa. Naturally the institution was even more important in itself—as an integral part of the West African way of life which was challenged by the arrival of the colonial powers.

Britain made the mistake of magnifying the institution of domestic slavery and assuming that if a satisfactory policy towards the institution could be found then Britain would easily solve the social and economic problems of the West African hinterlands which were being taken over by the British. Social and economic changes were not influenced as much by official policy as by factors outside official control. In the Sierra Leone Protectorate during the twentieth century the discovery of iron and diamonds, the Second World War and the withdrawal of the British have had far greater effects than the development of official policies towards domestic slavery.

NOTES

1. Already discussed in Chapter V.
2. S.L.A., M.P. C.S. 98/8 March 1915, Ronietta Report, 1913, p. 2.
3. Pim, *Economic History of Tropical Africa*, p. 41.
4. CO 267/580/10112, Wilkinson to CO, 30 January 1919. These figures were for domestic exports.
5. See administrative reports in CO 270 series.
6. CO 267/570/22293, Wilkinson to CO, 28 April 1916.
7. H. Labouret, "A Propos de l'esclavage: l'affaire de Sierra-Leone", *Renseignements coloniaux*, No. 11 (November 1927), pp. 405–8.
8. N. A. Cox-George, *Finance and Development in West Africa* (London 1961), pp. 181–2.
9. For examples of the official view of the eagerness of the Mende to serve see CO 267/564/12035, Merewether to CO, 23 February 1915, transmits Ronietta Report 1914 by Page, and CO 267/571/24882, Wilkinson to CO, 12 May 1916, transmits Ronietta Report 1915 by Stanley. For the runaway Mende see above Chapter V, p. 188 and Note 121.
10. Pujehun Archives, N. Sherbro Out Letter Book II, p. 178, 11 February 1917, Stanley to Col. Sec.
11. The problem of disgruntled ex-servicemen returning to a life of slavery has been discussed above, pp. 198–9.
12. H. C. Luke, *Cities and Men*, III (London 1953–56), p. 7.
13. CO 267/574/17212, Wilkinson to CO, 14 March 1917.
14. CO 267/572/42894, Wilkinson to CO, 23 August 1916; see above, p. 201.
15. *Ibid.*, Minutes. Apparently by some oversight the 1874 legislation abolishing slavery in the Gold Coast had not been made applicable to these territories. In 1924 Britain told the League of Nations that although slavery had not been abolished in these territories it had been so greatly modified that it was virtually not slavery, see P.R.O. 30/53/316, A. 25 (a) 1924 VI, 5 September 1924. Yet, in 1930 it was thought necessary to pass Gold Coast Ordinance No. 20, Ashanti Ordinance No. 10 and Northern Territories Ordinance No. 6 declaring slavery in any form whatsoever unlawful.
16. Ellis joined the Colonial Office as a clerk in 1895, in 1909 he was made a principal clerk and in 1920 an assistant secretary.
17. *Op. cit.*, Note 14, CO to Wilkinson, 17 October 1916.

18. For convenience I will refer to the parent body as the Anti-Slavery Society and to the Freetown society as the Sierra Leone Auxiliary, although it later changed its name to the Native Races Protection Society. In 1910 two humanitarian bodies had been formed in Freetown by C. D. Hotobah During and the Rev. J. T. Roberts; these combined to form the Sierra Leone Auxiliary in 1912.

19. Anti-Slavery Papers, MSS. Brit. Emp., S.22, G.244 (Sierra Leone Auxiliary, 1910–29). It protested against the retrospective nature of the Human Leopard Ordinance, the export duty on palm products, the trespass by Chief Inspector Rabbitt, *et al.*

20. *Ibid.*, S.20, Minute 2955, 4 July 1918.

21. Details of Banja Case from CO 267/580/7779, Wilkinson to CO, 22 January 1919 and CO 267/579/54710, Anti-Slavery Society to CO, 14 November 1918.

22. Pujehun Archives, N. Sherbro Out Letter Book II, 1916–17, Stanley to Williams, 17 October 1917.

23. CO 267/580/7779, Enclosure, Stanley to Col. Sec., 17 November 1917.

24. *Ibid.*, Solicitor General to Col. Sec., 23 November 1917 and Stanley to Col. Sec., 6 December 1917.

25. Anti-Slavery Papers, MSS. Brit. Emp., S.22, G 244, 21 August 1918, Secretary to Sierra Leone Auxiliary.

26. CO 267/580/7779, Wilkinson to CO, 22 January 1919; minutes by Ellis, 10 February 1919, Grindle, 11 February 1919 and Fiddes, date unclear.

27. *Ibid.*, draft replies to Anti-Slavery Society, 27 February 1919, and to Wilkinson, 31 March 1919.

28. CO 267/584/29476, Anti-Slavery Society to CO, 15 May 1919, Minute about the discussion, date unclear.

29. CO 267/584/40415, Anti-Slavery Society to CO, 8 July 1919; Anti-Slavery Papers, MSS. Brit. Emp. S.20, Min. 3072, 7 August 1919.

30. CO 267/588/57116, Wilkinson to CO, 28 October 1920.

31. *Sierra Leone Weekly News*, 26 June 1920, p. 8.

32. *Ibid.*, 12 November 1921, p. 8.

33. *Cmd. 3020, op. cit.*, Chapter V, Note 5, pp. 11–12, Governor Slater to CO, 20 June 1924, quoting Maxwell to CO, 18 October 1921.

34. *Idem*, Slater citing CO to Maxwell, 24 November 1921.

35. CO 267/594/55807, Maxwell to Ellis, 25 October 1921. The first part of the sentence is hidden in the binding. It is presumably something like "I may be".

36. Ransford Slater was Colonial Secretary of the Gold Coast from 1914 to 1922. He was knighted in 1924. In 1927 he was promoted from Sierra Leone to the Gold Coast, where he was Governor until 1932. From 1932 to 1934 he was Governor in Chief of Jamaica.

37. CO 270/50.

38. CO 267/598/36644, Liverpool C. of C. to CO, 25 July 1922.

39. CO 267/610/43608, Slater to CO, 13 September 1925.

40. CO 267/602/29162, Addison to CO, 9 June 1923. For more about Addison see above, p. 197 and Note 148.

41. CO 267/601/50043, Ag. Govr. to CO, 29 September 1923, Enc. 1, Report by Pillai, 26 October 1922 and Enc. 5, Comments by M. T. Dawe on Pillai's Report, 10 May 1923.

42. *Cmd. 3020*, p. 12, Slater quoting himself to the Colonial Office, 12 October 1922. He was referring to the newspaper leader of 30 September 1922, see above, p. 200.

43. *Sierra Leone Legislative Council Debates*, 20 November 1922, address by His Excellency. He told the Colonial Office that he had hoped this hint would get some response from unofficial opinion in Sierra Leone, but no opinion had been vouchsafed, *Cmd. 3020*, p. 21.

44. *Cmd. 3020*, pp. 21–2.

45. *Ibid.*, pp. 38–49, minute by Captain Stanley, 9 October 1923.

46. *Ibid.*, p. 22.

47. Greenidge, *Slavery*, p. 178.

48. P.R.O. 30/52/6, C. 252 M. 188. 1921 VI, Anti-Slavery and Aborigines' Protection Society to League of Nations, 2 August 1921.

49. P.R.O. 30/52/316, A. 25(a) 1924 VI, British Government to Secretary-General, 5 September 1924. Presumably pressure from the League could have helped the cause of abolition.

50. P.R.O. 30/52/312, A. 82 1922, 7 September 1922; Cecil of Chelwood, "The Final Blow at Slavery", *The Listener*, 14 June 1933, pp. 934–35.

51. P.R.O. 30/52/313, A. 82 1922, 18 September 1922.

52. P.R.O. 30/52/43, C. 408. 1923 VI, p. 2, Memorandum by the Secretary-General, "The Question of Slavery", followed by the various replies.

53. CO 267/606/60015, FO to CO, 23 December 1924, minute by Mr Harding, 18 February 1925.

54. P.R.O. 30/52/64, C. 258. 1924 VI.

55. Lugard, *Political Memoranda* (1906 ed.), pp. 136–7.

56. CO 267/572/42894, Wilkinson to CO, 23 August 1916, Minute by Calder.

57. P.R.O. 30/52/316, A. 17 1924 VI. Report to the Council, 12 July 1924.

58. *Cmd. 3020*, pp. 4–5, Secretary-General to Foreign Office, 22 December 1923.

59. *Ibid.*, pp. 5–6, Slater to CO, 30 April 1924. The three month delay in forwarding the questions seems excessive, particularly in view of the 1 June deadline.

60. *Idem.*

61. *Ibid.*, p. 28, Slater to CO, 24 June 1924.

62. See above, pp. 172 190–1, 201.

63. *Sierra Leone Legislative Council Debates*, 1925–1926, p. 58. The abolition of slavery was being debated.

64. *Cmd. 3020*, pp. 25–6, Slater to CO, 20 June 1924.

65. *Ibid.*, pp. 32–5.

66. CO 267/604/32037, Slater to CO, 20 June 1924, Minutes by Ellis and Read, 23 and 25 July 1924, Memo on Conference at CO, 7 August 1924, draft reply, CO to Slater, 26 September 1924. The League's questions and the Tanganyika Ordinance have been discussed above, pp. 232 and 230. For the earlier views of Ellis, see above, pp. 223 and 225.

67. Viscount Cecil of Chelwood, *A Great Experiment* (London 1941), p. 173; Cecil, "The Final Blow at Slavery"; see above, p. 230.

68. Cecil, *op. cit.*, Note 67; Greenidge, *Slavery*, p. 178.

69. CO 267/604/32037, Memorandum, *op. cit.*, Note 66.

70. CO 267/604/32038, Slater to CO, 21 June 1924, various minutes.

71. *Ibid.*, Extract from Slater to CO, 14 February 1927.

72. *Idem.* Slater was quoting para. 112 of the Temporary Slavery Commission Report of 25 July 1925.

73. *Idem.* The telegram referred to was XF 6678/26 S.L., Tel. from Secretary of State (Amery) to O.A.G., S.L. The telegram was apparently destroyed under statute.

74. CO 267/620/X4464, Slater to CO, 4 July 1927.

75. Fenton, *Outline of Native Law in Sierra Leone* (1948 ed.), p. 9; Sierra Leone, *Report of Commission of Inquiry into Disturbances in the Provinces, November 1955 to March 1956.* (Cox Report). Published in 1956. Chapter XV, paras. 20 and 21.

76. Bo Archives, Col. Sec. to Bowden, 24 December 1924, Bowden to Col. Sec., 3 January 1925.

77. Bo Archives, Copy of Slater to CO, 12 March 1925. It is odd that this despatch was excluded from *Cmd. 3020.* Bowden was the top official who supported abolition on the Tanganyika model.

78. Cited in *Cmd. 3020*, pp. 51–52, CO to Slater, 7 September 1925.

79. *Sierra Leone Legislative Council Debates*, No. I of 1925–1926 session, p. 71, 24 November 1925.

80. Hargreaves, *A Life of Sir Samuel Lewis*, p. 78 note.

81. *Sierra Leone Weekly News*, 28 November 1925, p. 12.

82. *Ibid.*, 5 December 1925, p. 9.

83. *Ibid.*, 12 December 1925, pp. 8 and 12.

84. *Ibid.*, 19 and 26 December 1925, pp. 5 and 9.

85. *Ibid.*, 9 January 1926, p. 11. He was one of the originators of the Sierra Leone Auxiliary, see above, Note 18.

86. *Ibid.*, 23 January 1926, p. 9.

87. *Ibid.*, 20 March 1926, p. 8.

88. *Sierra Leone Legislative Council Debates*, No. V of 1925–26 session, pp. 47–8, 24 March 1926.

89. *Cmd. 3020*, pp. 57–8, Report of Tour to Col. Sec. from Provincial Commissioner, Southern Province, 7 January 1926.

90. *Sierra Leone Legislative Council Debates*, No. V of 1925–26 pp. 49–51, 24 March 1926.

91. *Ibid.*, pp. 51–2.

92. *Ibid.*, No. VI of 1925–26, pp. 58–9, 29–30 March 1926.
93. *Idem.* The text of this Ordinance is in CO 269/10; see Appendix II for a copy of the Ordinance.
94. CO 323/957/CF 6069/26, FO to CO, 24 February 1926. Attorney-General's Opinion Book, p. 114, 4 April 1926. See also above, p. 235.
95. *Cmd. 3020*, pp. 60–1, 10 April 1926.
96. Anti-Slavery Papers, MSS. Brit. Emp. S. 20, E 2/15, minute 3864, p. 330, 7 January 1926; CO 267/604/32038, minute by Mac-Sweeney, 11 January 1927.
97. *Sierra Leone Weekly News*, 29 January 1927, p. 8.
98. Bo Archives, C 84/1924, Col. Sec. to Commissioner Central Province, 12 May 1926, Enclosure D.C. Karene to Commisisoner Northern Province, 29 April 1926.
99. *Ibid.*, minute by Attorney-General (McDonnell), 7 May 1926.
100. Bo Archives, C 13/1924, Commissioner Central Province to Commissioner Southern Province, 11 July 1927.
101. *Ibid.*, D.C. Kenema to D.C. Pujehun (Fenton), 30 May 1927.
102. *Ibid.*, D.C. Pujehun to Commissioner Southern Province, 16 June 1927.
103. *Ibid.*, Commissioner Central Province to Commissioner Southern Province, 11 July 1927.
104. *Manchester Guardian*, 27 August 1927, p. 11.
105. *Idem.* One indication that this was a test case is that in 1928 the new Governor of Sierra Leone asked, in vain, for approval of a payment of £100 to M'fa Nonko who had borne the costs of both cases. See CO 267/625/X9041/1928, No. 10, Byrne to Amery, 11 May 1928 and Amery to Byrne, 12 June 1928. This odd request may have been an expression of gratitude to M'fa Nonko who helped the Sierra Leone Government clarify the position as to the legality of domestic slavery in the Protectorate.
106. *Cmd. 3020*, pp. 62–6.
107. *Ibid.*, pp. 67–70. This Ordinance has been discussed above, see p. 183.
108. Bo Archives, Commissioner Northern Province File C289/10, No. C295/10, to Col. Sec., 12 August 1927.
109. *Ibid.*, Enclosure A, No. 283 (4), Commissioner Northern Province to District Commissioners, 7 October 1926.
110. *Ibid.*, Enclosure D, Extract from Commissioner Northern Province File 283 (17a), 1 November 1926.
111. *Ibid.*, para. 8 and Encl. C, Extract from C.N.P. File 295/10(5), Commissioner to D.C. Karene, 28 December 1926.
112. S.L.A., Karene District Decree Book, III, p. 126, 11 March 1927 and p. 127, 14 March 1927, the Sanda Loko and Sella Limba decrees.
113. *Sierra Leone Weekly News*, 17 September 1927, pp. 5 and 8.
114. Luke, *Cities and Men*, III, p. 10. Luke was Colonial Secretary in

Sierra Leone from 1924 to 1928 and at the time of the abolition crisis he was Acting Governor.

115. *Idem.*

116. Hansard, *Parliamentary Debates*, 209, p. 1454, 28 July 1927. The questioner was Mr. H. E. Crawford who apparently had no connections with humanitarian organizations. Mr. Ormsby-Gore was Acting Secretary of State. The autumn recess was from 19 July to 8 November.

117. *The Times*, 25 August 1927, p. 11. Sir John was a leading Liberal politician who had left the Cabinet in January 1916 in protest against conscription. He returned to high office in 1931. His wife Kathleen was on the Anti-Slavery Society Committee and his letter was at least partly due to her.

118. *Manchester Guardian,* 26 August 1927, pp. 8 and 9.

119. CO 267/621/X4483/27, No. 4, Harris to CO, 8 August 1927; No. 5, CO to Harris, 9 August 1927; No. 6, Harris to CO, 10 August 1927.

120. *Ibid.,* No. 11, CO to Harris, 30 August 1927; No. 16, Harris to CO, 3 September 1927.

121. Ibid., No. 17, Harris to *The Times*, minute. *The Times*, 7 September 1927, p. 8.

122. *The Times*, 14 September 1927, p. 10; *Manchester Guardian*, 15 September 1927.

123. CO 267/621/X4483/27, No. 33, Fiddian to Luke, 17 October 1927.

124. *The Times*, 27 August 1927, p. 11.

125. *The Observer*, 28 August 1927, pp. 13–14.

126. *Manchester Guardian*, 9 September 1927, p. 10. Bankole Bright had used similar arguments in the debate on Ordinance 9 of 1926, see above, p. 239. Presumably Bankole Bright was one of those whom Luke thought "found here a useful source of notoriety", see above, p. 245.

127. *Sierra Leone Legislative Council Debates*, No. VII of Session 1926–27, pp. 36–41 and 47–51, September 1927.

128. CO 267/621/X4483/27, No. 31, Luke to Fiddian, 25 September 1927. *Sierra Leone Legislative Council Debates*, No. VII of Session 1926–27, pp. 27–62. For the promise not to deprive living owners of slaves see above, p. 239.

129. *Cmd. 3020*, p. 78, CO to Governor, 17 October 1927.

130. Bo Archives, C.N.P. File C289/10, No. C295/10, C.N.P. to Col. Sec., 12 August 1927, para. 10.

131. Bo Archives, C 10/1927, C.C.P. to Col. Sec., 23 August 1927. I could not find any comments from the Commissioner of the Southern Province.

132. *Cmd. 3020*, p. 61, CO to Luke, 27 July 1927 and pp. 62–70, Luke to CO, 1 August 1927.

133. *Ibid.*, p. 70, CO to Luke, 30 August 1927. The sentence about the

case giving rise to comment was omitted from the Command Paper, but it can be found in CO 267/621/X4483/27, No. 10.

134. *Ibid.*, p. 70, Luke to CO, 31 August 1927 and p. 71, CO to Luke, 2 September 1927.

135. *Ibid.*, pp. 71–2, Luke to CO, 6, 10 and 15 September 1927 and CO to Luke, 8 and 14 September 1927.

136. *Ibid.*, pp. 73–7, Luke to CO, 22 and 23 September 1927. The text of the Ordinance is in Appendix III.

137. *League of Nations Printed Papers*, A. 24. 1928. VI. Slavery Convention, Annual Report, Letter from British Government, 30 July 1928 and A. 17. 1929. VI, Letters from British Government, 13 October 1928 and 29 May 1929.

138. *Ibid.*, A. 13. 1931. VI. Various letters from the British Government, referring to and giving the texts of these ordinances in the Gambia, the Somaliland Protectorate, the Protectorates of Nyasaland and Uganda, Northern Rhodesia, the Gold Coast Colony, Ashanti and the Northern Territories of the Gold Coast.

139. CO 267/621/X4483/37 Sub File "A", Buxton to Lovat, 11 November 1927. On 14 November Mr Pethick-Lawrence asked a question in the Commons but neither his question nor the answer were as comprehensive as those in the Lords.

140. Hansard, *Parliamentary Debates*, Vol. 69, pp. 199–214, 23 November 1927.

141. *The Times*, 2 January 1928, p. 13.

142. Hansard, *Parliamentary Debates*, Vol. 213, p. 1242, 20 February 1928.

143. CO 267/625/X9041/1928, Byrne to Amery, 30 May 1928, para. 9.

144. *Daily Mail*, 21 and 23 September 1927, pp. 9 and 11.

145. *Sierra Leone Weekly News*, 1 and 15 October 1927, pp. 8–9 and p. 8.

146. Bo Archives, Conf. Minute Paper No. 3, Minute No. 6, Conf. 1/29, D.C. Sumbuya to C.S.P., 11 January 1929; D.C. Mano River to C.S.P., 10 February 1929; and Conf. CCP 2/28, No. 5, C.C.P. to Col. Sec., 10 February 1928.

147. *Sierra Leone Legislative Council Debates*, No. 1 of 1928–29, pp. 17–18, 21 November 1928. Governor Byrne was quoting the Commissioner.

148. Roy Lewis, *Sierra Leone*, p. 67.

149. Bo Archives, Conf. No. 3/22/1929, D.C. Sembehun to C.S.P., 8 January 1929.

150. My informant is a lecturer at Fourah Bay College. Not unnaturally people in Sierra Leone were not forthcoming about the possibility of practices akin to slavery still surviving. As the Sierra Leone Archives still applies the fifty year rule, I was not able to see official papers later than 1920.

151. My informant is a lecturer at Njala University College.

152. H.M. Lynch Shyllon, "The Effect of the Ward System on the Schools in the Colony of Sierra Leone" (Dip. Ed. dissertation, Fourah Bay College, 1953).
153. Anti-Slavery Papers, MSS. Brit. Emp. S.22, G.498, 3 November 1945.
154. *Cox Report, op. cit.,* Note 75.
155. *Ibid.,* p. 98.
156. *Ibid.,* p. 165.

Bibliographical Notes

Plan of Bibliography

Unpublished Sources
A. Official British Archives
B. Sierra Leone Archives
C. Manuscript Collections
D. Unpublished Theses
E. Oral Evidence

Published Sources
F. Official
G. Newspapers
H. Unofficial sources containing primary material
J. Other unofficial sources

A. OFFICIAL BRITISH ARCHIVES

The records of the Colonial and Foreign Offices and the League of Nations papers are at the Public Record Office. The following were particularly useful—CO 267, Correspondence with the Governor of Sierra Leone; CO 269, Sierra Leone Ordinances; CO 270, Executive and Legislative Council Minutes and Administrative Reports; and CO 271, Sierra Leone Royal Gazette. I used these Sierra Leone papers from 1890 to 1930. Some volumes of FO 84 and 97, papers on the Slave Trade and Foreign Jurisdiction, were also useful. The League of Nations papers are collected in P.R.O. 30/52. I also used various Colonial Office Confidential Prints relating to West Africa.

B. SIERRA LEONE ARCHIVES

The national collection at Fourah Bay College includes the Attorney General's Opinion Books, the Government Interpreter's

Letter Books, the correspondence of the Department of Native Affairs, some Minute Papers and some of the Decree, Intelligence and Letter Books from the Districts. There are more Minute Papers and District Records at the Provincial and District Archives in Bo, Kenema and Pujehun. In footnotes I have stated whether the Sierra Leone Papers were at the national archives in Freetown (S.L.A.) or at Bo, Kenema or Pujehun.

C. Manuscript Collections

1. Anti-Slavery Papers at Rhodes House, Oxford.
2. Basel Mission: Abstracts from the Gold Coast Correspondence of the Basel Mission, taken by Paul Jenkins.
3. Sir David Chalmers MSS, University of Edinburgh.
4. Chamberlain Papers, University of Birmingham.
5. Church Missionary Society Papers, London.
6. Morel Papers, London School of Economics.
7. Nathan Papers, Rhodes House, Oxford.
8. United Brethren in Christ Papers (microfilmed) at Fourah Bay College Library, Freetown.
9. Wesleyan Methodist Missionary Society Papers, London.

D. Unpublished Theses

Etheridge, N. H. R., The Sierra Leone Frontier Police: a Study in the Functions and Employment of a Colonial Force (M.Litt. Aberdeen 1967).

Gertzel, C., John Holt: a British Merchant in West Africa in the Era of Imperialism (Ph.D. Oxford 1959).

Hopkins, A. G., An Economic History of Lagos 1880–1914 (Ph.D. London 1964).

Ijagbemi, E. Ade, A History of the Temne in the Nineteenth Century (Ph.D. Edinburgh 1968).

Miers, S., Great Britain and the Brussels Anti-Slave Trade Act of 1890 (Ph.D. London 1969).

Nworah, K. K. D., Humanitarian Pressure-groups and British Attitudes to West Africa, 1895–1915 (Ph.D. London 1966).

Oroge, E. A., The Institution of Slavery in Yorubaland with Particular Reference to the Nineteenth Century (Ph.D. Birmingham 1971).

Sesay, S. M., Transport in Relation to Social and Economic Development in Sierra Leone (Ph.D. Durham 1967).

E. ORAL EVIDENCE

Owing to the lack of time and money I was not able to gather much oral evidence in Sierra Leone, although I did have some interesting conversations with ex-slaves and ex-slaveholders. I am grateful to those former colonial officials who told me about their experiences—particularly Mr. N. C. Hollins.

F. OFFICIAL PUBLISHED SOURCES

1. Various Parliamentary Papers, cited as P.P. or by Command Numbers. Most important are the parts of the Chalmers Report—C.9388 and C.9391 and the Correspondence Relating to Domestic Slavery in the Sierra Leone Protectorate—Cmd. 3020.
2. Annual Reports on the Blue Book for Sierra Leone.
3. Sierra Leone, *Report of Commisson of Inquiry into Disturbances in the Provinces, November 1955 to March 1956.* Cox Report. 1956.
4. Hansard, *Parliamentary Debates.*
5. League of Nations Printed Papers.
6. *Sierra Leone Legislative Council Debates, 1922–1929.*
7. Various official and semi-official handbooks, pamphlets, reports and printed instructions:
   Foreign Office, *Peace Handbooks XV*, 90 and 92, "British West Africa General" and "Sierra Leone" (H.M.S.O. 1920).
   General Orders of the Colony of Sierra Leone (1918).
   Goddard, T. N., *The Handbook of Sierra Leone* (London 1925).
   Lugard, Sir F., *Memoranda on Subjects chiefly Political* (1906).
   Maxwell, J. C., *Land Tenure in the Protectorate* (London 1917).

G. NEWSPAPERS

I have read the available editions of the two Sierra Leone

newspapers for the relevant period and have used other papers rather more selectively.

Anti-Slavery Reporter
Church Missionary Intelligencer
Manchester Guardian
Sierra Leone Times
Sierra Leone Weekly News
The Times
West Africa

H. UNOFFICIAL PUBLISHED SOURCES CONTAINING PRIMARY MATERIAL

Alldridge, T. J., *The Sherbro and its Hinterland* (London 1901).

Alldridge, T. J., *A Transformed Colony. Sierra Leone: As it was, and as it is. Its progress, peoples, native customs and undeveloped wealth* (London 1910).

Beatty, K. J., *Human Leopards. An Account of the Trials of . . .* (London 1915).

Beck, Dr. G., "Eine neue Route nach dem obern Niger und dem Sudan". III. *Jahresbericht der Geographischen Gesellschaft in Bern 1880–1881*, pp. 35–53.

Burrows, D., "The Human Leopard Society of Sierra Leone", *Journal of the African Society*, XIII, No. 50, January 1914, pp. 143–51.

Burton, R. F., *A Mission to Gelele, King of Dahome* (London 1893).

Castle, Nina, *Extracts from her Letters and Journals from West Africa*, edited by E. Symons (London 1904).

Caulker, "The Caulker Manuscript", Part II, *Sierra Leone Studies*, o.s., No. 6 (November 1922).

Chalmers, J. A. (Lady), "In Defence of Sir David Chalmers", *The Nineteenth Century*, XLVII, pp. 485–97 (March 1900).

Crosby, K. H., "Polygamy in Mende Country", *Africa, Journal of the International Institute of African Languages and Cultures*, X, No. 3 (July 1937).

Cruickshank, B., *Eighteen Years on the Gold Coast of Africa, including an account of the native tribes and their intercourse with Europeans* (London 1853).

Bibliographical Notes

Davis, R. P. M., *History of the Sierra Leone Battalion of the Royal West African Frontier Force* (1929).

De Hart, J., "Notes on the Susuh Settlement at Lungeh, Bullom Shore", *Sierra Leone Studies*, o.s., No. 2 (March 1919).

Deherme, G., *L'Afrique occidentale française. Action politique, action économique, action social* (Paris 1908).

Dennett, R. E., *Nigerian Studies of the Religious and Political System of the Yoruba* (London 1910).

Ellis, A. B., *The Ewe-Speaking Peoples of the Slave Coast of West Africa. Their Religion, Manners, Customs, Laws, Languages, &c.* (Reprint of 1890 ed., the Netherlands 1966).

Faidherbe, General, *Le Sénégal* (Paris 1889).

Fenton, J. S., *Outline of Native Law in Sierra Leone* (Sierra Leone 1948, 1st ed. 1932).

Ferryman, A. F. M., *British West Africa: Its Rise and Progress* London 1900—2nd ed.).

Fiddes, G., *The Dominions and Colonial Offices* (London 1926).

Fitch-Jones, B. W. (ed.), "Extracts from the Diary of Lieut. J. Stewart of W. India Regiment during Rebellion of 1898", *Sierra Leone Studies*, o.s., No. 17 (February 1932).

Fitch-Jones, B. W., "A Victim of the '98 Rising", *Sierra Leone Studies*, o.s., No. 16 (August 1930).

Frere, N. G., "Notes on the History of Port Lokkoh and its Neighbourhood", *Sierra Leone Studies*, o.s., No. 2 (March 1919).

Geary, W. N. M., *Nigeria under British Rule* (London 1965— 1st ed. 1927).

Hollins, N. C., "Mende Law", I and II, *Sierra Leone Studies*, o.s., Nos. 12 and 15 (June 1928 and December 1929).

Hutchinson, T. J., "The Social and Domestic Slavery of Western Africa, and Its Evil Influence on Commercial Progress", *Journal of the Society of Arts*, 26 February 1875, pp. 310–21.

Luke, H. C., *Cities and Men* (London, 1953–56).

Moberly, F. J., *Military Operations, Togoland and the Cameroons, 1914–16* (London 1931).

Park, Mungo, *Travels in the Interior of Africa* (Edinburgh 1860).

Probyn, Leslie, "Address at Monthly Dinner, 6 Feb. 1907" *Journal of the African Society* (1907), VI, pp. 205–08.

Sarbah, J. M., *Fanti Customary Laws* (1968—1st ed. 1897).

Schlenker, Rev. C. F., *A Collection of Temne Traditions, Fables and Proverbs* (London 1861).

Talbot, P. A., *Tribes of the Niger Delta. Their Religions and Customs* (London 1932).

Temple, C. L., *Native Races and Their Rulers. Sketches and Studies of Official Life and Administrative Problems in Nigeria* (3rd ed., London 1968- -1st ed. 1918).

Temple, O., *Notes on the Tribes, Provinces, Emirates and States of the Northern Provinces of Nigeria* (London 1965, impression of 2nd ed. 1922).

Thomas, N. W., *Anthropological Report on Sierra Leone. Part I. Law and Custom of the Timne and Other Tribes* (London 1916).

Thomas, W. T., "Industrial Pursuits of the Yalunka People", *Sierra Leone Studies*, o.s., No. 1 (June 1918).

Trotter, J. K., *The Niger Sources and the borders of the new Sierra Leone Protectorate* (London 1898).

Vivian, Rev. W., *A Captive Missionary in Mendiland: The Story of The Rev. C. H. Goodman's Wonderful Deliverance from Death, and his Strange Experiences during the Sierra Leone Rebellion* (London 1899).

Vivian, Rev. W., "The Mendi Country", *The Journal of the Manchester Geog. Society*, XII, No. 1 (January 1896).

Vivian, Rev. W., *Mendiland Memories. Reflections and Anticipations* (London no date).

Waddell, Rev. H., *Twenty-nine years in the West Indies and Central Africa. A review of Missionary work and adventure, 1829-58* (2nd ed. London 1970).

Wallis, C. B., *The Advance of our West African Empire* (London 1903).

Wallis, C. B., "In the Court of the Native Chiefs in Mendiland", *Journal of the African Society*, 4 (1905), pp. 397-409.

Willans, Major R. H. K., "The Konnoh People", *Journal of the African Society*, 8, Nos. 30 and 31 (January and April 1909), pp. 130-44, 288-95.

J. OTHER UNOFFICIAL SOURCES

Abrahams, A., "Nyagua, the British and the Hut Tax War", *The International Journal of African Historical Studies*, Vol. 5 (1972), No. 1, pp. 94-98.

Ajayi, J. F. Ade, *Christian Missions in Nigeria 1841–1891. The Making of a New Elite* (London 1965).

Anene, J. C., *Southern Nigeria in Transition, 1885–1906. Theory and Practice in a Colonial Protectorate* (Cambridge 1966).

Anonymous, "A Guide to Pujehun District", *Sierra Leone Studies*, o.s., No. 17 (February 1932).

Ayandele, E. A., *The Missionary Impact on Modern Nigeria, 1842–1914. A Political and Social Analysis* (London 1966).

Baillaud, E., *La Politique indigène de l'Angleterre en Afrique Occidentale* (Paris 1912).

Balewa, Sir Abubakar Tafawa, *Shaihu Umar* (London 1967—translated and introduced by Mervyn Hiskett).

Batten, T. R., *Problems of African Development*, I and II (London 1947 and 1948).

Bouche, D., *Les Villages de liberté en Afrique noire française* (Paris 1968).

Buell, R. L., *The Native Problem in Africa*, I (New York 1928).

Butt-Thompson, F. W., *Sierra Leone, in History and Tradition* (London 1926).

Cambridge University Press, *Cambridge History of the British Empire*, II and III.

Campbell, O., *Mary Kingsley, a Victorian in the Jungle* (London 1957).

Cecil of Chelwood, Viscount, "The Final Blow at Slavery", *The Listener*, 14 June 1933.

Cecil of Chelwood, *A Great Experiment* (London 1941).

Cocks, F. S., *E. D. Morel. The Man and His Work* (London 1920).

Claridge, W. W., *A History of the Gold Coast and Ashanti* (2nd ed.—London 1964; 1st ed. 1915).

Coquery-Vidrovitch, Catherine, "La fête des coutumes au Dahomey: historique et essai d'interpretation", *Annales, Economies, Sociétés, Civilisations*, XIX, 4 (July–August 1964).

Couper, L., "Some Notes on West African Currency", *The Colonial Office Journal*, III (October 1909), No. 2.

Cox-George, N. A., *Finance and Development in West Africa. The Sierra Leone Experience* (London 1961).

Cross, C., *The Fall of the British Empire, 1918–1968* (London 1968).

Crowder, M. (ed.), *West African Resistance. The military responses to colonial occupation* (London 1971).

Curtin, P. D., *The Atlantic Slave Trade. A Census* (Madison 1969).

Curtin, P. D., *The Image of Africa: British ideas and action, 1780–1850* (Madison 1964).

Diké, K. O., *Trade and Politics in the Niger Delta* (Oxford 1956).

Dorjahn, V. R., "The Changing Political System of the Temne", *Africa*, 30, No. 2 (April 1960).

Dorjahn, V. R. and Tholley, A. S., "A Provisional History of the Limba", *Sierra Leone Studies*, n.s., 12 (1959).

Dunlop, J. S., "The Influence of David Livingstone on Subsequent Political Developments in Africa", *The Scottish Geographical Magazine*, 75, No. 3 (December 1959).

Elias, T. O., *The Nature of African Customary Law* (Manchester 1956).

Fage, J. D., *A History of West Africa. An introductory survey* (4th ed. Cambridge 1969).

Fage, J. D., "Slavery and the Slave Trade in the Context of West African History", *Journal of African History*, X, No. 3 (1969).

Finnegan, R. H., *Survey of the Limba People of Northern Sierra Leone* (London 1965).

Flint, J. E., "Mary Kingsley—a Reassessment", *Journal of African History*, IV, No. 1 (1963).

Forde, D. (ed.), *Efik Traders of Old Calabar* (London 1956).

Forde, D. and Jones, G. I., *The Ibo and Ibibio-speaking Peoples of South-eastern Nigeria* (London 1967—1st ed. 1950).

Fox Bourne, H. R., *The Claims of Uncivilised Races* (London 1900).

Fox Bourne, H. R., "Sierra Leone Troubles", *The Fortnightly Review*, No. CCCLXXX, N.S., 1 August 1898.

Fox Bourne, H. R., *Slavery and its Substitutes in Africa* (London 1900).

Furse, Sir R., *Aucuparius: Recollections of a Recruiting Officer* (London 1962).

Fyfe, C., *A History of Sierra Leone* (London 1962).

Gailey, H. A., *A History of the Gambia* (London 1964).

Garvin, J. L., *The Life of Joseph Chamberlain*, I-III (London 1932, 1933 and 1934).

George, C., *The Rise of British West Africa* (London 1903).

Gifford, P. and Louis, W. R. (eds.), *France and Britain in Africa. Imperial Rivalry and Colonial Rule* (Yale 1971).

Gorvie, M., *Old and New in Sierra Leone* (London 1945).

Gorvie, M., *Our People of the Sierra Leone Protectorate* (London 1944).

Gray, F., *My Two African Journeys* (London 1928).

Gray, J. M., *A History of the Gambia* (Cambridge 1940).

Greenidge, C. W. W., *Slavery* (London 1958).

Grenville, J. A. S., *Lord Salisbury and Foreign Policy: the Close of Nineteenth Century* (London 1964).

Gwynn, S., *The Life of Mary Kingsley* (London 1932).

Hargreaves, J. D., "The Establishment of the Sierra Leone Protectorate and the Insurrection of 1898", *Cambridge Historical Journal*, XII, No. 1 (1956).

Hargreaves, J. D., "The Evolution of the Native Affairs Department", *Sierra Leone Studies*, n.s., No. 3 (December 1954).

Hargreaves, J. D., Frontier Police Postings: The Growth of a Historical Legend", *Sierra Leone Studies*, n.s., No. 3 (December 1954).

Hargreaves, J. D., *A Life of Sir Samuel Lewis* (London 1958).

Hargreaves, J. D., *Prelude to the Partition of West Africa* (London 1963).

Harris, Sir John, *A Century of Emancipation* (London 1933).

Harris, Sir John, *Slavery or "Sacred Trust"?* (London 1926).

Harris, Rev. J. H., *Domestic Slavery in Southern Nigeria* (London 1911).

Harris, W. T. and Sawyerr, H., *The Springs of Mende Belief and Conduct* (Freetown 1968).

Haydon, A. P., "The Good Public Servant of the State", *Transactions of the Historical Society of Ghana*, XI (1970).

Heussler, R., *The British in Northern Nigeria* (London 1968).

Heussler, R., *Yesterday's Rulers. The Making of the British Colonial Service* (U.S.A. 1963).

Hofstra, S., "Personality and Differentiation in the Political Life of the Mendi", *Africa*, X, No. 4 (October 1937).

Hopkins, A. G., "The Currency Revolution in South-west Nigeria in the late Nineteenth Century", *Journal of the Historical Society of Nigeria*, III, No. 3 (December 1966).

Hopkins, A. G., "Economic Imperialism in West Africa: Lagos,

1880–92", *The Economic History Review*, XXI, No. 3 (December 1968).

Hopkins, A. G., "The Lagos Strike of 1897: an Exploration in Nigerian Labour History", *Past and Present*, No. 35 (December 1966).

Howard, C., *Mary Kingsley* (London 1957).

Hyam, R., *Elgin and Churchill at the Colonial Office, 1905–1908. The Watershed of the Empire-Commonwealth* (London 1968).

Ifemesia, C. C., "The 'Civilizing' Mission of 1841: Aspects of an Episode in Anglo-Nigerian Relations", *Historical Society of Nigeria Journal*, 2, No. 3 (1962).

Ikime, O., *Merchant Prince of the Niger Delta. The Rise and Fall of Nana Olomu, Last Governor of the Benin River* (London 1968).

Ingram, J. K., *A History of Slavery and Serfdom* (London 1895).

Jambouria, O., "Notes on the Foulah Tribe", *Sierra Leone Studies*, o.s., No. 1 (June 1918).

Jones, G. I., *The Trading States of the Oil Rivers* (London 1963).

Jordan, J. P., *Bishop Shanahan of Southern Nigeria* (Dublin 1946).

July, R. W., *The Origins of Modern African Thought* (London 1968).

Kimble, D., *A Political History of Ghana: the rise of Gold Coast Nationalism, 1850–1928* (Oxford 1963).

Kingsley, M. H., *Travels in West Africa* (London 1897).

Kingsley, M. H., *West African Studies* (London 1899).

Labouret, H., "A Propos de l'esclavage: l'affaire de Sierra-Leone", *Renseignements coloniaux*, 11 (November 1927).

Leonard, A. G., *The Lower Niger and Its Tribes* (London 1906).

Levtzion, N., *Muslims and Chiefs in West Africa: A Study of Islam in the Middle Volta Basin in the Pre-Colonial Period* (Oxford 1968).

Lewis, R., *Sierra Leone: A Modern Portrait* (London 1954).

Little, K. L., *The Mende of Sierra Leone* (Revised ed. London 1967—1st ed. London 1951).

Little, K. L., "The Political Function of the Poro", Part I, *Africa*, XXXV, 4 (1965).

Lugard, Lord, *The Dual Mandate* (5th ed. London 1965).

Lugard, Lord, "Slavery in all its Forms", *Africa*, VI, No. 1 (January 1933).

Lugard, Lord, "West Africa", in *The Empire and the Century*, edited by C. S. Goldman (London 1905).

Luke, H. C., *A Bibliography of Sierra Leone. Preceded by an Essay on the Origin, Character and Peoples of the Colony and Protectorate* (2nd ed. London 1925—1st ed. 1910).

McCulloch, M., *Peoples of the Sierra Leone Protectorate, Ethnographic Survey of Africa. Western Africa*, Part II (London 1950).

Marke, C., *Origin of Wesleyan Methodism in Sierra Leone. And History of Its Missions* (London 1913).

Meek, C. K., *A Sudanese Kingdom. An Ethnographical Study of the Jukun-Speaking Peoples of Nigeria* (London 1931).

Merriman-Labor, A. B. C., *Handbook of Sierra Leone* (1901 and 1902).

Metcalfe, G. E., *Great Britain and Ghana. Documents of Ghana, 1807–1957* (London 1964).

Metcalfe, G. E., *Maclean of the Gold Coast. The Life and Times of George Maclean, 1801–1847* (London 1962).

Meyerowitz, E. L., *The Akan of Ghana. Their Ancient Beliefs* (London 1958).

Migeod, F. W. H., "A View of the Colony of Sierra Leone", *Journal of the African Society*, XXV, No. XCVII (October 1925).

Migeod, F. W. H., *A View of Sierra Leone* (London 1926).

Milne, A. H., *Sir Alfred Lewis Jones K.C.M.G. A Story of Energy and Success* (Liverpool 1914).

Mitchell, P. K., "Trade Routes of the Early Sierra Leone Protectorate", *Sierra Leone Studies*, n.s., No. 16 (June 1962).

Morel, E. D., *Affairs of West Africa* (2nd ed. London 1968—1st ed. 1902).

Newbury, C. W., *British Policy towards West Africa*, II, Select Documents 1875–1914 (Oxford 1971).

Newland, G. H., "The Sofa Invasion", *Sierra Leone Studies*, o.s., No. 19 (December 1933).

Newland, H. O., *Sierra Leone: Its People, Products, and Secret Societies* (London 1916).

Nicolson, I. F., *The Administration of Nigeria, 1900–1960. Men, Methods and Myths* (Oxford 1969).

Nieboer, H. J., *Slavery as an Industrial System. Ethnological Researches* (2nd ed. 1910—1st ed. 1900).

Olivier, Lord, "Trusteeship in British West Africa", *West African Review*, 1932.

Olusanya, G. O., "The Freed Slaves' Homes—an Unknown Aspect of Northern Nigerian Social History", *Journal of the Historical Society of Nigeria*, III, No. 3 (December 1966).

Partridge, C., *Cross River Natives* (London 1905).

Pim, Sir Alan, *Economic History of Tropical Africa* (Oxford 1940).

Porter, B., *Critics of Empire. British Radical Attitudes to Colonialism in Africa 1895–1914* (London 1968).

Rattray, R. S., *Ashanti Law and Constitution* (London 1956—1st ed. 1929).

Renault, F., "L'abolition de l'esclavage au Sénégal: l'attitude de l'administration française 1848–1905", *Revue française d'histoire d'outre-mer*, LVIII, 210 (1971).

Robinson, R. and Gallagher, J., *Africa and the Victorians. The Official Mind of Imperialism* (London 1965—1st ed. 1961).

Rodney, W., "African Slavery and Other Forms of Social Oppression on the Upper Guinea Coast in the Context of the Atlantic Slave-Trade", *Journal of African History*, VII, 3 (1966).

Rodney, W., "A Reconsideration of the Mane Invasions of Sierra Leone", *Journal of African History*, VIII, 2 (1967).

Rolin, H., *Le Traitement des indigènes dans les Colonies anglaises. L'insurrection de Sierra-Leone en 1898* (Brussels 1903).

Root, J. W., "British Trade with West Africa", *Journal of the African Society*, No. 1 (October 1901).

Ryder, A. F. C., *Benin and the Europeans, 1485–1897* (London 1969).

Simon, K., *Slavery* (London 1929).

Smith, Adam, *The Wealth of Nations* (Oxford 1869).

Smith, M. G., "Slavery and Emancipation in Two Societies", *Social and Economic Studies*, 3, Nos. 3 and 4 (1954).

Suret-Canale, J., *La République de Guinée* (Paris 1970).

Thornton, A. P., *The Imperial Idea and its Enemies* (London 1966—1st ed. 1959).

Trimingham, J. S., *Islam in West Africa* (Oxford 1959).

Utting, F. A. J., *The Story of Sierra Leone* (London 1931).

Bibliographical Notes

Vansina, J., *Oral Tradition. A Study in Historical Methodology* (London 1965—1st ed. 1961).

Vansina, J., Mauny, H. and Thomas, L. (eds.), *The Historian in Tropical Africa*. Studies presented and discussed at the fourth international African seminar at the University of Dakar 1961 (London 1964).

Warren, H. G., "Notes on Yalunka Country", *Sierra Leone Studies*, o.s., No. 13 (September 1928).

Williams, E., *Capitalism and Slavery* (N. Carolina 1944).

Wylie, K. C., "Innovation and Change in Mende Chieftaincy 1880–1896", *Journal of African History*, X, No. 2 (1969).

APPENDIX I

THE ESCAPED SLAVES FORWARDED FROM THE CUSTOMS POST AT KIKONKEH, APRIL 1896–MAY 1897.
(Information extracted from Minute Papers in the Sierra Leone Archives)

MP	No.	Name	Sex	Age	Nation	Cause escape	Master	From
223	62	Fannah	M	25	Mendi	Ill treatment	Saidoo	Robally
	63	Danneh	F	40			Morlie	
	64	Morlie	M	18	Timani		Boccary	Matantoo
	65	Soribah	M	27			Alpha	Tarweah
	66	Almami	M	41	Mendi		Colleh	Binleh
	67	Sunkarry	F	40	Susu			
	68	Sunkarry	F	1				
	69	Serah	F	32	Korankoh		Setapha	
	70	Isatta	F	2				
	71	Gaindah	F	36	Mendi		Manyou	
	72	Sorie	M	35	Timani		Lamina Sama	Romarun
	73	Lompey	M	40				
	74	Mattar	F	20				
	75	Bye Marrow	M	38		Desire free		
	76	Yaincane	F	21		Ill treatment		
	77	Doncor	F	32				
	78	Dambee	F	24				
	79	Bassie	M	30	Mendi		Booboo	Mellacourie
	80	Macardee	F	30	Susu		Cerleymoody	Tarweah

276

MP	No.	Name	Sex	Age	Nation	Cause escape	Master	From
275	81	Gumboo	M	48	Mendi	Ill treatment	Combrah Bye	Rocoofru
	82	Yambah	M	38				
	83	Dossoo	F	36	Korankoh			
	84	Bundoo	F	1				
	85	Manmy	F	32	Timani		Sharkali	Rolale
	86	Foday	M	2				
	87	Boccary	M	48	Mendi		Bey Inga	Gbenti
	88	Bassia	M	36	Lokko			
	89	Gbassie	M	32	Mendi	Threat sale	Manga Yola	Barabara
	90	Mussoo	F	34		Ill treatment	Bey Inga	Gbenti
	91	Damaya	F	40	Timani		Gboleh	Maccaribate
	93	Kehmockoh	M	37		Threat sale	Fehrah	Mafallah
	94	Doncor	F	38		Ill treat	Yehroe	
	95	Damah	F	29			Fehrah	
	96	Saibay	F	43		Desire free		
	97	Yagua	F	33	Mendi	Ill treat		
	98	Damah	F	1				
	99	Rawfor	F	32	Timani		Yehroe	
	100	Faingray	F	3			Fehrah	
277	101	Allie	M	39				
	102	Foday	M	32		Desire free	Sharkzar	Robis
	103	Boye	F	25		Ill treat	Mambo	Tomboye

APPENDIX I—continued

MP	No.	Name	Sex	Age	Nation	Cause escape	Master	From
277	104	Macfie	M	37			Baccary Dooboo	Bongomarea
	105	Mussa	M	38	Susu	Threat sale	Colleh	Magbemma
	106	Koney	F	32	Temne	Ill treat	Bundoo	Tarweah.
	107	Nana	F	2				
	108	Konko	M	1				
301	109	Mormudoo	M	48	Susu		Colleh	Liha
	110	Bangalay	M	38				
	111	Gamah	F	26	Bullom			
	112	Kindoe	M	35	Temne		Morlie	Mangay
	113	Lamina	M	15			Colleh	Kabullor
	114	Succona	F	38			Gbonie	Robally
	115	Boye	F	28			Tamson	Rochain
	116	Kelpha	M	10			Lamina Seccoo	Maccassy
	117	Santiggy	M	27	Mendi	Desire free	Wongla	Fonkia
	118	Gbesseh	M	38	Temne	Ill treat	Lehrie	Contah
	119	Gbassie	M	42	Saffrocko	Lamina	Lamina	Robine
	120	Sallifoo	M	35			Foulah	
	121	Senloo	F	38	Limbah			
	122	Boarah	F	25	Saffro			
	123	Allie	M	25	Sankarah		Lamina	
337	124	Canray	M	35			Bullor	
	125	Yamgbah	M	37	Mendi		Sorie	Murricania

MP	No.	Name	Sex	Age	Nation	Cause escape	Master	From
337	126	Damoh	F	39	Temne			
	127	Allie	M	2				
	128	Musu	F	28	Mendi			
	129	Sorie	M	39				
	130	Gbessa	N	43				
	131	Seggor	F	32			Forey	Borroh
	132	Sorrie	M	3			Bye Marrow	
	133	Banger	M	32			Sharkar	Kabullor
	134	Mamy	F	27	Temne			
	135	Mawinney	F	1				
	136	Tinna	F	1				
	137	Coombah	F	43	Korankor			
	138	Barricah	M	40	Mendi			
	139	Yambah	M	48			Mormudoo	Cattick
	140	Canray	M	46			Tumgbah	Masamah
	141	Sorie	M	38	Lokko		Mormudoo	Cattick
	142	Bundee	F	40	Bullom	Threat sale		
	143	Mellay	F	1				
	144	Wonday	F	37	Mendi		Mormoh	Masamah
	145	Taryanday	F	37	Mendi	Ill treat	Yolah	Capesseh
	146	Mapelah	F	2				
	147	Kibbah	M	16	Temne	Threat sale	Borbor	Kartimp

MP	No.	Name	Sex	Age	Nation	Cause escape	Master	From
367	148	Saidoo	M	28	Temne	Ill treat	Bamp	Mambolo
	149	Lawanney	F	26				
	150	Musudee	F	38				Rolale
	151	Mormoh	M	1			Namina	
	152	Konkoray	M	2				
	153	Boondoo	M	4				
	154	Fairah	F	6				
	155	Tankoe	M	28	Temne	Desire free	Bubu	Kotrue
	156	Amarah	M	28			Moseray	Rolale
410	Nil	Yango	M	56	Mendi	Ill treat	Not given	—
	Nil	Marigbah	F	50				
	Nil	Kammanda	M	50				
	Nil	Foeserah	F	25	Susu			
406	157?	No details						
	158?	No details						
460	159	Ballachoo	M	46	Temne	Ill treat	Bokari	Robally
	160	Amara	M	24				
	161	Damoh	F	42				
	162	Yegee	F	10				
501	163	Seray-Dee	F	25	Susu	Threat sale	Yacooba	Robaviay
	164	Carpru	M	15	Timanee		Bubu	Patifoo
	165	Lamina	M	38	Mendi	Ill treat	Markeh	Foricaria

APPENDIX I—*continued*

MP	No.	Name	Sex	Age	Nation	Cause escape	Master	From
501	166	Jimmy	M	36		Threat sale	Keltigee	Campdee
	167	Yancane	F	38	Timanee		Sorie Tam	Kychom
529	168	Forankay	M	35	Koranko	Desire free	Konkoe	
	169	Sorie	M	40	Timanee	Ill treat	Santigee Foday	Kabullor
	170	Bearay	M	41			Sharkar	
	171	Gbannah	M	41	Mendi			
	172	Fudia	F	40	Susu	Threat sale		
	173	Mormoh	M	1				
	174	Namina	F	5				
	175	Carpru	M	3				
	176	Sailoh	F	2				
	177	Nancame	F	38	Mendi	Ill treat	Musu	
	178	Fudia	F	3				
	179	Talloma	F	2				
	180	Terree	M	$\frac{1}{4}$				
591	181	Barbardu	M	30			Morlie	Kabulo
	182	Bunkey	F	26	Temni			
	183	Myer	M	39	Lokko		Foodia	Mafallah
	184	Tierrah	M	42	Saffroko		Simrah	
	185	Yomboe I	F	30	Mendi	Threat sale	Foodia	
	186	Yomboe II	F	35	Temne		Ferah	
621	187	Sorie	M	28	Susu	Ill treat	Sharkah	Binleah

281

MP	No.	Name	Sex	Age	Nation	Cause escape	Master	From
621	188	Schree	M	30				
	189	Liho	M	26				
	190	Yemah	F	26	Mendi		Seray	Mambolo
	191	Tendeh	F	1				
44	1	Musu	F	38			Soko	
	2	Bearay	M	2				
	3	Morlie	M	39			Borbor	
	4	Sorie	M	42	Temni		Dick	
	5	Sye	F	39				
	6	Sarteah	F	40			Nankay	Nyack
	7	Capprah	M	12			Bengally	Benty
84	8	Foday	M	35			Ben Inga	Mangay
	9	Banger	M	36	Mendi		Yalliemoody	Malliegee
	10	Murmurdoo	M	42	Mandingo	Ill treat	Amsumana	Robis
	11	Dowdah	M	31	Temne	Desire free	Bambadee	Binleah
	12	Bingy	M	37		Ill treat		
	13	Coombah	F	32	Koranko	Desire free		
	14	Yallie	F	30	Limbah	Ill treat		
	15	Murmurdoo	M	1	Limbah			
	16	Barkahdee	F	2				
	17	Damour	F	36	Temne	Desire free	Allie	Mangay
	18	Bowl	F	2				

APPENDIX I—continued

MP	No.	Name	Sex	Age	Nation	Cause escape	Master	From
84	19	Colleah	M	32	Susu		Sorie	Mambolo
95	20	Benkah	M	36	Temne		Amarah	Mafallah
	21	Conteh	M	30		Threat sale		
	22	Marrie	F	40		Desire free		
	23	Ferrie	F	37				
	24	Whomarray	F	39		Ill treat		
	25	Dorah	F	35				
	26	Kofah	F	36				
	27	Monday	F	27				
	28	Lamina	M	43		Desire free		
	29	Murmoh	M	23				
	30	Borroh	F	38				
	31	None Chor	F	16			Murmurdoo	
	32	Coleoy	F	8				
	33	Murmurdoo	M	5				
	34	Bunkay	F	3				
	35	Mamy	F	2				
	36	Booyammah	F	38				
	37	Dady	M	2				
	38	Tanigray	F	1				
	39	Bormoh	M	27		Threat sale	Sorie	Mandon
122	40	Fahmah	F	32	Limbah	Desire free	Sabbroo	Benty

MP	No.	Name	Sex	Age	Nation	Cause escape	Master	From
122	41	Benty	F	6	Saffrocko			
	42	Sebbeh	M	28	Mendi	Ill treat	Alimamy	Cattomah
	43	Gobah	M	30	Susu	Ill treat	Liahi	Tombo
147	44	Soriebah	M	28	Kankor		Mamay Boye	Cartoma
	45	Sarrah	M	41	Temne		Saido	
	46	Coyah	F	25				
	47	Lamina	M	3				
	48	Foeday	M	1				
	49	Fahmatter	F	42	Mendi		Nordee	Carbanke
178	50	Goyanday	M	38	Temni		Borroh	Carhcorrah
	51	Sorie	M	36				
	52	Lamina	M	2				
	53	Ferrie	F	40		Desire free	Tekonkor	
	54	Dagbah	F	37			Borroh	
	55	Musu	F	1				
	56	Santiggee	M	28		Threat sale	Bamp	Yellie
	57	Morlie	M	5				Sanda
	58	Mima	F	32			Boccary	

284

Appendix I

Sex Ratio.

Males	94
Female	93

Distribution by Age.

0– 4	34
5– 9	9
10–14	3
15–19	5
20–24	5
25–29	27
30–34	24
35–39	48
40–44	25
45–49	7
50–+	3

Distribution by Tribe.

Temne	98
Mendi	47
Susu	18
Kankar ?	1
Limba	6
Saffroko	5
Koranko	7
Lokko	3
Bullom	3
Mandingo	1
Sankarah	1

Towns and Owners Losing Most Slaves.
1. Mafallah 28. Amara 11 at once, Murmurdoo 8 at once, Ferah 1 and 7.
2. Kabullor 20. Sharkar 7 and 6.
3. Binleah 15. Bambadee 6 at once.

Reasons Given for Escape.

Ill treatment	136
Desire freedom	31
Threat of sale	23

APPENDIX II

PROTECTORATE (No. 2) (AMENDMENT) ORDINANCE, 1926.
COLONY OF SIERRA LEONE. No. 9 of 1926.
In His Majesty's Name I assent to this Ordinance this
second day of April, 1926.

A. R. SLATER,
Governor.

An Ordinance to Amend the Protectorate Ordinance, 1924.

(14th April, 1926)

Date of com- mencement.	BE IT ENACTED by the Governor of the Colony of Sierra Leone, with the advice and consent of the Legislative Council thereof, as follows:
Short title	1. This Ordinance may be cited as the Protectorate (No. 2) (Amendment) Ordinance, 1926.
Substitution of a new section for Cap. 167, section 6.	2. Section six of the Protectorate Ordinance, 1924, shall be repealed and the following shall be substituted therefor:
Persons declared free.	"6. After the commencement of this Ordinance "(1) All persons born or brought into the Protectorate are hereby declared to be free. "(2) All persons treated as slaves or held in an manner of servitude shall be and become free on the death of their master or owner.
Claims relating to slaves not to be entertained.	"(3) No claim for or in respect of any slave shall be entertained by any of the Courts of the Protectorate".

Passed in the Legislative Council this twenty-ninth day of March, in
the year of our Lord One thousand nine hundred and twenty-six.

J. L. JOHN,
Clerk of Legislative Council.

APPENDIX III

LEGAL STATUS OF SLAVERY (ABOLITION) ORDINANCE, 1927. COLONY OF SIERRA LEONE. No. 24 of 1927.

(L.S.)   In His Majesty's name I assent to this Ordinance this twenty-second day of September, 1927.

H. C. LUKE,
Acting Governor.

An Ordinance to Abolish the Legal Status of Slavery in the Protectorate.
(1st January, 1928)

Date of commencement	Be it enacted by the Governor of the Colony of Sierra Leone, with the advice and consent of the Legislative Council thereof, as follows:
Short title, application and commencement	1. This Ordinance may be cited as the Legal Status of Slavery (Abolition) Ordinance, 1927; it shall apply to the Protectorate, and shall come into operation on the first day of January, 1928.
Abolition of legal status of slavery	2. The legal status of slavery is hereby declared to be abolished throughout the Protectorate.
Amendment of Cap. 167.	3. For the heading to Part II of the Protectorate Ordinance, 1924, namely "Slave Dealing, etc." there shall be substituted the heading "Dealing in Persons, etc."
Repeal of sections 5 and 7 of Cap. 167.	4. Sections five and seven of the Protectorate Ordinance, 1924, are hereby repealed.

5. Section eight of the Protectorate Ordinance, 1924, shall be amended in the following particulars:

(a) In paragraph (1) for the word "slave" there shall be substituted the word "person";

(b) Paragraph (2) shall be deleted;

Amendment of section 8 of Cap. 167.

(c) In paragraph (3) for the word "servitude" there shall be substituted the words "any service";

(d) In paragraph (4) the words "or becoming a slave" shall be deleted, and for the word "servitude" there shall be substituted the words "any service";

287

(e) In paragraph (5) the words "or in any service" shall be inserted between the words "in servitude" and the words "as a pledge";

(f) In paragraph (7) for the words "slaves or other" there shall be substituted the word "any".

Repeal of No. 9 of 1926.

6. The Protectorate (No. 2) (Amendment) Ordinance, 1926, is hereby repealed.

Amendment of Cap. 169.

7. The Protectorate Courts Jurisdiction Ordinance, 1924, shall be amended in the following particulars:

(a) Section four shall be repealed;

(b) In paragraph (2) (a) of section seven and in paragraph (2) (a) of section twenty-four for the word "slaves" there shall be substituted the word "persons".

Passed in the Legislative Council this twenty-second day of September, in the year of Our Lord One thousand nine hundred and twenty-seven.

J. L. JOHN,
Clerk of Legislative Council.

Index

Index